Cassell's

SPELLING
Dictionary

Compiled by David Firnberg

New and expanded edition

Cassell
London

CASSELL LTD
1 Vincent Square, London SW1P 2PN

First published 1976
Second edition 1985
Reprinted 1986

ACKNOWLEDGEMENTS

Cliff Parfit of the National Association for Remedial Education and
teacher adviser to the ILEA gave helpful advice on the project at all stages.

We were able to prepare this dictionary and set the final version in type –
all with the aid of a computer system developed by Hamish Carmichael.
His skill in devising the system and in adapting it to our special needs was
of great value and we are grateful for his contribution. Our thanks are also
due to two major British companies, ICL and Plessey, for the provision of
computer facilities and for much technical assistance.

Adele Barclay prepared the American spelling entries; and Christopher
White helped us with the usage of 'who' and 'whom'.

We are also grateful to Colston Sanger for several suggestions which
have been incorporated in the introductory pages of the revised edition of
the dictionary.

British Cataloguing in Publication Data

Firnberg, D.
    Cassell's spelling dictionary – 2nd ed.
    1. English language – Orthography and spelling
    – Dictionaries
    I. Title   II. Firnberg, Leopold Bernald.
    Cassell's new spelling dictionary
    428.1 PE1146

    ISBN 0–304–31137–5

Printed in Great Britain by Richard Clay (The Chaucer Press) Ltd,
Bungay, Suffolk

ABOUT THIS DICTIONARY

This dictionary is not just an English dictionary with the definitions missing; the words in it have been chosen especially because they may not be easy to spell. For this reason some common words will not be found in it.

However, to have included all the words in the language which are difficult to spell would have made the dictionary too long, so we decided to limit ourselves to words likely to be used by the general reader or writer. This meant that only the commonest legal, medical and musical terms could be included. Very few proper names are given, and foreign words are included only if they have passed into common use. Thus 'chauffeur' and 'debut' are included, but not 'habitué' or 'parvenu'. A few common slang words have also been given.

This dictionary does not set out to define words. But when there is similarity in the spelling or sound of words, a brief definition is given in brackets: for example:

    complement (to add to)
    compliment (praise)
    principal (chief)
    principle (moral code)

HOW TO USE THIS DICTIONARY

Layout

The entries in this dictionary are arranged in two ways. Root words are listed in strict alphabetical order. Under each root word will be found its derived form. To make finding a word as clear and easy as possible, the derived forms are given in full. They are arranged alphabetically after their root word, except that plurals follow immediately after the singular.

ROOT WORD	fun	ROOT WORD	divine (God-like)
DERIVED FORMS	funnier	DERIVED FORMS	divinely
	funnily		divinity
	funny		divinities (*pl.*)

It has not been possible to include every derived form but, when a derived form in common usage is not given, you can make it by adding to the unchanged root the ending that you want. For instance, when you can form the past form of verbs by adding 'd' or 'ed' to the root, this does not appear in the dictionary.

One problem in English is the inconsistent way that these past forms are made. Many words ending in a vowel and single consonant double the consonant when an ending such as 'ed', 'ing' or 'er' is added; for example, 'jog, jogging', 'besot, besotted'. But others do not follow this pattern; for example, 'benefit, benefited', 'budget, budgeted'. This dictionary will enable you to learn the patterns each word follows.

In the case of adjectives the basic form is given but the forms in 'er' and 'est' have been omitted whenever they can be made by simply adding the endings to the root. Even when the root changes, only the 'er' or comparative form is given because the 'est' or superlative form behaves in the same way. For example, 'blunt' is given, but not 'blunter' or 'bluntest'; 'creamy' and 'creamier' are given, but not 'creamiest'.

Plurals

Plurals are given in all cases where the root word is changed to make the plural:

> gallery
>> galleries (*pl.*)

They are not given when they are formed by adding 's' to the root.

Possessives

The possessive forms of nouns give many people trouble. They do not know where to put the apostrophe. This edition of *Cassell's Spelling Dictionary* includes many examples of possessives. You should find an example to guide you wherever you open the book. In addition, tricky examples are always given, for example, under 'brother':

> brother-in-law
>> brothers-in-law (*pl.*)
>> brother-in-law's (of the brother-in-law)
>> brothers-in-law's (of the brothers-in-law)

There are further notes on forming the possessive and using the apostrophe on page viii.

Spelling adopted

Although many dictionaries have been consulted during the compilation of this one, the Oxford series of dictionaries was adopted as the authority for British spelling and the Webster series for American spellings.

Both these sources sometimes recognise several alternative spellings for the same word. Where more than one spelling exists, the alternatives are given.

bale, bail (out of aeroplane)

American spellings

In writing you may need to be aware of words with different British or American spelling. Where the American spelling is commonly different from the British, the American variant is given and printed like this:

epaulette
epaulet

Sometimes only a derived word is spelled differently:

abstract
abstraction
abstractor
abstracter

Sometimes the root and all the derived forms are different:

aesthete
esthete
aesthetic
esthetic
aesthetical
esthetical
aestheticism
estheticism

In cases where an American variant exists but the British spelling is acceptable to Americans, then only the British version is given.

-ise or -ize?

In British usage verbs and their associated forms ending in '-ise' can also be spelt '-ize'. Some people opt for one form and some for the other.

Americans always use '-ize', except in a few cases which are listed below. If you prefer '-ize', follow the American spellings of these words. Where a word is given ending in '-ise' and no American spelling is given, be careful: the Americans spell these words with '-ise' too, e.g.:

advertise	advise	afranchise
apprise	arise	braise
chastise	circumcise	comprise
compromise	concise	demise
despise	devise	disfranchise
disguise	emprise	enfranchise
enterprise	excise	exercise
expertise	franchise	guise
improvise	incise	merchandise
misadvise	misprise	mortise
precise	premise	prise
reprise	revise	supervise
surmise	surprise	televise
	treatise	

Foreign words

When a foreign word has been taken into common usage, American and British spellings sometimes differ. The two versions are shown in the usual way. However, if it is only a matter of accents – British 'abbé', American 'abbe' – then only the British version is given. Sometimes only the plural is affected:

château
    châteaux, *châteaus* (*pl.*)

COMMON SPELLING RULES (AND EXCEPTIONS)

English spelling is notoriously inconsistent. Here are some rules of thumb, with examples – and exceptions.

1. 'i before e, except after c.' This rule works well in most cases – 'believe', 'chief', 'diesel', 'friend', 'receive' – but watch out for exceptions such as 'counterfeit', 'either', 'neither', 'weird', 'sleight' and proper names such as 'Keith' and 'Sheila'.

2. In compound words such as 'almighty', 'fulfil', 'until', 'welfare', the double 'll' of 'all', 'full' and 'fill', 'till' and 'well' becomes a single 'l'. Exceptions include 'farewell', 'fullness', 'illness' and 'wellbeing'.

3. Verbs whose roots end in a vowel + single consonant + 'e', e.g. 'bake', 'chase', drop the 'e' when 'ed', 'ing' or 'er' is added: 'baker', 'chasing'. As always, there are exceptions, such as 'ageing'.

4. The silent 'e' is also dropped before a vowel in compound words but retained before a consonant, for example:

valueless	valuable
pursue	pursuing

Some exceptions are 'argument', 'awful', 'duly', 'truly' and 'wholly'.

5. Nouns ending in 'y' form their plurals by substituting 'ies' for 'y', except where 'y' is preceded by a vowel, for example:

ambiguity	ambiguities
category	categories
penny	pennies
BUT	
array	arrays
key	keys
chimney	chimneys

6. Many words have alternative spellings, either of which is correct. The important thing is to be consistent in your use of a particular spelling. Examples are:

abridgment	abridgement
disk	disc
despatch	dispatch
hullo	hallo (or hello)
inquire	enquire
loth	loath
mediaeval	medieval
ratable	rateable
spelt	spelled
Welsh rabbit	Welsh rarebit

How to use the apostrophe

Possessives

The apostrophe is used mainly to indicate possession or relationship as, for example, in:

> the child's mother (the mother of the child)
> the boys' school (the school of the boys)

Most people hesitate for a moment when forming the possessive of names ending in 's'. The usual practice with short names is to add another 's' as well as the apostrophe – 'St James's Street'. But with longer names the final 's' is often omitted; 'Mr Jenkins' office' is perfectly acceptable.

Whether an apostrophe is needed in phrases such as 'a week's holiday' or 'six weeks' work' is really a matter of style. Grammarians would say that it depends on whether 'six weeks' is regarded as a descriptive genitive or an adjectival phrase, for example: 'three minutes' rest' or 'the three-minute rule'.

Possessive pronouns

Possessive pronouns do not have an apostrophe:

> mine, his, hers, its, ours, yours, theirs, whose

The exception is 'one's'.

Be careful of 'it's' which has the same form as the corresponding possessive adjective. It never has an apostrophe. ('It's' is short for 'it is' and should be used only in sentences such as 'It's raining today.')

The apostrophe to show omission

The 'It's raining' example shows this use of the apostrophe. It is used to show that something has been left out of a word. An extreme example is 'fo'c's'le' which is a shortening of 'forecastle'. You will also find the apostrophe used in this way in verse where the poet uses it to shorten words to fit the metre.

Plurals

The apostrophe is also used occasionally to indicate the plural of a word or symbol that does not ordinarily have a plural, for example:

There are two m's and two t's in committee.

If the meaning is clear without the apostrophe, then you can leave it out: '1830s' rather than '1830's', 'MPs' rather than 'MP's' which could be taken as a possessive.

SOURCES OF CONFUSION

To lay or lie

lay (laid, laying) – to place, set or arrange something (this verb always has an object)

> I laid the table before I left home.
> They were still laying the carpet at four o'clock.
> He had laid the matter before the committee.

lie (lay, lying, lain) – to be in a horizontal position (as in bed) or to take that position

> I lie down on my bed every afternoon.
> The book was lying on the table.
> The dog had lain in the same position all day.
> The apples lay in the long grass.

lie (lied, lying) – to tell untruths

> Do not lie to me.
> I lied to you about the money.
> The accused is lying about his actions.

To raise or rise

Similar confusion affects the meaning of these two words, although luckily their actual forms do not lead to confusion.

> Like 'lay', 'raise' always has an object.

raise – to lift

> I raise my hand in a salute.
> The Customs officer opened the suitcase by raising the lid.
> She raised herself in bed.

rise – to get up, get higher

> In May the sun rises at four o'clock.
> Get up, the sun has risen.
> The water in the river is rising.
> The star slowly rose above the horizon.

Who or whom

The rule is that 'who' is the subject and 'whom' the object:

> The man who came to dinner is my cousin.
> The man whom I invited to dinner was late.

However, 'whom' is rarely used in spoken English. We say: 'Who did you meet there?' and 'Who did you hear that from?' 'The person it belongs to' sounds more natural than 'the person to whom it belongs'.

In general, 'whom' is rarely used without a preceding preposition, as in 'to whom', 'from whom', 'by whom', 'with whom', 'of whom':

> The author of whom I had heard a great deal was at the dinner.

Note that 'whose' is sometimes used instead of 'of whom':

> Whose is this coat?

A

aback
abacus
  abacuses (*pl.*)
  abaci (*pl.*)
abandon
  abandoned
  abandoning
  abandonment
abase (to humiliate)
  abasement
  abasing
abash (to embarrass)
abate (to decrease)
  abatement
  abating
abattoir
abbé (priest)
abbess (*fem.*)
  abbesses (*pl.*)
  abbess's (of the abbess)
  abbesses'
      (of the abbesses)
abbey (building)
abbot
  abbot's (of the abbot)
  abbots' (of the abbots)
abbreviate
  abbreviating
  abbreviation
abdicate
  abdicating
  abdication
abdomen
  abdominal
abduct
  abduction
  abductor
aberration
abet (to encourage)

abets
abetted
abetter
abetting
abettor (legal)
abeyance
abhor (to hate)
  abhorred
  abhorrence
  abhorrent
  abhorring
  abhors
abide
  abidance
  abiding
  abode
ability
  abilities (*pl.*)
abject (miserable)
  abjection
  abjectly
abjure
  abjuration
  abjuring
ablative (*grammar*)
ablaze
able
  able-bodied
  ably
ablution (washing)
abnegate
  abnegating
  abnegation
abnormal
  abnormality
  abnormalities (*pl.*)
  abnormally
  abnormity
  abnormities (*pl.*)
aboard
abode (dwelling)
abolish
  abolishes
  abolition
  abolitionary

abominable
  abominably
abominate
  abominating
  abomination
aboriginal
  aboriginally
  aborigine
abort
  abortion
  abortionist
  abortive
abound
about
  about-face
above
  above-board
abracadabra
abrade (to scrape)
  abrading
abrasion
  abrasive
abreast
abridge
  abridgement
  abridging
  abridgment
abroad
abrogate
  abrogating
  abrogation
abrupt
abscess
  abscesses (*pl.*)
abscissa (geometry)
  abscissas, abscissae (*pl.*)
abscond
absent
  absence
  absented
  absentee
  absenteeism
  absently
  absent-minded
  absents (he, she)

absinth
  absinthe
absolute
  absolutely
absolve
  absolution
  absolving
absorb (to take into)
  absorbency
  absorbent
  absorption
  absorptive
abstain
  abstainer
  abstention
abstemious
  abstemiously
abstinence
  abstinent
abstract
  abstraction
  abstractor
  abstracter
abstruse
  abstrusely
  abstruseness
absurd
  absurdity
  absurdities (*pl.*)
  absurdly
abundance
  abundant
  abundantly
abuse
  abusing
  abusive
  abusively
abut
  abutment
  abuts
  abutted
  abutting
abysmal
  abysmally
abyss

abysses (*pl.*)
acacia
academy
  academies (*pl.*)
  academia
  academic
  academical
  academically
  academician
  academies'
    (of the academies)
  academy's
    (of the academy)
accede
  acceding
  accession
accelerate
  accelerating
  acceleration
  accelerator
accent
  accent's (of the accent)
  accents' (of the accents)
accentuate
  accentuating
  accentuation
accept
  acceptability
  acceptable
  acceptance
access (approach)
  accesses (*pl.*)
  accessibility
  accessible
  accessibly
accession (*from* accede)
accessory, accessary
  accessories (*pl.*)
accidence (*grammar*)
accident
  accidents (*pl.*)
  accidental
  accidentally
acclaim
  acclamation

acclimatise
  acclimatize
  acclimatisation
  acclimatization
  acclimatising
  acclimatizing
accolade
accommodate
  accommodating
  accommodation
accompany
  accompanied
  accompanies
  accompaniment
  accompanist
  accompanist's
    (of the accompanist)
  accompanists'
    (of the accompanists)
  accompanying
accomplice
    (partner in crime)
accomplish
  accomplished
  accomplishes
  accomplishment
accord
  accordance
  according
accordion
    (musical instrument)
accost
account
  accountability
  accountable
  accountancy
  accountant
  accountant's
    (of the accountant)
  accountants'
    (of the accountants)
accoutrements
  accouterments
accredit
  accreditation

accredited
accrediting
accretion
accrue
  accrual
  accruing
accumulate
  accumulating
  accumulation
  accumulator
accurate
  accuracy
  accurately
accursed, accurst
accusative (*grammar*)
accuse
  accusation
  accusatory
  accuser
  accusing
accustom
  accustomed
ace
acerbate (to embitter)
  acerbating
  acerbic
  acerbity (bitterness)
acetate
  acetic (acid)
acetylene
ache
  aching
achieve
  achievable
  achievement
  achieving
achromatic
acid
  acidic
  acidified
  acidify
  acidifying
  acidity
acidosis
acknowledge

acknowledgement
acknowledging
acknowledgment
acme (top)
acne (pimple)
acolyte (attendant)
aconite (plant, drug)
acorn
acoustic
  acoustical
  acoustically
  acoustics
acquaint
  acquaintance
  acquaintanceship
acquiesce
  acquiescence
  acquiescent
  acquiescing
acquire
  acquirement
  acquiring
  acquisition
  acquisitive
acquit (to pardon)
  acquits
  acquittal
  acquitted
  acquitting
acre
  acreage
acrid
  acridity
acrimonious
  acrimoniously
  acrimony
acrobat
  acrobatic
  acrobatically
acronym
acrophobia
    (dread of heights)
acropolis
across
acrostic

acrylic
act
  actable
  acting
action
  actionable
activate
  activating
  activation
active
  actively
  activism
  activist
  activity
  activities (*pl.*)
actor
  actor's (of the actor)
  actors' (of the actors)
actress
  actresses (*pl.*)
  actress's (of the actress)
  actresses'
      (of the actresses)
actual
  actuality
  actualities (*pl.*)
  actually
actuary
  actuaries (*pl.*)
  actuarial
  actuaries'
      (of the actuaries)
  actuary's
      (of the actuary)
actuate
  actuating
  actuation
acumen
acupuncture
acute
  acuity
  acutely
  acuteness
adage (proverb)
adagio

adagios (*pl.*)
adamant
adapt (to make suitable)
adaptability
adaptable
adaptation
adaption
adaptive
adaptor (device)
adapter (person)
add
addendum
addenda (*pl.*)
adder (snake)
addict
addiction
addictive
addition
additional
additionally
additive
addle
addled
addling
address
addresses (*pl.*)
addressed
addressee
addresses
adduce
adducing
adenoid
adenoidal
adept (clever)
adequate
adequacy
adequately
adhere
adherence
adherent
adhering
adhesion
adhesive
ad hoc
adieu

adieus, adieux (*pl.*)
ad infinitum
adipose (fat)
adiposity
adjacent
adjacency
adjacencies (*pl.*)
adjacently
adjective (*grammar*)
adjectival
adjectivally
adjoin (to be next to)
adjoining
adjourn (to postpone)
adjournment
adjudicate
adjudicating
adjudication
adjudicator
adjunct
adjust
adjustable
adjuster
adjustment
adjutant (officer)
adjuvant (helpful)
ad-lib (to improvise)
ad-libbed
ad-libbing
ad-libs
adman
admen (*pl.*)
administer (an oath)
administered
administering
administrate
(to manage)
administrating
administration
administrative
administrator
admiral
admiral's
(of the admiral)

admirals'
(of the admirals)
admiralty
admire
admirable
admirably
admiration
admirer
admiring
admission
admissibility
admissible
admissibly
admit
admits
admittance
admitted
admitting
admixture
admonish
admonished
admonishes
admonition
admonitory
ad nauseam
ado (fuss)
adolescent
adolescents (*pl.*)
adolescence
adolescent's
(of the adolescent)
adolescents'
(of the adolescents)
adopt
adopter
adoption
adoptive
adore
adorable
adorably
adoration
adorer
adoring
adorn
adornment

adrenalin
adrift
adroit (clever)
adsorb (on surface)
adsorbent
adsorption
adulate (to flatter)
adulating
adulation
adult (grown up)
adulterate
(to make less pure)
adulterant
adulterating
adulteration
adultery
adulterer
adulterer's
(of the adulterer)
adulterers'
(of the adulterers)
adulteress (*fem.*)
adulteresses (*pl.*)
adulteress's
(of the adulteress)
adulteresses'
(of the adulteresses)
adulterous
adulterously
advance
advancement
advancing
advantage
advantageous
advantageously
advent (arrival)
Advent
(time before Christmas)
adventitious (accidental)
adventitiously
adventure
adventurer
adventuring
adventurous
adventurously

adverb
adverbial
adversary (enemy)
adversaries (*pl.*)
adversary's
(of the adversary)
adversaries'
(of the adversaries)
adverse (unfavourable)
adversely
adversity (misfortune)
advertise
advertisement
advertiser
advertising
advice (suggestion)
advise (to give advice)
advisability
advisable
advisedly (deliberately)
adviser, advisor
advising
advisory
advocate (lawyer)
advocate's
(of the advocate)
advocates'
(of the advocates)
advocate (to recommend)
advocacy
advocating
advocation
aegis
aegises (*pl.*)
aeon
aerate
aerating
aeration
aerator
aerial (in the air)
aerially
aerial (radio)
aerobatics
aerodrome
airdrome

aerodynamics
aerofoil
airfoil
aeronaut
aeronaut's
(of the aeronaut)
aeronauts'
(of the aeronauts)
aeronautical
aeronautics
aeroplane
airplane
aerosol
aerospace
aesthete
esthete
aesthetic
esthetic
aesthetically
esthetically
aestheticism
estheticism
afar (distant)
affable
affability
affably
affair
affect (to influence)
affectation (pretence)
affection (love)
affectionate
affectionately
affidavit
affiliate
affiliating
affiliation
affinity
affinities (*pl.*)
affirm
affirmation
affirmative
affirmatively
affix
afflict
affliction

affluent
affluence
afford
afforest
afforestation
affray
affrays (*pl.*)
affront
aficionado
afield
afloat
aforesaid
afraid
afresh
Afrikaans
after
aftermath
afternoon
afterthought
afterwards
again
against
agape
agate
age
aged
ageing
ageless
agelessness
aging
agency
agencies (*pl.*)
agency's
    (of the agency)
agencies'
    (of the agencies)
agenda
agent
agglomerate
agglomeration
aggrandise
aggrandize
aggrandisement
aggrandizement
aggrandising

aggrandizing
aggravate
aggravating
aggravation
aggregate (total)
aggregation
aggregate
    (used in concrete)
aggression
aggressive
aggressively
aggressiveness
aggressor
aggrieve
aghast
agile
agilely
agility
agitate
agitating
agitation
agitator
aglow
agnostic
agnosticism
ago
agog
agony
agonies (*pl.*)
agonise
agonize
agonising
agonizing
agoraphobia
    (dread of open spaces)
agrarian
agree
agreeable
agreeably
agreed
agreeing
agreement
agriculture
agricultural
agriculturist

agriculturalist
aground
ague
ahead
ahoy
aid
aide (helper)
aiding
aide-de-camp
aides-de-camp (*pl.*)
ail (to be ill)
ailing
ailment
aileron
aim
aimless
aimlessly
aimlessness
air
airborne
air-conditioned
aircraft
aircraftman
airfield
air force
air hostess
air hostesses (*pl.*)
airing
airless
airlessness
airlift
air line
airline
airlock
airmail
airman
airmen (*pl.*)
airplane (*see* aeroplane)
airport
air raid
airspace
airtight
airworthiness
airworthy
airy

6

airily
airiness
airy-fairy
aisle (church gangway)
ajar
akimbo
akin
alabaster
à la carte
alacrity
à la mode
alarm
  alarmist
alas
albatross
  albatrosses (*pl.*)
albeit
albino
  albinos (*pl.*)
  albinism
album
albumen (white of egg)
albumin (protein)
alchemy
  alchemist
alcohol
  alcoholic
  alcoholism
alcove
alderman
  aldermen (*pl.*)
  aldermanic
  aldermanry
  alderman's
      (of the alderman)
  aldermanship
  aldermen's
      (of the aldermen)
ale (beer)
alert
  alertly
  alertness
alfresco
alga
  algae (*pl.*)

algebra
  algebraic
  algebraical
  algebraically
alias
  aliases (*pl.*)
alibi
  alibis (*pl.*)
alien
  alienable
  alienate
  alienating
  alienation
  alienator
alight (to get down)
alight (lit up, on fire)
align, aline
  alignment, alinement
alike
aliment (food)
  alimentary canal
alimony
alive
alkali
  alkalis (*pl.*)
  alkalies (*pl.*)
  alkaline
  alkalinity
all-American
allay (to reduce, lessen)
allege
  allegation
  alleged
  allegedly
  alleging
allegiance (loyalty)
allegory (story)
  allegories (*pl.*)
  allegorical
  allegorically
allegro (in music)
  allegretto
alleluia, halleluiah,
          hallelujah
allergy (reaction)

allergies (*pl.*)
allergic
alleviate
  alleviating
  alleviation
alley
  alleys (*pl.*)
alliance
alligator
  alligator's
      (of the alligator)
  alligators'
      (of the alligators)
alliteration
allocate
  allocating
  allocation
allocution (speech)
allot
  allotment
  allots
  allotted
  allotting
allow
  allowable
  allowance
alloy
  alloys (*pl.*)
all right
allude (to mention)
  alluding
allure (to tempt)
  allured
  allurement
  alluring
allusion (*from* allude)
alluvial
ally
  allies (*pl.*)
  alliance
  allied
  allies' (of the allies)
  allying
  ally's (of the ally)
alma mater

almanac
almighty
almond
almoner
almost
alms (charity)
aloe (plant)
aloft
alone
along
aloof
  aloofly
  aloofness
aloud
alp
  alpine
alpaca
alphabet
  alphabetical
  alphabetically
already
also
  also-ran
altar (in church)
alter (to change)
  alterable
  alteration
  altered
  altering
altercate (to quarrel)
  altercating
  altercation
alternate
  alternating
  alternation
  alternator
alternative
  alternatively
although
altimeter
altitude
alto
  altos (*pl.*)
altogether
altruism

altruist
altruistic
altruistically
alum
aluminium
  aluminum
always
amalgam
  amalgamate
  amalgamating
  amalgamation
amanuensis
  amanuenses (*pl.*)
amass
amateur
  amateurish
  amateurishly
  amateurishness
  amateurism
amaze
  amazement
  amazing
ambassador
  ambassadorial
  ambassador's
    (of the ambassador)
  ambassadors'
    (of the ambassadors)
  ambassadress (*fem.*)
  ambassadresses (*pl.*)
  ambassadress's
    (of the ambassadress)
  ambassadresses'
  (of the ambassadresses)
amber
ambi- (both)
  ambidextrous
  ambience
  ambient
  ambiguity
  ambiguous
  ambiguously
  ambit (extent)
  ambition
  ambitious

  ambitiously
ambivalence
  ambivalent
amble
  ambling
ambulance
  ambulant (able to walk)
ambush
  ambushes (*pl.*)
ameliorate
  ameliorating
  amelioration
amen
amenable
  amenably
amend (to correct)
  amendment
amenity
  amenities (*pl.*)
American
  Americana
  Americanise
  Americanize
  Americanising
  Americanizing
  Americanism
amethyst
amiable (good tempered)
  amiability
  amiably
amicable (friendly)
  amicability
  amicably
amid
  amidships
  amidst
amiss
amity
ammeter
ammonia
ammunition
amnesia (loss of memory)
amnesty (pardon)
  amnesties (*pl.*)
amoeba

amoebas, amoebae (*pl.*)
amoebic
amok, amuck
among
  amongst
amoral (not moral)
  amorally
amorous (loving)
  amorously
  amorousness
amorphous
amortise
  amortize
  amortising
  amortizing
  amortisation
  amortization
amount
amour
ampere
  ammeter
  amperage
ampersand (and sign)
amphetamine
amphibia
  amphibian
  amphibious
amphitheatre
  amphitheater
ample
  amplitude
  amply
amplify
  amplification
  amplified
  amplifier
  amplifies
  amplifying
ampoule
  ampul
amputate
  amputating
  amputation
  amputee
amuck, amok

amulet
amuse
  amusement
  amusing
anachronism
  anachronistic
anaemia
  anaemic
anaesthetic
  anesthetic
anaesthesia
  anesthesia
anaesthetisation
  anesthetization
anaesthetise
  anesthetize
anaesthetising
  anesthetizing
anaesthetist
  anesthetist
anagram
anal (*from* anus)
analgesic (pain-killer)
  analgesia
analogous
  analog (computer)
  analogical
  analogue
  analogy
  analogies (*pl.*)
analyse
  analyze
  analysing
  analyzing
  analysis
  analyses (*pl.*)
  analyst
  analyst's
    (of the analyst)
  analysts'
    (of the analysts)
  analytic
  analytical
  analytically
anarchist

anarchic
anarchical
anarchism
anarchist's
  (of the anarchist)
anarchists'
  (of the anarchists)
anarchy
anathema
anathemas (*pl.*)
anatomy
anatomical
anatomic
anatomically
anatomise
anatomize
anatomised
anatomized
anatomising
anatomizing
anatomist
ancestor
  ancestor's
    (of the ancestor)
  ancestors'
    (of the ancestors)
  ancestral
  ancestress
  ancestresses (*pl.*)
  ancestress's
    (of the ancestress)
  ancestresses'
    (of the ancestresses)
  ancestry
anchor
  anchorage
  anchored
  anchoring
anchovy
  anchovies (*pl.*)
ancient
ancillary
anecdote
anecdotal
anemometer (wind gauge)

anemone (flower)
aneroid
aneurysm
anew
angel
  angelic
  angelical
  angelically
  angel's (of the angel)
  angels' (of the angels)
anger
  angered
  angering
  angrier
  angrily
  angry
angina
angle (corner)
angle (to fish)
  angler
  angling
Anglican
  Anglicanism
anglice (in English)
anglicise
  anglicize
  anglicism
Anglomania
Anglophile
Anglophobe
  Anglophobia
angostura
anguish
angular
  angularity
anhydrous
aniline
animal
  animalcule
  animal's (of the animal)
  animals'
      (of the animals)
animate
  animatedly
  animating

animation
animosity (dislike)
  animosities (*pl.*)
animus (hostility)
aniseed
ankle
  anklet
annal (story of one year)
  annals
  annalist
anneal
  (to toughen metal, etc.)
annex (to join)
  annexation
annexe (of house)
  annex
annihilate
  annihilating
  annihilation
anniversary
  anniversaries (*pl.*)
annotate
  annotating
  annotation
  annotator
announce
  announcement
  announcer
  announcing
annoy
  annoyance
annual (yearly)
  annually
annuity
  annuities (*pl.*)
  annuitant
annul
  annulled
  annulling
  annulment
  annuls
annular (ring-like)
  annularity
annunciate
  annunciating

annunciation
anode
anodyne
anoint
anomalous (irregular)
  anomalously
  anomaly
  anomalies (*pl.*)
anon. (anonymous)
anon (soon)
anonymous (unnamed)
  anonymity
  anonymously
anorak
another
answer
  answerable
  answered
  answering
antacid
antagonise
  antagonize
  antagonising
  antagonizing
  antagonism
  antagonist
antarctic
antecedent
  antecedents (*pl.*)
  antecedence
antechamber
antedate
  antedating
antediluvian
antelope
antenatal
antenna (of insect)
  antennae (*pl.*)
antenna (radio)
  antennas (*pl.*)
anterior
  anteriority
  anteriorly
ante-room
anthem

anther
anthology
  anthologies (*pl.*)
  anthologist
anthracite
anthrax
anthropo- (man)
anthropoid
anthropology
  anthropological
  anthropologist
anthropomorphic
  anthropomorphism
anti-aircraft
antibiotic
antibody
  antibodies (*pl.*)
antic
antichrist
anticipate
  anticipating
  anticipation
  anticipative
  anticipatory
anticlimax
  anticlimaxes (*pl.*)
  anticlimactic
anticyclone
  anticyclonic
antidepressant
antidote
antifreeze
antigen
antihistamine
antilogarithm
antimacassar
antimony
antipathy
  antipathies (*pl.*)
  antipathetic
antipodes
  antipodean
antiquary
  antiquaries (*pl.*)
  antiquarian

antiquarian's
    (of the antiquarian)
  antiquarians'
    (of the antiquarians)
antique (very old)
  antiquated
  antiquity
  antiquities (*pl.*)
antirrhinum
  antirrhinums (*pl.*)
anti-Semitism
  anti-Semite
  anti-Semitic
antiseptic
  antisepsis
  antiseptically
antisocial
  antisocially
antithesis
  antitheses (*pl.*)
antitoxin
  antitoxic
antler
  antlered
antonym
anus
  anal
anvil
anxious
  anxiety
  anxiously
any
  anybody
  anybody's (of anybody)
  anyhow
  anyone
  anyone's (of anyone)
  anything
  anyway
  anywhere
aorta
apace (quickly)
apart
  apartheid
  apartment

apathy
  apathetic
  apathetically
ape
  ape's (of the ape)
  apes' (of the apes)
  apery (monkey-house)
ape (to imitate)
  aping
  apery (imitation)
aperient (laxative)
aperitif (cocktail)
aperture
apex
  apexes (*pl.*)
  apices
aphis (greenfly)
  aphides (*pl.*)
aphorism
  aphoristic
aphrodisiac
apiary (for bees)
  apiaries (*pl.*)
  apiarist
apiculture
apiece (each)
aplomb
apocalypse
  apocalyptic
apocrypha
  apocryphal
apogee
apologia (written excuse)
apology
  apologies (*pl.*)
  apologetic
  apologetically
  apologise
  apologize
  apologising
  apologizing
apophthegm (witticism)
apoplexy
  apoplectic
  apoplectically

11

apostasy
  apostate
  apostatise
  apostatize
a posteriori
apostle
  apostolate
  apostolic
apostrophe
  apostrophise
  apostrophize
  apostrophising
  apostrophizing
apothecary
  apothecaries (*pl.*)
  apothecary's
    (of the apothecary)
  apothecaries'
    (of the apothecaries)
apotheosis
appal
  appall
  appalled
  appalling
  appals (it)
apparatus
  apparatuses (*pl.*)
  apparatus (*pl.*)
apparel
  apparelled
  appareled
apparent
  apparently
apparition (*from* appear)
appeal
  appealing
  appellant
appear
  appearance
  appeared
  appearing
appease
  appeasement
  appeaser
appellation

append
  appendage
appendix
    (addition to a book)
  appendices (*pl.*)
appendix (in anatomy)
  appendixes (*pl.*)
  appendicitis
appertain
  appertaining
appetite
  appetiser
  appetizer
  appetising
  appetizing
applaud
  applause
apple
  apple-cart
  apple-pie
appliqué
apply
  appliance
  applicable
  applicant
  application
  applied
  applying
appoint
  <u>appointment</u>
apportion
  apportioning
apposite (apt)
appraise
  appraisal
  appraisement
  appraising
appreciate
  appreciable
  appreciably
  appreciating
  appreciation
  appreciative
apprehend
  apprehension

apprehensive
apprentice
  apprentice's
    (of the apprentice)
  apprentices'
    (of the apprentices)
  apprenticeship
apprise (to inform)
  apprising
apprize (to value)
  apprizing
appro. (approval)
approach
  approaches (*pl.*)
  approachable
approbation
appropriate
  appropriately
  appropriateness
  appropriating
  appropriation
  appropriator
approve
  approval
  approving
approximate
  approximately
  approximating
  approximation
appurtenance (accessory)
apricot
a priori
apron
apropos
apt
  aptitude
  aptly
  aptness
aqua-, aque- (water)
aqualung
aquarium
aquatic
aquatint
aqueduct
aqueous

aquiline (eagle-like)
arabesque
Arabian
  Arabic
arable
arbiter
  arbitrage
arbitrary
  arbitrarily
  arbitrariness
arbitrate
  arbitrating
  arbitration
  arbitrator
arbour (garden bower)
  arbor
arc
  arced
  arcked
  arcing
  arcking
arcade
arch (cheeky)
  archly
  archness
arch (of building)
  arches (*pl.*)
archaeology
  archaeological
  archaeologically
  archaeologist
archaic
  archaism
  archaistic
archangel
archbishop
  archbishopric
  archbishop's
    (of the archbishop)
  archbishops'
    (of the archbishops)
archdeacon
  archdeaconry
archdiocese
archduke

archducal
archduchess
  archduchesses (*pl.*)
  archduchy
arch-enemy
archer
  archery
archetype
  archetypal
archiepiscopal
  archiepiscopate
archipelago
  archipelagos,
    archipelagoes(*pl.*)
architect
  architect's
    (of the architect)
  architects'
    (of the architects)
  architectural
  architecturally
  architecture
architrave
archive
  archivist
arctic
ardent
  ardently
  ardour
  ardor
arduous
  arduously
are
  aren't (are not)
area (space)
arena
argosy
argot (slang)
argue
  arguable
  arguably
  arguing
  argument
  argumentative
aria (song)

arid
  aridity
aright
arise
  arisen
  arising
  arose
aristocracy
  aristocrat
  aristocratically
arithmetic
  arithmetical
  arithmetically
  arithmetician
ark (Noah's)
arm (of body)
  armchair
  armful
  armlet
  arm's (of the arm)
  arms' (of the arms)
armada
Armageddon
armament
armature
armistice
armour
  armor
  armourer
  armorer
  armoury
  armory
  armouries (*pl.*)
  armories (pl.)
arms (coat of)
  armorial
arms (weapons)
army
  armies (*pl.*)
  army's (of the army)
  armies' (of the armies)
aroma
  aromatic
arose (*from* arise)
around

13

arouse
  arousal
  arousing
arraign (to accuse)
  arraignment
arrange (to put in order)
  arranged
  arrangement
  arranging
arrant (thorough)
array
arrears
arrest
arrive
  arrival
  arriving
arrogant (proud)
  arrogance
  arrogantly
arrogate
      (to claim unduly)
  arrogating
  arrogation
arrow
arrowroot
arsenal
arsenic
  arsenical
  arsenious
arson
  arsonist
art
  artist
  artiste (performer)
  artistic
  artistically
  artistry
  artist's (of the artist)
  artists' (of the artists)
artefact, artifact
artery
  arteries (pl.)
  arterial
artesian
artful

artfully
artfulness
arthritis
arthritic
artichoke
article
articulate
  articulating
  articulation
  articulately
artifact, artefact
artifice
artificer
artificial
  artificiality
  artificially
artillery
  artilleryman
  artillerymen (pl.)
  artilleryman's
    (of the artilleryman)
  artillerymen's
    (of the artillerymen)
artisan
artist (see art)
artiste (performer)
artless
  artlessly
  artlessness
arty
Aryan
asbestos
  asbestosis
ascend (to go up)
  ascendancy,
                    ascendency
  ascendant
  ascension
  ascent (going up)
ascertain
  ascertainable
  ascertainment
ascetic (abstinent)
  ascetically
  asceticism

ascribe
  ascribable
  ascribing
  ascription
aseptic (surgically clean)
  asepsis
ash (cinders)
  ashes (pl.)
  ashen
  ashy
ash (tree)
ashamed
ashore
Asia
  Asiatic
aside
asinine
  asininity
ask
askance
askew
asleep
asp (snake)
asparagus
  asparagus (pl.)
aspect
aspen (tree)
asperity (harshness)
  asperities (pl.)
aspersion (slander)
asphalt
asphyxia
  asphyxiant
  asphyxiate
  asphyxiating
  asphyxiation
aspic (jelly)
aspidistra
aspirate (letter H)
aspire (to seek to attain)
  aspirant
  aspiration
  aspired
  aspiring
aspirin

ass
  asses (*pl.*)
  ass's (of the ass)
  asses' (of the asses)
assail
  assailant
assassin
  assassin's
    (of the assassin)
  assassins'
    (of the assassins)
  assassinate
  assassinating
  assassination
  assassinator
assault
  assaulter
assay (to test)
  assayer
assemble
  assemblage
  assembling
assembly
  assemblies (*pl.*)
assent (agreement)
assert (to insist)
  assertion
  assertive
assess (to fix amount)
  assessable
  assessment
  assessor
asset (possession)
assiduous
  assiduity
  assiduously
assign
  assignable
  assignation
  assignee
  assignment
assimilate
  assimilating
  assimilation
assist

assistance (help)
assistant (helper)
assize
associate
  associate's
    (of the associate)
  associates'
    (of the associates)
  associating
  association
assort
  assortment
assuage
  assuagement
  assuaging
assume
  assuming
  assumption
assure
  assurance
  assuredly
  assurer
  assuring
aster (plant)
asterisk
asteroid (planet)
astern
asthma
  asthmatic
astir (moving about)
astigmatism
  astigmatic
astonish
  astonishment
astound
astral
astrakhan
astray
astride
astringent
  astringency
astrology
  astrologer
astronaut
  astronautics

astronomy
  astronomer
  astronomic
  astronomical
  astronomically
astute
  astutely
  astuteness
asunder
asylum
asymmetry
  asymmetric
  asymmetrical
  asymmetrically
atheist
  atheism
athlete
  athlete's (of the athlete)
  athletes'
    (of the athletes)
  athletics
atlas
  atlases (*pl.*)
atmosphere
  atmospheric
atoll
atom
  atomic
  atomically
  atomisation
  atomization
  atomise
  atomize
  atomiser
  atomizer
  atomising
  atomizing
atone
  atonement
  atoning
atrocious
  atrociously
  atrocity
  atrocities (*pl.*)
atrophy

atrophied
atrophies
atrophying
attach (to fix)
  attachable
  attachment
attaché
  attaché case
attack (to fight against)
  attacker
attain
  attainable
  attainment
attempt
attend
  attendance
      (being present)
  attendant
      (person present)
  attendants (*pl.*)
  attention
  attentive
  attentively
attenuate
  attenuating
  attenuation
  attenuator
attest
  attestation
  attestor
  attestator
attic
attire (clothes, to clothe)
  attiring
attitude
attorney
  attorneys (*pl.*)
  attorney's
      (of the attorney)
  attorneys'
      (of the attorneys)
attract
  attraction
  attractive
  attractiveness

attribute
  attributable
  attributing
  attribution
  attributive
  attributively
attrition
attune
atypical (not typical)
  atypically
aubergine
auburn
auction
  auctioneer
  auctioneer's
      (of the auctioneer)
  auctioneers'
      (of the auctioneers)
  auctioning
audacious
  audaciously
  audacity
audible
  audibility
  audibly
audience
audio- (hearing)
  audiometer
  audiometric
  audiometry
  audio-typist
  audio-visual
audit
  audited
  auditing
  auditor
  auditor's
      (of the auditor)
  auditors'
      (of the auditors)
  audition
  auditorium
au fond
auger (tool)
aught (anything)

augment
  augmentation
au gratin
augur (to predict)
  augured
  auguring
  augurs
  augury
  auguries (*pl.*)
August (month)
august (noble)
auk (sea-bird)
aunt
  auntie, aunty
  aunt's (of the aunt)
  aunts' (of the aunts)
au pair
aura
  aurae (*pl.*)
  auras (*pl.*)
aural (by ear)
  aurally
au revoir
auspices
auspicious (favourable)
  auspiciously
austere
  austerely
  austerity
  austerities (*pl.*)
autarchy (absolute power)
  autarchies (*pl.*)
autarky (self-sufficiency)
authentic
  authentically
  authenticate
  authenticating
  authentication
  authenticity
author
  author's (of the author)
  authors'
      (of the authors)
  authoress (*fem.*)
  authoresses (*pl.*)

authoress's
(of the authoress)
authoresses'
(of the authoresses)
authorship
authorise
authorize
authorisation
authorization
authorising
authorizing
authority
authorities (*pl.*)
authoritarian
authoritative
authoritatively
autism
autistic
auto- (self)
autobiography
autobiographies (*pl.*)
autobiographic
autobiographical
autobiographically
autocrat
autocracy
autocracies (*pl.*)
autocratic
autocratically
autogenous
autogiro, autogyro
autograph
automation
automatic
automatically
automatism
automaton
automatons, automata
(*pl.*)
automobile
automotive
autonomous
autonomy
autopilot
autopsy

autopsies (*pl.*)
autostrada
autostrade (*pl.*)
auto-suggestion
autumn
autumnal
auxiliary
avail
availability
available
avalanche
avant-garde
avarice
avaricious
avenge
avenger
avenging
avenue
aver
averred
averring
avers
average
averaging
averse (opposed)
aversion (dislike)
avert (to prevent)
avertable
avertible
aviary (for birds)
aviaries (*pl.*)
aviation
aviator
aviator's
(of the aviator)
aviators'
(of the aviators)
avid
avidity
avidly
avocado
avocation
avoid
avoidable
avoidably

avoidance
avuncular
await
awaited
awaiting
awake
awaken
awakening
awaking
awoke
awaked
award
aware
awareness
away
awe
awesome
awful
awfully
awfulness
aweigh (anchor lifted)
awhile
awkward
awkwardly
awkwardness
awl (tool)
awning
awry (crooked)
axe
ax
axing
axial
axially
axiom
axiomatic
axiomatically
axis
axes (*pl.*)
axle
ayah
ay, aye (yes)
azalea
azimuth
azimuthal
azure

B

babble (of voices)
  babbler
  babbling
babe
Babel (tower of)
baboon
baby
  babies (*pl.*)
  baby's (of the baby)
  babies' (of the babies)
  babyish
  baby-sitter
bachelor
  bachelor's
      (of the bachelor)
  bachelors'
      (of the bachelors)
  bachelorhood
bacillus
  bacilli (*pl.*)
  bacillary
back
  backache
  back bench
  back benches (*pl.*)
  back-bencher
  backbone
  back-breaking
  backed
  backer
  backgammon
  background
  backstairs
  backwater
backbite
  backbiter
  backbiting
backdate
  backdating

backfire
  backfiring
backward
  backwardness
bacon
bacterium
  bacteria (*pl.*)
  bacterial
  bacteriological
  bacteriologist
  bacteriology
bad
  badly
  bad-tempered
bade (from bid)
badge
badger (animal)
badger (to pester)
  badgered
  badgering
badminton
baffle
  baffling
bag
  bagged
  baggier
  bagging
  baggy
bagatelle
baggage
bagpipe
bail (cricket)
bail (security)
bail (*see* bale)
bailiff
  bailiff's (of the bailiff)
  bailiffs' (of the bailiffs)
bairn
bait (for fish)
bait (to torment)
baize
bake
  baker
  baker's (of the baker)
  bakers' (of the bakers)

bakery
  bakeries (*pl.*)
  baking
baksheesh (tip)
  bakshish
balalaika
balance
  balancing
balcony
  balconies (*pl.*)
bald
  bald-headed
  baldness
balderdash
bale, bail
      (out of aeroplane)
  baling, bailing
bale, bail
    (to pump out a boat)
bale (of merchandise)
  baling
baleful (evil)
  balefully
balk, baulk
       (billiards, timber)
balk, baulk (to hinder)
ball
  ball-bearing
  ball bearing
  ball-point
ballad
ballast
ballerina
  ballerina's
      (of the ballerina)
  ballerinas'
      (of the ballerinas)
ballet
  ballet dancer
ballistic
balloon
ballot (to vote)
  balloted
  balloting
ballyhoo

balm
  balmy (fragrant)
baloney, boloney
balsam
baluster
  balustrade
bamboo
bamboozle
  bamboozling
ban
  banned
  banning
  bans
banal
  banality
  banalities (*pl.*)
  banally
banana
band
  bandsman
  bandsmen (*pl.*)
  bandsman's
      (of the bandsman)
  bandsmen's
      (of the bandsmen)
bandage
  bandaging
bandit
  banditry
bandoleer, bandolier
bandy (crooked)
  bandy-legged
bandy
  (to exchange remarks)
  bandied
  bandies
  bandying
bane (ruin)
  baneful
  banefully
bang
bangle
banish
  banishment
banister, bannister

banjo
  banjos (*pl.*)
bank
  banker
  bank holiday
  banknote
bankrupt
  bankruptcy
  bankruptcies (*pl.*)
  bankrupt's
      (of the bankrupt)
  bankrupts'
      (of the bankrupts)
banner
banns (for wedding)
banquet
  banqueting
bantam
  bantam-weight
banter (to tease)
  bantered
  bantering
baptise
  baptize
  baptising
  baptizing
  baptism
bar (of pub)
  barmaid
  barmaid's
      (of the barmaid)
  barmaids'
      (of the barmaids)
  barman
  barmen (*pl.*)
  barman's
      (of the barman)
  barmen's
      (of the barmen)
  bartender
bar (to prevent)
  barred
  barring
  bars
bar (of metal, etc.)

bar (except)
bar (law court)
barb
  barbed wire
barbarian
  barbaric
  barbarism
  barbarous
  barbarously
barbecue
barber
  barber's (of the barber)
  barbers' (of the barbers)
barbitone
  barbiturate
  barbituric
bard
bare (uncovered)
  bareback
  barefaced
  barefoot
  bareheaded
  barelegged
  bareness
barely (scarcely)
bargain
barge (boat)
  bargee
  barge-pole
barge (to push)
  barging
baritone
  baritone's
      (of the baritone)
  baritones'
      (of the baritones)
barium
bark (dog's)
bark (of tree)
bark, barque (ship)
barley
  barley sugar
barmy (silly)
  barmier
  barmily

19

barn
barnyard
barnacle
barometer
barometric
baron
baron's (of the baron)
barons' (of the barons)
baroness (*fem.*)
baronesses (*pl.*)
baroness's
(of the baroness)
baronesses'
(of the baronesses)
baronet
baronial
barony
baroque
barque, bark (ship)
barrack (for soldiers)
barrack (to jeer)
barrage
barrel
barrelled
barreled
barren
barrenness
barricade
barricading
barrier
barrister
barrister's
(of the barrister)
barristers'
(of the barristers)
barrow
barter
bartered
barterer
bartering
basalt
base
baseless
basely
baseness

basing
basement
bashful
bashfully
bashfulness
basic
basically
basin
basis
bases (*pl.*)
bask
basket
basketball
bas-relief
bass, bast (fibre)
bass (fish)
bass (music)
basses (*pl.*)
bass's (of the bass)
basses' (of the basses)
bass clef
basset (hound)
bassoon
bast, bass (fibre)
bastard
bastardy
baste (cooking or sewing)
basting
bastion
bat
batsman
batsman's
(of the batsman)
batsmen's
(of the batsmen)
batted
batting
batch
batches (*pl.*)
bate (to restrain)
bated breath
bating
bath
bathing
bathe (to go swimming)

bather
bathing
bathos
batik
batman (soldier servant)
batmen (*pl.*)
batman's
(of the batman)
batmen's
(of the batmen)
baton (conductor's)
battalion
batten (to close)
battened
battening
batter (to beat)
battered
battering
batter (for pastry)
battery
batteries (*pl.*)
battle
battleaxe
battleax
battledress
battleship
battling
battlement
batty (crazy)
battier
bauble (cheap jewel)
baulk, balk
(billiards, timber)
baulk, balk (to hinder)
bauxite
bawd (debauched person)
bawdier
bawdiest
bawdy
bawl (to shout)
bay (laurel)
bay-leaf
bay (gulf)
bay (of a hound)
baying

bay (compartment)
  bay window
bayonet
  bayoneted
  bayoneting
bazaar
bazooka
be
  been
  being
beach (shore)
  beachcomber
  beachhead
beacon
bead
  beady
beadle
beagle
  beagling
beak
beaker (cup)
beam
bean (vegetable)
  beanfeast
  beanstalk
bear (animal)
  bear's (of the bear)
  bears' (of the bears)
bear (to carry)
  bearable
  bearer
  bore
  born (of a baby)
  borne (carried)
beard
bearing (of a machine)
beast
  beastlier
  beastliness
  beastly
beat (to hit)
  beaten
  beater
beat (rhythm)
beatific

beau
  beaux (*pl.*)
beauty
  beauties (*pl.*)
  beauteous
  beautician
  beautified
  beautiful
  beautifully
  beautify
  beautifying
beaver
becalm
because
beckon (to signal)
become
  became
  becoming
bed
  bedclothes
  bedded
  bedding
  bedridden
  bedrock
  bed-sitter
  bed-sitting-room
bedaub
bedevil
  bedevilled
  bedeviled
  bedevilling
  bedeviling
bedlam
  bedlamite
bedouin
bedraggle
bee
  bee's (of the bee)
  bees' (of the bees)
  beehive
  beeswax
beech (tree)
beef
  beefeater
  beefier

  beefsteak
  beefy
beeline
been (*from* be)
beer (drink)
  beeriness
  beery
beet (vegetable)
  beetroot
beetle (insect)
  beetle's (of the beetle)
  beetles' (of the beetles)
befall
  befallen
  befell
befit
  befitted
  befitting
before
  beforehand
befoul
befriend
beg
  beggar
  beggared
  beggaring
  beggarliness
  beggarly
  beggar's (of the beggar)
  beggars'
      (of the beggars)
  beggary
  begged
  begging
  begs
beget
  begetter
  begot
  begotten
begin
  began
  beginner
  beginner's
      (of the beginner)

beginners'
  (of the beginners)
beginning
begins
begun
begone (go away)
begonia
begrudge
  begrudging
beguile
  beguilement
  beguiler
  beguiling
behalf
behave
  behaving
  behaviour
  behavior
behead
  beheaded
behind
  behindhand
behold
  beheld
  beholden
    (under obligation)
  beholder
  beholding
behove (to be necessary)
beige
being
belabour
  belabor
  belaboured
  belabored, belabord
  belabouring
  belaboring
belated
belay (nautical term)
belch
  belched
beleaguer
  beleaguered
  beleaguering
belfry

belfries (*pl.*)
belie
  belying
belief
  believable
  believe
  believer
  believing
belittle
  belittler
  belittling
bell (for ringing)
belladonna
belle (pretty girl)
belles lettres
bellicose
  bellicosity
belligerent
  belligerence
bellow (to shout)
bellows (air pump)
belly
  bellies (*pl.*)
  bellyful
belong
beloved
below (under)
belt
bemoan
bemuse
bench
  benches (*pl.*)
  bencher
bend
  bent
beneath
benediction (blessing)
benefaction (doing good)
benefactor
  benefactor's
    (of the benefactor)
  benefactors'
    (of the benefactors)
  benefactress (*fem.*)
  benefactresses (*pl.*)

benefice (church living)
beneficence (kindness)
  beneficent
beneficial (advantageous)
  beneficially
  beneficiary
  beneficiaries (*pl.*)
benefit
  benefited
  benefiter
  benefiting
benevolent
  benevolence
  benevolently
benighted
benign
  benignancy
  benignant
benison (blessing)
bent (skill)
benumb
  benumbed
benzene (petroleum fluid)
benzine (cleaning fluid)
bequeath
  bequest
berate
  berating
bereave
  bereavement
  bereft
  bereaved
beret (cap)
berry (fruit)
  berries (*pl.*)
berserk, berserker
berth (nautical)
beryl
beseech
  beseeched
  beseeches
  besought
beset
  besetting
beside

besides
besiege
  besieging
besom (broom)
besotted
besought (*from* beseech)
bespeak
  bespoke
  bespoken
best
bestial
  bestialism
  bestiality
  bestialities (*pl.*)
  bestially
bestir
  bestirred
  bestirring
  bestirs
bestow
  bestowal
bestride
  bestriding
  bestrode
bet
  betted
  better
  betting
bête noire
  bêtes noires (*pl.*)
betel (leaf)
betide
betimes
betoken
betray
  betrayal
  betrayed
betroth
  betrothal
  betrothed
better
  best
better (to improve)
  bettered
  bettering

betterment
between
betwixt
bevel
  bevelled
  beveled
  bevelling
  beveling
beverage
bevy
  bevies (*pl.*)
bewail
beware
bewilder
  bewildered
  bewildering
  bewilderment
  bewilders
bewitch
  bewitched
  bewitches
beyond
biannual (half-yearly)
  biannually
bias
  biased
  biases (*pl.*)
  biasing
bible
  biblical
bibliography
  bibliographies (*pl.*)
  bibliographer
  bibliographic
  bibliographical
  bibliographically
bibliophile, bibliophil
bibulous
bicarbonate
bicentenary
  bicentenaries (*pl.*)
  bicentennial
biceps
bicker
  bickered

bickering
bicycle
  bicycling
  bicyclist
bid
  bidden
  bidder
  bidding
  bade
bide (to wait)
  biding
bidet
biennial (every two years)
  biennially
bier (coffin stand)
bifocal
bifurcate
  bifurcating
  bifurcation
big
  bigger
bigamy
  bigamies (*pl.*)
  bigamist
  bigamist's
      (of the bigamist)
  bigamists'
      (of the bigamists)
  bigamous
  bigamously
bigot
  bigoted
  bigotry
bigwig
bijou
  bijoux (*pl.*)
bike (bicycle)
bikini
bilateral
  bilaterally
bilberry
  bilberries (*pl.*)
bile
  biliary
bilge

bilingual
  bilingualism
  bilinguist
bilious
  biliousness
bilk (to cheat)
bill
  bill of fare
bill (beak)
billet
  billeted
  billetee
  billeter
  billeting
billet doux
  billets doux (*pl.*)
billiards
billion (UK million million)
billion
  (US thousand million)
  billionaire
billow
  billowy
bimonthly
  (every two months)
  bimonthly
  (twice a month)
bin
binary
binaural
bind
  binder
  bindery
  bound
binge
bingo
binnacle
binocular
binomial
bio- (*life*)
biochemist
  biochemical
  biochemistry
biography
  biographies (*pl.*)

biographer
biographical
biographically
biology
biological
biologically
biologist
biologist's
    (of the biologist)
biologists'
    (of the biologists)
bionics
biopsy
  biopsies (*pl.*)
bipartite
bipartisan
biped
biplane
bipolar
birch (tree)
birch (whip)
bird
  bird's (of the bird)
  birds' (of the birds)
  bird's-eye
  birdie (golf)
birth
  birthday
  birthplace
  birthrate
  birthright
biscuit
bisect
  bisection
  bisector
bisexual
  bisexually
bishop
  bishopric
  bishop's (of the bishop)
  bishops'
    (of the bishops)
bismuth
bison
bistro

bitch
  bitches (*pl.*)
bite
bit
biter
bites
biting
bitten
bitter (beer)
bitter (sour)
  bitterer
  bitterly
  bitterness
bittern (bird)
bitumen
  bituminous
bivalve
bivouac
  bivouacked
  bivouacking
bizarre (unusual)
  bizarrely
  bizarreness
blab
  blabbing
  blabbed
  blabs
black
  blackberry
  blackberries (*pl.*)
  blackbird
  blackbird's
    (of the blackbird)
  blackbirds'
    (of the blackbirds)
  blackboard
  blacken
  blackened
  blackening
  black market
  black marketeer
  blackness
  blackout
  blacked out
  blackguard

blackguardly •
blackguard's
  (of the blackguard)
blackguards'
  (of the blackguards)
blackmail
 blackmailed
 blackmailer
blacksmith
 blacksmith's
  (of the blacksmith)
 blacksmiths'
  (of the blacksmiths)
bladder
blade
blame
 blameless
 blamelessly
 blaming
blanch (to whiten)
blancmange
bland (gentle)
 blandly
blandish (to flatter)
 blandishment
blank
 blank cheque
 blank check
blanket
 blanketed
 blanketing
blare
 blaring
blarney
blasé
blaspheme
 blasphemer
 blaspheming
 blasphemous
 blasphemously
 blasphemy
 blasphemies (*pl.*)
blast
 blast-off
blatant

blatancy
blatantly
blaze
blazing
blazer
blazon (coat of arms)
bleach
bleak
 bleaker
 bleakly
 bleakness
blear
 blear-eyed
 blearily
 bleariness
 bleary
 bleary-eyed
bleat
bleed
 bled
 bleeder
blemish
 blemishes (*pl.*)
blench
 blenched
 blenches
blend
 blender
bless
 blessed (sacred)
 blest
 blesses
 blessing
blew (*from* blow)
blight
 blighter
blind
 blind alley
 blindfold
 blindly
 blindness
blink
 blinkered
bliss
 blissful

blissfully
blissfulness
blister
 blistered
 blistering
blithe
 blithely
 blitheness
blithering
blizzard
bloat
 bloated
 bloater
blob
bloc (group)
block
 blockage
 blockbuster
blockade
 blockading
blockhead
bloke
 bloke's (of the bloke)
 blokes' (of the blokes)
blond (*male*)
blonde (*fem.*)
blood
 bloodcurdling
 bloodhound
 blood pressure
 bloodshed
 bloodshot
 bloodthirsty
 blood vessel
 bloody
bloom
 bloomer
blossom
blot
 blots
 blotted
 blotter
 blotting
blotch
 blotches (*pl.*)

blotchy
blouse
blow
  blew
  blower
  blown
  blows
blowzy (red-faced)
blub (to cry)
  blubbed
  blubbing
  blubs
blubber (of whale)
  blubbery
blubber (to sob)
  blubbered
bludgeon
  bludgeoned
  bludgeoning
blue
  bluebell
  blueberry
  blueberries (*pl.*)
  blue-chip
  blue-collar
  blue-eyed
  blueness
  blue-pencil
  blue-pencilled
  blue-penciled
bluff (to deceive)
bluff (hearty)
  bluffness
blunder
  blundered
  blunderer
  blundering
  blunders
blunderbuss
blunt
  bluntly
  bluntness
blur
  blurred
  blurriness

blurs
blurb
blurt
blush
  blushes (*pl.*)
  blushed
  blushes
bluster
  blustered
  blustering
  blusters
  blustery
boa (fur wrap)
boa (snake)
  boa-constrictor
boar (male pig)
  boar's (of the boar)
  boars' (of the boars)
board
  boarder
board (of wood)
boast
  boaster
  boastful
  boastfully
  boastfulness
boat
  boat's (of the boat)
  boats' (of the boats)
  boatswain (bosun)
bob
  bobbed
  bobbing
  bobs
bobbin
bobby
  bobbies (*pl.*)
  bobby's (of the bobby)
  bobbies'
      (of the bobbies)
bob-sled, bobsleigh
bode
  boding
bodice
bodkin

body
  bodies (*pl.*)
  bodied
  bodies' (of the bodies)
  bodiless
  bodily
  bodyguard
  body's (of the body)
bogey (golf)
boggle
  boggling
bogie (undercarriage)
bogus
bogy, bogey (goblin)
  bogeys, bogies (*pl.*)
boil
  boiler
boisterous
  boisterously
bold
  boldly
bole (clay)
bole (of tree)
bollard
boloney, baloney
Bolshevik
  Bolshevism
  Bolshevist
bolster
  bolstered
  bolstering
bolt
bomb
  bomber
  bombshell
bombard
  bombardier
  bombarding
  bombardment
bombast
  bombastic
  bombastically
bona fide (in good faith)
  bona fides (good faith)
bonanza

bond
bondage
bone
boneless
bony
bonfire
bonhomie
bonnet
bonneted
bonny
bonnier
bonus
bonuses (*pl.*)
bon voyage
boo
booed
booing
booby
boobies (*pl.*)
book
bookable
booklet
book's (of the book)
books' (of the books)
book token
bookie (bookmaker)
bookies (*pl.*)
bookie's (of the bookie)
bookies'
(of the bookies)
bookkeeper
bookkeeping
boom
boomerang
boor (lout)
boorish
boost (to strengthen)
booster
boot
bootee
bootlace
bootless (profitless)
bootleg
bootlegged
bootlegger

bootlegging
booth
booty
booze
boozer
boozing
borax
boracic
border (edge)
bordered
bordering
bore (to weary)
boredom
boring
bore (*from* to bear)
bore (to pierce)
boring
born (of a baby)
borne (carried)
borough (town)
borrow (money, etc.)
borrower
bosh (nonsense)
bosom
boss
bosses (*pl.*)
bosses' (of the bosses)
bossier
bossiness
bossily
boss's (of the boss)
bossy
bosun (boatswain)
botany
botanical
botanist
botch
both
bother
botheration
bothered
bothering
bothersome
bottle
bottling

bottleneck
bottom
bottomless
bottommost
botulism
boudoir
bough (branch)
bought (purchased)
boulder (large stone)
boulevard
bounce
bouncing
bound (to jump)
bound (*from* bind)
boundary
boundaries (*pl.*)
bounder (rascal)
boundless
bounteous
bounty
bounties (*pl.*)
bountiful
bouquet
bourbon
bourgeois
bourgeoisie
bout
boutique
bovine
bow (to bend forward)
bow (for violin, etc)
bow (knot)
bow-tie
bow (forepart of ship)
bow (weapon)
bowdlerise
bowdlerize
bowdlerising
bowdlerizing
bowel (intestine)
bower (summer-house)
bowl (in cricket)
bowler
bowler's (of the bowler)

bowlers'
     (of the bowlers)
bowling
bowl (basin)
bow-legs
  bow-legged
box
  boxer
  boxer's (of the boxer)
  boxers' (of the boxers)
box
  boxes (*pl.*)
box-office
boy
  boys (*pl.*)
  boyhood
  boy-friend
  boyish
  boyishly
  boyishness
  boy's (of the boy)
  boys' (of the boys)
boycott
  boycotted
  boycotting
brace
  bracing
bracelet
braces
bracken
bracket
  bracketed
  bracketing
brackish
brad
  bradawl
brag
  brags
  braggart
  bragged
  bragging
braid
Braille
brain
  brainier

brainless
brain's (of the brain)
brains' (of the brains)
brainwashed
brainwashing
brainwave
brainy
braise (to cook)
  braising
brake (to slow down)
  braking
brake (vehicle)
bramble
bran
branch
  branches (*pl.*)
brand
  brand-new
brandy
  brandies (*pl.*)
brash
brass
  brasses (*pl.*)
brassard
brassière
brat
bravado
brave
  bravely
  bravery
  braving
bravo (cry of approval)
  bravos (*pl.*)
bravo (ruffian)
  bravoes (*pl.*)
bravura
brawl
brawn
  brawny
bray
braze (to weld)
  brazing
brazen (impudent)
  brazenness
brazen (made of brass)

brazen
  (out, to be unashamed)
brazier (brass-worker)
brazier (pan)
breach
bread (food)
breadth
break
  breakable
  breakage
  breakfast
  breakthrough
bream
breast
  breast-feeding
  breast-fed
breath
  breathalyser
  breathalyzer
  breathing
  breathless
  breathtaking
breathe (to take breaths)
  breather
  breathing
breech (of gun)
  breech-loader
  breech-loading
breeches (trousers)
breed
  bred
breeze
  breezily
  breezy
brethren
brevity
  brevities (*pl.*)
brew
  brewer
  brewer's (of the brewer)
  brewers'
     (of the brewers)
  brewery
  breweries (*pl.*)
briar, brier

bribe
 bribable
 bribery
 bribing
bric-à-brac
brick
 brickbat
 bricklayer
 bricklayer's
  (of the bricklayer)
 bricklayers'
  (of the bricklayers)
 bricklaying
bride
 bridal
 bridegroom
 bridesmaid
bridge
 bridging
 bridgehead
bridle
 bridle-path
 bridling
brief
 brief-case
 briefly
brier, briar
brigade
 brigadier
 brigadier's
  (of the brigadier)
 brigadiers'
  (of the brigadiers)
brigand
bright
 brighten
  (to make bright)
 brightened
 brightening
 brightly
Brighton
brilliant
 brilliance
 brilliantly
brim

brim-full
 brimful
brimstone
brine
 briny
bring
 brought
brink
brisk
 briskly
brisket
bristle
 bristling
 bristly
Britain
 British
 Briton (British subject)
Britannia
 Britannic
Brittany (in France)
brittle
 brittleness
broach (to open, begin)
 broached
 broaches
broad
 broaden
 broadened
 broadening
 broadly
broadcast
 broadcaster
 broadcaster's
  (of the broadcaster)
 broadcasters'
  (of the broadcasters)
broadminded
 broadside
brocade
broccoli
brochure
brogue
broil
 broiler
broke (*from* break)

broke (bankrupt)
broken
 broken-hearted
broker
 brokerage
bromide
bronchial
 bronchitic
 bronchitis
bronco (horse)
 broncos (*pl.*)
bronze
brooch (jewel)
 brooches (*pl.*)
brood
 broody
brook (stream)
 brooklet
brook (to tolerate)
broom (brush)
broom (shrub)
broth
brothel
brother
 brothers (*pl.*)
 brotherhood
 brother-in-law
 brothers-in-law (*pl.*)
 brother-in-law's
  (of the brother-in-law)
 brothers-in-law's
 (of the brothers-in-law)
 brotherliness
 brotherly
 brother's
  (of the brother)
 brothers'
  (of the brothers)
brougham (carriage)
brought (*from* bring)
brow
 browbeaten
brown
Brownie (junior Guide)
browse

29

browsing
bruise
  bruiser
  bruising
brunette
brunt
brush
  brushes (*pl.*)
  brushing
brusque
  brusquely
  brusqueness
Brussels
  Brussels sprouts
brute
  brutal
  brutalisation
  brutalization
  brutalise
  brutalize
  brutalising
  brutalizing
  brutality
  brutalities (*pl.*)
  brutally
  brute's (of the brute)
  brutes' (of the brutes)
bubble
  bubbling
  bubbly
buccaneer
buck (male deer, rabbit)
buck (to jump)
buck (up, to hurry)
buck (in card-game)
  buck-passer
  buckpassing
  pass the buck
buck rarebit (food)
bucket
  bucketful
  bucketfuls (*pl.*)
buckle
  buckling
buckram

bucolic
bud
  buds
  budded
  budding
Buddha
  Buddhism
  Buddhist
buddleia
budge
  budging
budgerigar
budget
  budgetary
  budgeted
  budgeting
buff
buffalo
  buffaloes (*pl.*)
  buffalo's
              (of the buffalo)
  buffaloes'
              (of the buffaloes)
buffer
  buffered
  buffering
buffet (to knock)
  buffeted
  buffeting
  buffets
buffet (for food)
buffoon
  buffoonery
  buffooneries (*pl.*)
bug (to listen in)
  bugged
  bugging
bug (insect)
bugbear
buggy (small cart)
  buggies (*pl.*)
  buggy's (of the buggy)
  buggies' (of the buggies)
bugle
  bugler

bugling
build
  builder
  building
  built
bulb
  bulbous
bulge
  bulging
bulk
  bulkier
  bulky
  bulkhead
bull
  bullfighter
  bullish
  bullock
  bull's (of the bull)
  bulls' (of the bulls)
bulldoze
  bulldozer
  bulldozing
bullet
  bullet-proof
bulletin
bullfinch
  bullfinches (*pl.*)
bullion
bullock
bull's-eye
bully
  bullied
  bullies (*pl.*)
  bullies' (of the bullies)
  bullying
  bullyrag
  bully's (of the bully)
bulrush
bulwark
bum
bumble-bee
bump
  bumper
  bumpier
  bumpily

bumpiness
bumpy
bumpkin
bumptious
  bumptiously
  bumptiousness
bun
bunch
  bunches (*pl.*)
bundle
  bundling
bung
  bunged up
bungalow
bungle
  bungler
  bungling
bunion
bunk (bed in ship)
bunk (to run away)
bunker (in golf)
  bunkered
  bunkering
bunkum
bunny
  bunnies (*pl.*)
  bunny's (of the bunny)
  bunnies'
    (of the bunnies)
Bunsen burner
bunting
buoy (float)
  buoyancy
  buoyant
  buoyantly
  buoyed (up)
  buoying
bur, burr (of a plant)
burble
  burbling
burden
  burdened
  burdening
  burdensome
bureau

bureaux (*pl.*)
bureaus (*pl.*)
bureaucracy
bureaucrat
bureaucratic
bureaucratically
burgeon
  burgeoning
burgle
  burglar
  burglary
  burglaries (*pl.*)
  burgling
burgomaster
burgundy
burial
burlesque
burly
  burlier
  burliness
burn
  burned
  burner
  burning
  burnt
burnish
  burnished
  burnisher
  burnishing
burr (sound)
burrow
bursar
  bursary
  bursaries (*pl.*)
burst
bury
  burial
  buried
  buries
  burying
bus
  buses (*pl.*)
  bussed
  bussing
busby

busbies (*pl.*)
bush
  bushes (*pl.*)
  bushy
bushel
business
  businesses (*pl.*)
  business-like
bust
bustle
  bustling
busy
  busier
  busily
  busybody
  busybodies (*pl.*)
  busying
  busyness (being busy)
but
butcher
  butchers (*pl.*)
  butchered
  butcherer
  butchering
  butcher's
    (of the butcher)
  butchers'
    (of the butchers)
  butchery
  butcheries (*pl.*)
butler
  butlers (*pl.*)
  butler's (of the butler)
  butlers' (of the butlers)
butt (to push)
butts (for shooting)
butt (thick end)
butt (barrel)
butter
  buttered
  butter-fingered
  butter fingers
  buttering
  buttery
buttercup

butterfly
  butterflies (*pl.*)
  butterfly's
    (of the butterfly)
  butterflies'
    (of the butterflies)
buttery (food store)
  butteries (*pl.*)
buttock
button
  buttoned
buttress
  buttresses (*pl.*)
buxom
  buxomness
buy
  bought
  buyer
  buyer's (of the buyer)
  buyers' (of the buyers)
  buying
buzz
buzzard
by
  by and by
bye (in cricket)
by-election
bygone
by-law
byline
bypass
  bypasses (*pl.*)
bypath
by-play
by-product
byre (cow-house)
byroad
bystander
byword

C

cab
  cabby
  cabbies (*pl.*)
  cabby's (of the cabby)
  cabbies' (of the cabbies)
cabaret
cabbage
cabin
cabinet
cable
  cablegram
  cabling
cache (hiding place)
cackle
  cackling
cacophony (ugly noise)
  cacophonous
cactus
  cacti, cactuses (*pl.*)
cad
  caddish
  caddishly
  cad's (of the cad)
  cads' (of the cads)
cadaver
  cadaverous
caddie (golf)
  caddying
caddis
  caddis-worm
caddy (tea)
  caddies (*pl.*)
cadence (rhythm)
cadenza (in music)
cadet
  cadet corps
  cadet's (of the cadet)
  cadets' (of the cadets)
cadge

cadging
cadmium
Caesarean (birth)
café
  cafés (*pl.*)
cafeteria
caffeine
cage
cagey (shrewd)
  cagier
  cagiest
  cagily
  caginess
cairn
caisson
cajole
  cajolery
  cajoling
cake
  cake's (of the cake)
  cakes' (of the cakes)
  caking
calabash
calamine (ointment)
calamity
  calamities (*pl.*)
  calamitous
calcify
  calcification
  calcified
  calcifying
calcium
calculate
  calculable
  calculating
  calculation
  calculator
calculus
calendar (table of dates)
calender (machine)
  calendered
  calendering
calends, kalends
calf
  calves (*pl.*)

calving
calf (of leg)
  calves (*pl.*)
calibre
  caliber
  calibrate
  calibrating
  calibration
calico
caliph
  caliphate
call
  caller
  caller's (of the caller)
  callers' (of the callers)
calligraphy
  calligrapher
  calligraphic
  calligraphist
calliper
  caliper
callisthenic
  calisthenic
callous (unfeeling)
  callously
  callousness
callow (inexperienced)
callus (hardened skin)
  calluses (*pl.*)
  callosity
calm
  calmly
  calmness
calomel
calorie
  calories (*pl.*)
  calorific
  calorimeter
  calorimetric
  calorimetry
calumny
  calumnies (*pl.*)
  calumniate
  calumniating
  calumniator

calumnious
calve
  calving
calypso
calyx
  calyxes, calyces (*pl.*)
cam
camaraderie
camber
  cambered
cambric
came (*from* come)
camel
  camel-hair
camellia
Camembert
cameo
  cameos (*pl.*)
camera
  camera's
      (of the camera)
  cameras'
      (of the cameras)
camisole
camomile (herb)
camouflage
  camouflaging
camp
campaign
camphor
  camphorated
campus
  campuses (*pl.*)
can
  canned
  cannery
  canning
can
  can't (cannot)
canal
  canalisation
  canalization
  canalise
  canalize
canary (bird)

canaries (*pl.*)
canary's (of the canary)
canaries'
     (of the canaries)
can-can
cancel
  cancellation
  cancelled
  canceled
  cancelling
  canceling
  cancels
cancer
  cancerous
candelabra, candelabrum
  candelabra,
        candelabras,
        candelabrums(*pl.*)
candid (outspoken)
  candidly
  candour
  candor
candidate
  candidacy
  candidacies (*pl.*)
  candidature
candle
  candlelight
  candlestick
candour (frankness)
  candor
candy (sweetmeat)
  candies (*pl.*)
  candied (sugared)
  candying
cane
  caning
canine
canister
canker
cannabis
cannery
  canneries (*pl.*)
cannibal
  cannibalisation

cannibalization
cannibalise
cannibalize
cannibalising
cannibalizing
cannibalism
cannibal's
    (of the cannibal)
cannibals'
    (of the cannibals)
cannon (gun)
  cannonade
  cannon's
    (of the cannon)
  cannons'
    (of the cannons)
cannot, can't
canny (shrewd)
  cannier
  cannily
  canniness
canoe
  canoes (*pl.*)
  canoeing
  canoeist
canon
  (Church law, dignitary)
  canonical
  canonisation
  canonization
  canonise
  canonize
  canonising
  canonizing
  canonry
canon (music)
canopy
  canopies (*pl.*)
  canopied
cant (jargon)
cant (hypocrisy)
cantabile
  (with singing tone)
cantaloup, cantaloupe
    (melon)

cantankerous
  cantankerously
cantata
  cantatas (*pl.*)
canteen
canter (easy gallop)
  cantered
  cantering
cantilever
  cantilevered
canto (part of poem)
  cantos (*pl.*)
canton (Swiss county)
  cantonal
cantonment
cantor (singer)
canvas (cloth)
  canvases (*pl.*)
canvass (for votes)
  canvassed
  canvasser
  canvasses
  canvassing
canyon
caoutchouc
cap
  capped
  capping
  caps
capable
  capability
  capabilities (*pl.*)
  capably
capacious
capacity
  capacities (*pl.*)
  capacitance (*electr.*)
  capacitive
  capacitor (*electr.*)
cape
caper (to jump)
  capered
  capering
caper (spice)
  caper-sauce

capillary
  capillaries (*pl.*)
capital
  capitalisation
  capitalization
  capitalise
  capitalize
  capitalising
  capitalizing
  capitalism
  capitalist
  capitalistic
  capitally
capitation
    (counting people)
Capitol (building)
capitulate (to give in)
  capitulating
  capitulation
capon
caprice
  capricious
  capriciously
capsize
  capsizable
  capsizing
capstan
capsule
  capsular
captain
  captaincy
  captaincies (*pl.*)
  captain's
    (of the captain)
  captains'
    (of the captains)
caption
  captioned
captious (peevish)
  captiously
  captiousness
captivate (to delight)
  captivating
  captivation
captive

captivity

capture

  captor

  capturing

car

  car's (of the car)

  cars' (of the cars)

carabiniere

  carabinieri (*pl.*)

carafe

caramel

carat (weight)

caravan

  caravanning

  caravaning

caraway (seed)

carbide (chemical)

carbine (rifle)

carbohydrate

carbolic

carbon

  carbonaceous

  carbonate

  carbon dioxide

  carbonic

  carbonisation

  carbonization

  carbonise

  carbonize

  carbonising

  carbonizing

carborundum

carboy (large jar)

carbuncle

carburettor

  carburetor

carcass, carcase

  carcasses, carcases (*pl.*)

carcinoma

  carcinogenic

card

  cardboard

  card-carrying

cardiac

cardigan

cardinal (of Church)

cardinal (most important)

cardio- (heart)

  cardiogram

  cardiograph

  cardiographer

  cardiographic

  cardiography

care

  carefree

  careful

  carefully

  careless

  carelessly

  carelessness

  careworn

  caring

careen

  (to turn ship on side)

  careened

  careening

career (in life)

  careerist

career (to rush about)

  careering

caress

  caresses (*pl.*)

  caressed

  caresses

  caressing

caretaker

  caretaker's

    (of the caretaker)

  caretakers'

    (of the caretakers)

  caretaking

cargo

  cargoes (*pl.*)

caricature

  caricaturing

  caricaturist

caries (tooth decay)

carillon

carminative (drug)

carmine (colour)

carnage

carnal

  carnally

carnation

carnival

carnivore (flesh-eater)

  carnivorous

carol

  carolled

  caroled

  caroller

  caroler

  carolling

  caroling

carotid (artery)

carouse

  carousal

  carousing

carousel (roundabout)

carp (to grumble)

carp (fish)

carpenter

  carpentering

  carpenter's

    (of the carpenter)

  carpenters'

    (of the carpenters)

  carpentry

carpet

  carpeted

  carpeting

carriage

carrier

carrion

carrot (vegetable)

  carroty

carry

  carried

  carrier

  carries

  carrying

cart

  cartage

  carter

carte blanche

cartel
cartilage
  cartilaginous
cartography
  cartographer
  cartographic
carton (cardboard)
cartoon (drawing)
  cartoonist
cartridge
carve (to cut up)
  carving
  carving knife
caryatid (pillar)
cascade
  cascading
cascara
case
  casing
casein (basis of cheese)
casement
cash
  cashed
  cashes
cash and carry
cashew (nut)
cashier (of a bank, etc.)
  cashier's
        (of the cashier)
  cashiers'
        (of the cashiers)
cashier (to dismiss)
  cashiered
  cashiering
cashmere
casino
  casinos (*pl.*)
cask
casket
casserole
cassette
cassock
cast (to throw)
  cast-off
cast (of actors)

castanet
castaway
caste (social class)
  casteless
castellated
castigate
  castigating
  castigation
castle
castor, caster (of chairleg)
castor, caster (sugar)
castor oil
castrate
  castrating
  castration
  castrato (singer)
  castrati (*pl.*)
casual
  casually
  casualness
casualty
  casualties (*pl.*)
casuist (arguer)
  casuistry
cat
  catcall
  catnap
  cat's (of the cat)
  cats' (of the cats)
  cat's eye
  cattish
  cattily
  catty
catabolism
cataclysm (upheaval)
  cataclysmal
  cataclysmic
  cataclysmically
catacomb
catalepsy
  cataleptic
catalogue
  catalog
  cataloguer
  cataloger

cataloguing
  cataloging
catalyse
  catalyze
catalysation
  catalyzation
catalyser
  catalyzer
catalysis
catalyses (*pl.*)
catalyst
catalytic
catamaran
catapult
cataract
catarrh
  catarrhal
catastrophe
  catastrophic
  catastrophically
catch
  catches
  catchment
  catchy
  caught
catechise
        (to ask questions)
  catechize
  catechising
  catechizing
  catechism
categoric
  categorical
  categorically
category
  categories (*pl.*)
categorise
        (to make a list)
  categorize
  categorising
  categorizing
cater
  catered
  caterer
  catering

caterpillar
  caterpillar's
    (of the caterpillar)
  caterpillars'
    (of the caterpillars)
caterwaul
catgut
catharsis
  cathartic
cathedral
catheter
cathode
  cathodic
catholic
  catholicism
  catholicity
catkin
catsup
  ketchup
cattle
caucus
  caucuses (*pl.*)
caught (*from* catch)
caul (of a baby)
cauldron
cauliflower
caulk
    (to make watertight)
cause
  causal
  causation
  causative
  causing
causeway
caustic
  caustically
cauterise
  cauterize
  cauterisation
  cauterization
  cauterising
  cauterizing
cautery
  (surgical instrument)
  cauteries (*pl.*)

caution
  cautionary
  cautious
  cautiously
cavalcade
cavalier
  cavalier's
    (of the cavalier)
  cavaliers'
    (of the cavaliers)
cavalry
cave
  caving
caveat (warning)
cavern
  cavernous
caviare
  caviar
cavil (to object)
  cavilled
  caviled
  cavilling
  caviling
  cavils
cavity
  cavities (*pl.*)
cavort
caw
cayenne
cease
  ceaseless
  ceaselessly
  ceasing
  cessation
cedar
cede (to yield)
  ceding
  cession
cedilla
ceiling (of a room)
celandine
celebrate
  celebrant
  celebrating
  celebration

  celebrator
celebrity
  celebrities (*pl.*)
celerity (speed)
celery (vegetable)
  celeriac
celestial
  celestially
celibate (unmarried)
  celibacy
cell
cellar
  cellarage
cello
  cellos (*pl.*)
  cellist
  cellist's (of the cellist)
  cellists' (of the cellists)
cellophane
cellular
celluloid
cellulose
Celsius (centigrade)
Celt
  Celtic
cement
cemetery
  cemeteries (*pl.*)
cenotaph
censer (for incense)
censor (official)
  censored
  censoring
  censorious
  censorship
censure (blame)
  censured
  censuring
census (count of people)
  censuses (*pl.*)
cent (money)
centaur (mythical horse)
centenary
  (hundredth anniversary)
  centenaries (*pl.*)

centenarian
   (person aged ddd)
centennial
centigrade
centigram
centilitre
  centiliter
centime (money)
centimetre
  centimeter
centipede
central
  centralisation
  centralization
  centralise
  centralize
  centralising
  centralizing
  centrally
centre
  center
  centred
  centered
  centre-forward
  centre-piece
  centerpiece
  centring
  centering
centrifugal
  (away from centre)
  centrifugally
  centrifuge
centripetal
  (towards centre)
centrist
centuple (hundredfold)
centurion
century
  centuries (*pl.*)
  century's
    (of the century)
  centuries'
    (of the centuries)
cephalic
  cephalitis

ceramic
cereal (corn)
cerebellum
cerebral
  cerebration
    (working of brain)
  cerebro-spinal
  cerebrum
    (part of brain)
ceremony
  ceremonies (*pl.*)
  ceremonial
  ceremonially
  ceremonious
  ceremoniously
cerise (cherry-coloured)
certain
  certainly
  certainty
  certainties (*pl.*)
  certitude
certify
  certifiable
  certificate
  certification
  certified
  certifies
  certifying
certitude
cervix
  cervical
cessation (ceasing)
cession (yielding)
cesspit
  cesspool
chafe (to rub)
  chafing
chaff (to tease)
chaff (husks)
chaffinch
  chaffinches (*pl.*)
chagrin
  chagrined
chain
chair

chaired
chairing
chairman
chairmen (*pl.*)
chairman's
  (of the chairman)
chairmen's
  (of the chairmen)
chairwoman
chairwomen (*pl.*)
chairwoman's
  (of the chairwoman)
chairwomen's
  (of the chairwomen)
chaise longue
  chaises longues (*pl.*)
chalcedony
chalet
chalice
chalk
  chalky
challenge
  challenger
  challenging
chamber
  chambermaid
  chambermaid's
    (of the chambermaid)
  chambermaids'
    (of the chambermaids)
chamberlain
chameleon
chamfer
  chamfered
  chamfering
chamois
champ (to munch)
champagne
champion
  championed
  championing
  championship
chance
  chancing
  chancy

chancel (part of church)
chancellor (official)
  chancellery
      (of an embassy)
  chancelleries (*pl.*)
chancery (law court)
  chanceries (*pl.*)
chandelier
chandler
change
  changeable
  changing
changeling
channel
  channelled
  chaneled
  channelling
  chaneling
chant
chantry
  chantries (*pl.*)
chaos .
  chaotic
  chaotically
chap (fellow)
chap
  chapped
chapel
chaperon
  chaperonage
  chaperoned
  chaperoning
chaplain
  chaplaincy
chaplet (wreath)
chapter
char (house work)
  charred
  charlady
  charladies (*pl.*)
  charlady's
      (of the charlady)
  charladies'
      (of the charladies)
  charring

charwoman
charwomen (*pl.*)
charwoman's
  (of the charwoman)
charwomen's
  (of the charwomen)
char (to scorch)
  charred
  charring
charabanc
character
  characterisation
  characterization
  characterise
  characterize
  characterising
  characterizing
  characteristic
  characteristically
charade
charcoal
charge
  chargeable
  charging
chargé d'affaires
  chargés d'affaires (*pl.*)
chariot
  charioteer
charisma
  charismatic
charity
  charities (*pl.*)
  charitable
  charitably
charlatan
charlotte
  charlotte russe
charm
  charmer
chart
charter
  chartered
  charterer
  chartering
charwoman

charwomen (*pl.*)
chary (careful)
  charily
  chariness
chase
  chaser
  chasing
chasm
chassis
  chassis (*pl.*)
chaste
  chastely
  chasten
  chastened
  chastening
  chastity
chastise
  chastisement
  chastising
chat
  chats
  chatted
  chatter
  chatterbox
  chattering
  chatting
  chatty
château
  châteaux, *châteaus (pl.)*
chattel
chatelaine
chauffeur
  chauffeurs (*pl.*)
  chauffeur's
      (of the chauffeur)
  chauffeurs'
      (of the chauffeurs)
  chauffeuse (*fem.*)
chauvinism
  chauvinist
  chauvinistic
cheap
  cheaper
  cheaply
  cheapness

cheat
check (to restrain or test)
  checkmate
  checkmating
cheek
  cheekier
  cheekily
  cheekiness
  cheeky
cheep (chick's chirp)
cheer
  cheerily
  cheerless
  cheery
cheerful
  cheerfully
  cheerfulness
cheese
  cheese-paring
cheetah (animal)
chef
  chef's (of the chef)
  chefs' (of the chefs)
chef-d'oeuvre
  chefs-d'oeuvre (pl.)
chemical
  chemically
chemise
chemist
  chemistry
  chemist's
    (of the chemist)
  chemists'
    (of the chemists)
cheque (order on bank)
  check
chequer
  (to mark with squares)
  checker
  chequered
  checkered
chequered (varied)
  checkered
cherish
cheroot

cherry
  cherries (pl.)
cherub
  cherubic
  cherubically
chess
  chessboard
chest
  chestnut
chevalier
chevron
  chevroned
chevy, chivy, chivvy
  chevied, chivied,
          chivvied
chew
  chewy
Chianti
chic (elegant)
chicanery (trickery)
chichi
chick
  chicken
  chickenpox
  chicken's
    (of the chicken)
  chickens'
    (of the chicken)
  chickweed
chicory
chide (to scold)
  chided
  chid
  chidden
  chiding
chief
  chief's (of the chief)
  chiefs' (of the chiefs)
  chieftain
  chieftaincy
chiffon
chilblain
child
  children (pl.)
  childbirth

childhood
childish
children's
  (of the children)
child's (of the child)
chill
chilled
chillier
chilly
chilli (spice)
  chili
  chillies (pl.)
  chilies (pl.)
chime
  chiming
chimney
  chimneys (pl.)
chimpanzee
chin
China
  Chinese
china (porcelain)
chink
chintz
  chintzes (pl.)
chip
  chipped
  chipping
  chips
chipmunk
chiropodist
  chiropodist's
    (of the chiropodist)
  chiropodists'
    (of the chiropodists)
chiropody
chiropractic
chiropractor
chiropraxy
chirp
chirrup
  chirruped
  chirruping
chisel (tool)
chisel (to cheat)

chiselled
chiseled
chiseller
chiseler
chiselling
chiseling
chisels
chit (short note)
chit (young child)
chit-chat
chivalry
  chivalrous
  chivalrously
chive
chivvy, chivy, chevy
  chivvied, chivied,
         chevied
chlorate
    (chem. compound)
chloride
    (chem. compound)
chlorine (chem. element)
  chlorinate
  chlorinating
  chlorination
chlorodyne
chloroform
chlorophyll
chock
  chock-a-block
  chock-full
chocolate
choice
  choicely
  choiceness
  choicest
choir
choke
  choker (high collar)
  choking
choler (anger)
  choleric
cholera (disease)
cholesterol
choose

choosing
choosy, choosey
chose
chosen
chop
  chopped
  chopper
  chopping
  chopstick
  choppy (of sea, rough)
chop-suey
choral
  chorally
chorale (hymn)
  choral
chord (music)
chord (maths)
chore (task)
choreography
  choreographer
  choreographic
chorister
chortle
  chortling
chorus
  choruses (*pl.*)
chosen (*from* choose)
chow (dog)
Christ
  Christendom
  Christian
  Christianity
  Christmas
  Christmassy
christen
  christened
  christening
chromate
chrom- (colour)
  chromatic
  chromatin
  chrome
  chromic
  chromium
  chromosome

chromosphere
chron- (time)
  chronic (continuous)
  chronically
  chronicle
  chronology
  chronologies (*pl.*)
  chronological
  chronologically
  chronometer
chrys- (gold)
  chrysalis
  chrysalises (*pl.*)
  chrysanthemum
  chrysanthemums (*pl.*)
chub (fish)
chubby
  chubbier
chuck
  chucker-out
chuckle
  chuckling
chug
  chugging
chukker, chukka,
        chukkar(polo)
chum
  chummed
  chumming
  chummy
chump
chunk
  chunky
Church
  church-goer
  churchwarden
churlish (sulky)
churn
chute (sloping passage)
chutney
cicada
cicatrice (scar)
cicatrise (to heal)
  cicatrize
  cicatrising

cicatrizing
cider
cigar
  cigarette
  cigaret
cinder
  Cinderella
cinema
  cinematic
  cinematograph
  cinematography
cineraria (plant)
cinerary (for ashes)
  cinerarium
  cinerary urn
cinnamon
cipher, cypher
circa (approximately)
circle
  circling
circuit
  circuitous
  circuitry
  circuitries (*pl.*)
circular
  circularising
  circularizing
circulate
  circulating
  circulation
circum- (around)
  circumcise
  circumcising
  circumcision
  circumference
  circumflex
  circumlocution
  circumnavigate
  circumnavigation
  circumscribe
  circumscribing
  circumscription
  circumspect
  circumspection
  circumstance

circumstantial
circumstantially
circumvent
circumvention
circus
  circuses (*pl.*)
cirrhosis
cirrus (cloud)
cist (tomb)
cistern
citadel
cite (to quote)
  citation
  citing
citizen
  citizen's (of the citizen)
  citizens' (of the citizens)
  citizenship
citron (tree)
  citrate
  citric (acid)
  citrus
    (orange, lemon, etc.)
city
  cities (*pl.*)
  city's (of the city)
  cities' (of the cities)
civet
civic
  civic centre
  civic center
civil
  civilian
  civilian's
    (of the civilian)
  civilians'
    (of the civilians)
  civility
  civilities (*pl.*)
  civilly
civilise
civilize
civilisation
civilization
civilising

civilizing
civvies (civilian clothes)
clad (clothed)
  cladding
claim
  claimable
  claimant
    (one who claims)
clairvoyance
  clairvoyant
clam (shellfish)
clamant (noisy)
clamber
  clambered
  clambering
clammy
  clamminess
clamour
  clamor
  clamorous
clamp
clan
  clannish
clandestine
  clandestinely
clang
  clanger (bad mistake)
  clangour (noise)
  clangor
clap
  clapped
  clapping
  claps
claptrap
claret
clarify
  clarification
  clarified
  clarifies
  clarifying
clarinet
  clarinettist,   clarinetist
  clarinetist
clarion (loud)

clarity (clearness)
clash
clasp
class (in school)
  classroom
class (social position)
  classless
  classy
classic
  classical
  classically
  classicism
  classicist
  classics
classify
  classifiable
  classification
  classified
  classifies
  classifying
clatter
  clattered
  clattering
clause
claustral
claustrophobia
  claustrophobic
clavichord
clavicle (collar-bone)
  clavicular
claw
clay
clean
  cleanable
  cleaner (more clean)
  cleaner (person)
  cleanliness
  cleanly
cleanse
  cleansing
clear
  clearance
  clearly
clear-cut
cleave (to stick to)

clave
  cleaved
  cleaving
cleave (to split)
  cleavage
  cleaved
  cleaving
  cleft
  clove
  cloven
clef
clematis
clement
  clemency
clench (to close tightly)
clergy
  clergyman
  clergymen (*pl.*)
  clergyman's
      (of the clergyman)
  clergymen's
      (of the clergymen)
cleric
  clerical
clerk
  clerk's (of the clerk)
  clerks' (of the clerks)
clever
  cleverer
  cleverly
clew, clue (thread)
cliché
click
client
  clientele
  client's (of the client)
  clients' (of the clients)
cliff
climacteric
climate (weather)
  climatic
  climatically
  climatology
climax
  climaxes (*pl.*)

climactic
climb
  climbable
  climber
clime (region)
clinch (boxing, settling)
cling
  clung
clinic
  clinical
  clinically
clink
  clinker
clip
  clipped
  clipping
  clips
clipboard
clipper (sailing ship)
clique
  cliquey
  cliquish
clitoris
cloak
  cloakroom
clobber
  clobbered
  clobbering
cloche
clock
  clockwise
  clockwork
clod
  clodhopper
clog
  clogged
  clogging
  clogs
cloister
  cloistered
  cloistral
close (near)
close (to shut)
  closing
  closure

closet
  closeted
clot
  clots
  clotted
  clotting
cloth (material)
clothe (to dress)
  clad
  clothed
  clothes (garments)
  clothier
  clothing
cloud
  cloudier
  cloudy
clout (to hit)
clove (*see* cleave)
  cloven
clove (spice)
clover
  clover-leaf
clown
cloy
club (to hit)
  clubbed
  clubbing
club (association)
cluck
clue (to mystery)
  clueless
clue, clew (thread)
clump
clumsy
  clumsier
  clumsily
  clumsiness
clung (*from* cling)
cluster
  clustered
  clustering
clutch
clutter
  cluttered
  cluttering

coach (carriage)
  coaches (*pl.*)
  coachman
coach (to teach)
coagulate
  coagulating
  coagulation
coal
coalesce
  coalescence
  coalescent
  coalescing
coalition
coarse (rough)
  coarsely
  coarsen
  coarsened
  coarseness
  coarsening
coast
  coastal
  coaster
  coastguard
coat (garment)
coat (to cover)
coax
coaxial
cob
cobalt
cobble
  cobbler
  cobbling
cobra
cobweb
  cobwebbed
cocaine
  cocain
coccyx (base of spine)
  coccygeal
cochineal
cochlea (of the ear)
cock (bird)
  cockcrow
  cockerel
  cock-eyed

cockade
cockatoo
  cockatoos (*pl.*)
cockchafer
cockle
cockney
  cockneys (*pl.*)
  cockney's
    (of the cockney)
  cockneys'
    (of the cockneys)
cockpit
cockroach
cocksure
cocktail
cocky (conceited)
  cockier
  cockily
coco (tree)
  coconut
cocoa (drink)
cocoon
cocotte
cod
  codling (small cod)
  cod's roe
coda (music)
coddle
  coddling
code
  coding
codeine (drug)
codger
codicil
codify
  codification
  codified
  codifying
coeducation
  coeducational
coefficient
coerce
  coercing
  coercion
coexist

coexistence
coffee
coffer (box)
coffin
cog
  cog-wheel
cogent
  cogency
  cogently
cogitate
  cogitating
  cogitation
cognac
cognate (related)
cognisance (knowledge)
  cognizance
  cognisant
  cognizant
cognition (knowing)
  cognitive
cognomen (nickname)
cohabit
  cohabitation
  cohabited
  cohabiting
cohere
  coherence
  coherent
  coherently
  coherer
  cohering
  cohesion
  cohesive
cohort
coiffeur (hairdresser)
  coiffeurs (*pl.*)
  coiffeuse (*fem.*)
  coiffeuses (*pl.*)
  coiffure (hair style)
coil
coin
  coinage
  coiner
coincide
  coincidence

coincident
coincidental
coincidentally
coinciding
coir (fibre)
coition, coitus
coke
  coking
col (mountain pass)
colander (strainer)
cold
  cold-blooded
  colder
  coldly
  cold-shoulder
  cold-shouldered
cole (cabbage)
  coleslaw
colic
  colicky
Coliseum (in London)
  Colosseum (in Rome)
colitis
collaborate
  collaborating
  collaboration
  collaborator
collage
  (patchwork picture)
collapse
  collapsible
  collapsing
collar
  collared
  collarette
  collaret
  collaring
collate
  collating
  collation
  collator
collateral
collation (meal)
colleague
collect

collection
collector
collector's
  (of the collector)
collectors'
  (of the collectors)
collect (prayer)
collective
  collectively
  collectivism
  collectivist
colleen
college
  collegial
  collegian
  collegiate
collide
  colliding
  collision
collie (dog)
collier
  colliery
  collieries (*pl.*)
collision
collocate (to arrange)
  collocating
  collocation
colloid
  colloidal
colloquial
  colloquialism
  colloquially
  colloquy
  colloquies (*pl.*)
collude
  colluding
  collusion
  collusive
cologne
colon (gut)
  colitis
colon (punctuation mark)
colonel
  colonelcy

colonel's
    (of the colonel)
colonels'
    (of the colonels)
colonnade
colony
  colonies (*pl.*)
  colonial
  colonialism
  colonisation
  colonization
  colonise
  colonize
  coloniser
  colonizer
  colonising
  colonizing
  colonist
coloration (*from* colour)
coloratura (singer)
colossal
  colossally
  colossus (large statue)
colour
  color
  coloration
  coloured
  colored
  colourful
  colorful
  colourfully
  colorfully
  colouring
  coloring
  colourless
  colorless
colt
  coltish
columbine
column
  columnar
  columnist
coma (unconsciousness)
  comatose (unconscious)
comb

combat
combatant
combative
combe, coomb (valley)
combine
  combinable
  combination
  combining
combustion
  combustible
come
  came
  coming
comedy
  comedies (*pl.*)
  comedian
  comedian's
    (of the comedian)
  comedians'
    (of the comedians)
  comedienne (*fem.*)
comely (pretty)
  comelier
  comeliness
comestible
comet
come-uppance
comfit (sweetmeat)
comfort
  comfortable
  comfortably
  comforter
comic
  comical
  comicality
  comicalities (*pl.*)
  comically
comity (friendship)
  comities (*pl.*)
comma
    (punctuation mark)
command
  commandant
  commander
  commandment

commandeer (to seize)
  commandeered
  commandeering
commando
  commandos (*pl.*)
commemorate
  commemorating
  commemoration
  commemorative
commence
  commencement
  commencing
commend (to praise)
  commendable
  commendably
  commendation
commensurate
  commensurable
  commensurably
  commensurately
comment (remark)
  commentary
  commentaries (*pl.*)
  commentator
commerce
  commercial
  commercialisation
  commercialization
  commercialise
  commercialize
  commercialising
  commercializing
  commercialism
  commercially
commiserate (to pity)
  commiserating
  commiseration
commissar (political boss)
commissariat
    (food supply)
commission
  commissionaire
  commissioner
commit
  commitment

commits
committal
committed
committing
committee
commode
commodious
commodity
commodities (pl.)
commodore
common
commoner
Common Market
commonplace
commonwealth
commotion
communal
communally
commune (to discuss)
communing
commune (settlement)
communicate
communicable
communicating
communication
communicative
communion
communicant
communiqué
communism
communist
community
communities (pl.)
commute
commutable
commutation
commutator (electr.)
commuter (traveller)
commuter's
(of the commuter)
commuters'
(of the commuters)
commuting
compact
companion

companionable
company
companies (pl.)
company's
(of the company)
companies'
(of the companies)
compare
comparable
comparably
comparative
comparatively
comparing
comparison
compartment
compartmentalisation
compartmentalization
compartmentalise
compartmentalize
compass
compasses (pl.)
compassion
compassionate
compatible
compatibility
compatibly
compatriot
compel
compelled
compelling
compels
compendious
compendium
compensate
compensating
compensation
compensator
compensatory
compère
compèring
compete
competing
competition
competitive
competitively

competitor
competitor's
(of the competitor)
competitors'
(of the competitors)
competent (capable)
competence (skill)
competently
compile
compilation
compiler
compiling
complacent (smug)
complacency
complacently
complain
complainant
complainer
complaint
complaisant (willing)
complaisance
(willingness)
complement (to add to)
complementary
complete
completely
completing
completion
complex
complexity
complexities (pl.)
complexion
complicate
complicacy
complicating
complication
complicity
(sharing in crime)
compliment (praise)
complimentary
compline (church service)
comply
compliance
compliant
complied

complies
complying
component
comport (to behave)
  comportment
      (behaviour)
compose
  composer (of music)
  composing
  composition
  composure (calmness)
composite
  compositely
compositor (in printing)
compos mentis
compost (garden refuse)
compote (of fruit)
compound
comprehend
  comprehensibility
  comprehensible
  comprehensibly
  comprehension
  comprehensive
  comprehensively
compress
  compressibility
  compressible
  compression
  compressor
comprise
  comprising
compromise
  compromising
comptometer
comptroller
compulsory
  compulsion
  compulsive
  compulsively
  compulsorily
compunction
compute
  computable
  computation

computer
computerisation
computerization
computerise
computerize
computerising
computerizing
computing
comrade
  comradely
  comradeship
con (to cheat)
  conned
  conning
  cons
con (to inspect)
  conned
  conning
con (to steer a ship)
  conning-tower
concave
  concavity
  concavities (*pl.*)
conceal (to hide)
  concealed
  concealing
  concealment
concede (to yield)
  conceding
  concession
conceit (pride)
  conceited
conceive (to imagine)
  conceivable
  conceivably
  conceiving
conceive
  (to become pregnant)
  conceiving
  conception
concentrate
  concentrating
  concentration
  concentrator
concentric

concentrically
concentricity
concept
  conception
  conceptual
  conceptualise
  conceptualize
  conceptualising
  conceptualizing
concern
concert
  concertina
  concerto
  concertos (*pl.*)
concert (to plan together)
concession
  concessionaire
  concessionnaire
  concessionary
concierge
  concierge's
    (of the concierge)
  concierges'
    (of the concierges)
conciliate
  conciliating
  conciliation
  conciliator
  conciliatory
concise
  concisely
  conciseness
conclave
conclude
  concluding
  conclusion
  conclusive
  conclusively
concoct
  concoction
concomitant
  concomitance
concord
  concordance
  concordant

concourse
concrete
  concretely
  concreteness
concubine
  concubinage
concur
  concurred
  concurrence
  concurrent
  concurrently
  concurring
  concurs
concuss
  concussed
  concussion
condemn
  condemnation
  condemnatory
condense
  condensation
  condenser
  condensing
condescend
  condescension
condign (severe)
  condignly
condiment
condition
  conditional
  conditionally
condole (to sympathise)
  condolatory
  condolence
  condoler
  condoling
condom
condone (to forgive)
  condonation
  condoning
conduce
  conducing
  conducive
conduct (behaviour)
conduct (electr.)

conductance
conductivity
conductor
conductor (of orchestra)
  conductor's
    (of the conductor)
  conductors'
    (of the conductors)
conductor (bus)
  conductress (fem.)
  conductresses (pl.)
conduit
cone
coney, cony (rabbit)
  coneys, conies (pl.)
confabulate
  confabulating
  confabulation
confection
  confectioner
  confectioner's
    (of the confectioner)
  confectioners'
    (of the confectioners)
  confectionery
confederate
  confederacy
  confederacies (pl.)
  confederating
  confederation
confer
  conference
  conferment
  conferred
  conferring
  confers
confess
  confession
  confessional
  confessor
confetti
confidant (person)
  confidante (fem.)
confide
  confidence

confident
confidential
confidentiality
confidentially
confidently
confiding
configuration
confine
  confinement
  confining
confirm
  confirmable
  confirmation
  confirmative
  confirmatory
confiscate
  confiscating
  confiscation
  confiscator
conflagration
conflict
conform
  conformable
  conformance
  conformation (shape)
  conformity
confound
confrère, confrere
confront
  confrontation
confuse
  confusing
  confusion
confute (to prove wrong)
  confutation
  confuting
congeal (to freeze)
  congealed
  congealing
  congelation
congenial (sympathetic)
  congeniality
  congenially
congenital (inborn)
  congenitally

conger
  conger-eel
congest
  congestion
  congestive
conglomerate
  conglomerating
  conglomeration
congratulate
  congratulating
  congratulation
  congratulatory
congregate
  congregating
  congregation
  congregational
congress
  congresses (*pl.*)
  congressional
congruent
  congruence
congruous (suitable)
  congruity
conic (*from* cone)
  conical
  conically
conifer
  coniferous
conjecture
  conjecturable
  conjecturably
  conjectural
  conjecturing
conjoin
  conjoint
  conjointly
conjugal
conjugate (*grammar*)
  conjugating
  conjugation
conjunction
conjunctive (*grammar*)
  conjunctival
conjunctivitis (eye disease)
conjure

conjurer, conjuror
conjuring
conkers (chestnuts)
connect
  connection, connexion
  connective
  connector, connecter
conning-tower
connive
  connivance
  conniving
connoisseur
  connoisseur's
    (of the connoisseur)
  connoisseurs'
    (of the connoisseurs)
connote
  connotation
  connoting
connubial
  connubially
conquer
  conquerable
  conquered
  conqueror
  conquest
consanguinity
  consanguineous
conscience
  conscientious
    (painstaking)
  conscientiously
  conscientiousness
conscious
  consciously
  consciousness
conscript
  conscription
  conscript's
    (of the conscript)
  conscripts'
    (of the conscripts)
consecrate
  consecrating
  consecration

consecutive
  consecutively
consensus
consent
consequence
  consequential
  consequently
conservatoire
conserve
  conservancy
  conservation
  conservatism
  conservative
  conservatory
  conservatories (*pl.*)
  conserving
consider
  considerable
  considerably
  considerate
  considerately
  considerateness
  consideration
  considered
  considering
consign
  consignee (receiver)
  consignment
  consignor (sender)
  consigner
consist
  consistence
  consistency
  consistencies (*pl.*)
  consistent
console
    (to sympathise with)
  consolable
  consolation
  consolatory
  consoler
  consoling
console (cabinet)
consolidate
  consolidating

consolidation
consols (Govt. securities)
consommé
consonant
consort (husband or wife)
consort
    (to come together)
consortium
  consortia (*pl.*)
conspicuous
  conspicuously
  conspicuousness
conspire
  conspiracy
  conspiracies (*pl.*)
  conspirator
  conspiratorial
  conspiring
constable
  constable's
    (of the constable)
  constables'
    (of the constables)
  constabulary
  constabularies (*pl.*)
constant
  constancy
  constantly
constellation
    (cluster of stars)
consternation
constipate
  constipated
  constipating
  constipation
constituency
  constituencies (*pl.*)
  constituent
constitute
  constituting
  constitution
  constitutional
  constitutionally
constrain
  constrained (repressed)

constraint (repression)
constrict
  constriction
  constrictive
  constrictor
construct
  construction
  constructional
  constructive
  constructively
  constructor
construe
  construing
consul
  consular
  consulate
  consul's (of the consul)
  consuls' (of the consuls)
consult
  consultant
  consultation
  consultative
consume
  consumable
  consumer
  consumer's
    (of the consumer)
  consumers'
    (of the consumers)
  consuming
consumption
  consumptive
consummate
  consummately
  consummation
contact
  contactor
contagion
  contagious
contain
  container
  containerisation
  containerization
  containerise
  containerize

containment
contaminate
  contaminant
  contaminating
  contamination
contemplate
  contemplating
  contemplation
  contemplative
  contemplatively
contemporaneous
  contemporary
  contemporaries (*pl.*)
contempt
  contemptible
  contemptibly
  contemptuous
  contemptuously
contend
 (to compete or struggle)
  contention
  contentious
content
    (amount contained)
content (satisfied)
  contentment
contention (dispute)
  contentious
contest
  contestable
  contestant
context
contiguous
  contiguously
  contiguity
continence (restraint)
  continent
continent (mainland)
  continental
contingent
  contingency
    (chance happening)
  contingencies (*pl.*)
contingent
    (group of soldiers)

continue
continual
continually
continuance
continuation
continuing
continuity
continuous
continuously
contort
contortion
contortionist
contour
contraband
contraception
contraceptive
contract
contraction
contractor
contractor's
    (of the contractor)
contractors'
    (of the contractors)
contractual
contractually
contradict
contradiction
contradictory
contralto
contraltos (*pl.*)
contralto's
    (of the contralto)
contraltos'
    (of the contraltos)
contraption
contrary
contrarily
contrariness
contrast
contravene
contravening
contravention
contretemps (mishap)
contribute
contributing

contribution
contributor
contributory
contrite (penitent)
contritely
contrition
contrive
    (to plan or invent)
contrivance
contriving
control
controllable
controlled
controller
controlling
controls
controversial
controversially
controversy
controversies (*pl.*)
controvert
controvertible
contumacy
contumacious
contumely
contuse
contusion
conundrum
conurbation
convalesce
convalescence
convalescent
convalescing
convection
convector
convene
convener
convening
convention
convenient
convenience
conveniently
convent
convention
conventional

conventionality
conventionally
converge
convergence
convergent
converging
conversant
    (acquainted with)
converse (opposite)
conversely
converse (to talk)
conversation
conversational
conversationalist
conversationally
conversazione
conversaziones (*pl.*)
conversazioni (*pl.*)
conversing
convert
conversion
converter
convertor (*alt.*)
convertibility
convertible
convex
convexity
convey
conveyance
conveyancer (lawyer)
conveyancing
conveyor, conveyer
conveyor belt
belt conveyer
convict
conviction
convict's
    (of the convict)
convicts'
    (of the convicts)
convince
convincing
convincingly
convivial
conviviality

convivially
convocation
convoke
  convoking
convolute
  convolution
convolvulus
  convolvuluses (*pl.*)
convoy
convulse
  convulsing
  convulsion
  convulsive
  convulsively
cony, coney (rabbit)
  conies, coneys (*pl.*)
coo
  cooed
  cooing
cook
  cooker
  cookery
  cook's (of the cook)
  cooks' (of the cooks)
cool
  coolant
  cooler
  cool-headed
  cooling
  coolly
  coolness
coolie (labourer)
coomb, combe (valley)
coop (to enclose)
  cooped (up)
co-op (society or store)
co-operate
  cooperate
  co-operating
  co-operation
  co-operative
  co-operator
co-opt
  co-option
co-ordinate

co-ordinating
co-ordination
cop (policeman)
  cop's (of the cop)
  cops' (of the cops)
cope (to manage)
  coping
cope (cloak)
copeck (Russian money)
  kopek, kopeck
co-pilot
  copilot
copious (abundant)
  copiously
copper (metal)
  copperplate
copper (policeman)
coppice, copse
       (small wood)
copra
copse (coppice)
copulate
  copulating
  copulation
copy
  copies (*pl.*)
  copied
  copier
  copies
  copying
  copyright
  copyrighted
coquette
  coquetry
  coquetted
  coquetting
  coquettish
coral
cord (string)
  cordage
  cordite
cordial (drink)
cordial (friendly)
  cordiality
  cordially

cordon
  cordon bleu
  cordoned
  cordoning
corduroy
core
co-respondent
    (in divorce case)
  corespondent
cork
  corkage
  corkscrew
corm
cormorant
corn
  cornflour (in cooking)
  cornflower (blue flower)
  cornstarch
cornea (of the eye)
  corneal
cornelian (cherry)
cornelian (precious stone)
corner
  cornered
  cornering
cornet
cornice
corny (old-fashioned)
corollary
  corollaries (*pl.*)
corona
  coronae, coronas (*pl.*)
  coronation
coronary (thrombosis)
coroner
coronet
  coroneted
corporal (soldier)
  corporal's
    (of the corporal)
  corporals'
    (of the corporals)
corporal (of the body)
  corporal punishment
corporate

corporation
corporeal (not spiritual)
corps (group of people)
   corps de ballet
corpse (dead body)
corpulent
   corpulence
corpuscle
   corpuscular
corral (to enclose cattle)
   corralled
   corralling
correct
   correction
   corrective
   correctly
   correctness
   corrector
correlate
   correlating
   correlation
   correlative
   correlativity
correspond
   correspondence
   correspondent
corridor
corrigendum
   corrigenda (*pl.*)
corroborate (to confirm)
   corroborating
   corroboration
   corroborative
corrode
   corrodible
   corroding
   corrosion
   corrosive
corrugate
   corrugated
   corrugation
corrupt
   corrupter
   corruptibility
   corruptible

corruption
corruptive
corruptly
corruptness
corsage
corset
cortège
   cortege
cortex
   cortical
cortisone
corundum (mineral)
corvée (hard task)
corvette (small ship)
cosecant, cosec (*maths.*)
cosh
co-signatory
   cosignatory
   co-signatories (*pl.*)
cosine, cos (*maths.*)
cos lettuce
cosmetic
   cosmetician
cosmic
   cosmically
cosmonaut
cosmopolitan
cosmos
cossack
cosset
   cosseted
   cosseting
cost
   costlier
   costly
co-star
   costar
costard (apple)
coster
   costermonger
   costermonger's
   (of the costermonger)
   costermongers'
   (of the costermongers)
costive (constipated)

costume
costumier
cosy
   cozy
   cosier
   cozier
   cosily
   cozily
   cosiness
   coziness
cosy (for teapot)
   cozy
   cosies (*pl.*)
   cozies (*pl.*)
cot (baby's)
cotangent, cot (*maths.*)
coterie
cottage
   cottager
cotton
   cottonwool
cotyledon (botany)
couch
   couches (*pl.*)
couch-grass
cough
could (*from* can)
   couldn't (could not)
council (County, etc.)
   councillor
counsel
   (lawyer or advice)
   counselled
   counseled
   counselling
   counseling
   counsellor
   counselor
   counsels
count
   countless
count (nobleman)
   count's (of the count)
   counts' (of the counts)
   countess (*fem.*)

countesses (*pl.*)
countess's
    (of the countess)
countesses'
    (of the countesses)
countdown
countenance
counter (of shop)
counter (to oppose)
  countered
  countering
counteract
  counteracting
  counteraction
counter-attraction
  counterattraction
counterbalance
  counterbalancing
counter-clockwise
counterfeit
counterfoil
counter-irritant
  counterirritant
countermand
countermine
  countermining
counterpane
counterpart
counterpoint
counterpoise
countersign
countersink
  countersunk
counterweight
country
  countries (*pl.*)
  country's
    (of the country)
  countries'
    (of the countries)
countrified
countrify
countryman
countrymen (*pl.*)

countryman's
  (of the countryman)
countrymen's
  (of the countrymen)
county
  counties (*pl.*)
  county council
  county councillor
coup
  coup d'état
  coup de grace
couple
  couplet (poetry)
  coupling
coupon
courage
  courageous
  courageously
courier
course (lectures, etc.)
course (of a meal)
course (golf)
course (direction)
court (tennis, etc.)
court (to woo)
  courtier
  courting
  courtship
court
  courtyard
courtesan
courtesy (politeness)
  courtesies (*pl.*)
courteous
courteously
courtly (polite)
court-martial
  court-martials (*pl.*)
  courts-martial (*pl.*)
  court-martialled
  court-martialed
  court-martialling
  court-martialing
cousin
  cousinly

cousin's (of the cousin)
cousins' (of the cousins)
couture
  couturier
  couturière (*fem.*)
cove (bay)
cove (fellow)
coven (of witches)
covenant
cover
  coverage
  covered
  covering
  coverlet
  cover-up
covert (small wood)
covert (secret)
  covertly
covet (to wish for)
  coveted
  coveting
  covetous
covey (flock of birds)
  coveys (*pl.*)
cow
  cowboy
  cowherd
  cowhide
  cowman
  cowmen (*pl.*)
cow (to subdue)
  cowed
coward
  cowardice
  cowardliness
  cowardly
cower (to crouch)
  cowered
  cowering
cowl (hood)
cowrie, cowry (shell)
cowslip
cox
  coxswain
coxcomb (fop)

coy

coyly

coyness

cozen (to cheat)

cozenage

crab

crabbed

crabby

crack

cracker

crackle

crackling

cradle

cradling

craft (boat)

craft (guile)

craftier

craftily

crafty (sly)

craft (skilled trade)

craftsman

craftsmen (*pl.*)

craftsmanship

crag

craggy

crake

cram

crammed

crammer

cramming

crams

cramp

cranberry

cranberries (*pl.*)

crane (hoisting machine)

cranage

crane (bird)

crane (to stretch neck)

craning

cranium

cranial

crank (engine part)

crankcase

crankshaft

crank (odd person)

crankier

crankiness

cranky

cranny

crannies (*pl.*)

crape (black crêpe)

crapulent

crapulence

crapulous

crash

crash-land

crass (stupid)

crate (packing case)

crater (of volcano)

cravat

crave (to long for)

craving

craven (cowardly)

crawfish, crayfish

crawl

crawler

crayon

craze

crazier

crazily

craziness

crazy

creak (noise)

creaky

cream

creamery

creameries (*pl.*)

creamier

creaminess

creamy

crease

creasing

create

creating

creation

creative

creatively

creativity

creator

creature

creature's

(of the creature)

creatures'

(of the creatures)

crèche

credence

credential

credible

credibility

credibly

credit

creditable

creditably

credited

crediting

creditor

creditor's

(of the creditor)

creditors'

(of the creditors)

credo

credulity

credulous

creed

creek (small stream)

creep

creeper

creepier

creepily

creepiness

creepy

crept

cremate

cremating

cremation

crematorium

crematory

crematoria,

crematoriums(*pl.*)

crematories

Creole

creosote

crêpe (fabric)

crepe

crepitate (to creak)

crepitating
crepitation
crepuscular
crescendo
crescendos (*pl.*)
crescent
cress
crest
crestfallen
cretin (idiot)
cretinism
cretinous
cretonne (cloth)
crevasse (in glacier)
crevice (crack)
crew (*from* crow)
crew (of a ship)
crib (child's cot)
crib (to cheat)
cribbed
cribber
cribbing
cribs
cribbage (game)
crick
cricket
cricketer
cricketer's
(of the cricketer)
cricketers'
(of the cricketers)
cricket (insect)
cried (*from* cry)
crier
cries
crime
criminal
criminally
criminologist
criminology
crimson
cringe
cringing
crinkle
crinkling

crinkly
crinoline
cripple
crippling
crisis
crises (*pl.*)
crisp
crispness
criss-cross
criss-crossed
criss-crossing
criterion
criteria (*pl.*)
critic
critical
critically
criticise
criticize
criticising
criticizing
criticism
critic's (of the critic)
critics' (of the critics)
critique (critical essay)
croak
crochet (knitting)
crocheted
crocheting
crock
crockery
crocodile
crocodile's
(of the crocodile)
crocodiles'
(of the crocodiles)
crocus
crocuses (*pl.*)
croft
crofter
croissant
crony
cronies (*pl.*)
crony's (of the crony)
cronies' (of the cronies)
crook (to bend)

crooked
crookeder
crookedly
crook (criminal)
croon
crooner
crop (of corn, etc.)
crop (to cut)
cropped
cropping
cropper (fall)
croquet (game)
croquette (rissole)
crore (of rupees)
crosier (bishop's staff)
cross (angry)
crossly
crossness
cross
crosses (*pl.*)
crossing
cross-breed
cross-bred
cross-examine
cross-examination
cross-examiner
cross-examining
cross-eyed
cross-legged
cross-purpose
cross-question
cross-questioned
cross-questioner
cross-questioning
cross-reference
crossroad
cross-section
crossword (puzzle)
crotch
(of body or trousers)
crotchet (music)
crotchety (peevish)
crouch
croup
croupier

57

croûton, crouton
crow
  crowing
crow (bird)
crowed (*from* to crow)
crowbar
crowd (of people)
crown
crucial
  crucially
crucible
crucify
  crucified
  crucifix
  crucifixes (*pl.*)
  crucifixion
  crucifying
crude
  crudely
  cruder
  crudity
  crudities (*pl.*)
cruel
  crueller
  cruelly
  cruelty
  cruelties (*pl.*)
cruet
cruise
  cruiser
  cruising
crumb
  crumby
crumble
  crumbling
  crumbly
crumpet
crumple
  crumpling
crunch
  crunchy
crupper
crusade
  crusader
  crusading

crush
  crushed
crust
  crustily
  crusty
crustacea (shellfish)
  crustacean
  crustaceous
crutch
  crutches (*pl.*)
crux
  cruxes, cruces (*pl.*)
cry
  cries (*pl.*)
  cried
  crier
  crying
crypt- (hidden)
  crypt (under church)
  cryptic (obscure)
  cryptically
  cryptogam (plant)
  cryptogram (code)
  cryptograph
  cryptographer
  cryptographic
  cryptography
crystal
  crystalline
  crystallisation
  crystallization
  crystallise
  crystallize
  crystallographer
  crystallography
cub
cubby-hole
cube
  cubic
cubicle
cuckold
cuckoo
  cuckoo's
          (of the cuckoo)

cuckoos'
          (of the cuckoos)
cucumber
cuddle
  cuddling
  cuddly
cudgel
  cudgelled
  cudgeled
  cudgelling
  cudgeling
  cudgels
cue (actor's)
cue (billiards)
cuff (of coat)
cuff (to hit)
cuisine
cul-de-sac
  culs-de-sac (*pl.*)
culinary
cull (to pick flowers)
cull (to kill animals)
culminate
  culminating
  culmination
culottes
culpable
  culpability
  culpably
culprit
  culprit's (of the culprit)
  culprits' (of the culprits)
cult
cultivate
  cultivatable
  cultivating
  cultivation
  cultivator
culture
  cultural
  culturally
  culturing
culvert
cumbersome
cummerbund

cumulative
  cumulatively
cumulus (cloud)
cunning
  cunningly
cup
  cupful
  cupfuls (*pl.*)
  cupped
  cupping
cupboard
cupidity
cupola
cur
  currish
curaçao
curate
  curate's (of the curate)
  curates' (of the curates)
  curacy
  curacies (*pl.*)
curator
curb, kerb (road edge)
  curbstone, kerbstone
curb (harness)
curb (to restrain)
curd
  curdle
  curdling
cure
  curability
  curable
  curative
  curing
curé (priest)
curette (knife)
curfew
curio
  curios (*pl.*)
curious
    (inquisitive, peculiar)
  curiosity
  curiosities (*pl.*)
  curiously
curl

curler
curly
curlew (bird)
curmudgeon
currant (fruit)
currency (money)
  currencies (*pl.*)
current (*electr.*)
current (at present)
  currently
current (flow)
curriculum
  curricula (*pl.*)
  curriculums (pl.)
  curriculum vitae
curry (spice)
  curried
curry (to groom)
  curried
  curries
  curry-comb
  currying
curse
  cursing
cursive (handwriting)
cursor
  (of slide rule, computer)
cursory (rapid)
  cursorily
curt
  curtly
  curtness
curtail
  curtailed
  curtailment
curtain
  curtained
  curtaining
curtsy, curtsey
  curtsies, curtseys (*pl.*)
  curtsied, curtseyed
  curtsies, curtseys
  curtsying, curtseying
curve
  curvature

curving
cushion
cuss
  cussed
  cussedness
custard
custody (imprisonment)
  custodial
  custodian
custom
  customarily
  customary
  custom-built
  customisation
  customization
  customise
  customize
  customising
  customizing
  custom-made
customer
  customer's
    (of the customer)
  customers'
    (of the customers)
cut
  cutter
  cutting
cutaneous
cutback
cute
  cutely
  cuteness
cuticle
cutlass
  cutlasses (*pl.*)
cutler
  cutlery
cutlet
cuttlefish
cyanide (chem.)
cyanosis (disease)
cybernetics
cyclamen
cycle

cycling
cyclist
cyclist's (of the cyclist)
cyclists' (of the cyclists)
cyclometer
cyclic
  cyclical
  cyclically
cyclone
  cyclonic
cygnet (young swan)
cylinder
  cylindrical
  cylindrically
cymbal (gong)
  cymbalist
cynic
  cynical
  cynically
  cynicism
cynosure
cypher, cipher
cypress (tree)
  cypresses (*pl.*)
cyst (bladder)
  cystitis
cytology
Czech
  Czechoslovakia

D

dab
  dabbed
  dabbing
  dabs
dab (fish)
dab (clever person)
dabble
  dabbler
  dabbling

da capo
  (from the beginning)
dace (fish)
dachshund
dad
  daddy
  daddies (*pl.*)
  daddies' (of daddies)
  dad's (of dad)
  dads' (of dads)
  daddy's (of daddy)
dado
  dados (*pl.*)
  dadoes (*pl.*)
daffodil
daft
  dafter
dagger
dago
  dagos (*pl.*)
dahlia
  dahlias (*pl.*)
daily (every day)
  dailies (*pl.*)
dainty
  daintier
  daintily
  daintiness
dairy
  dairies (*pl.*)
  dairymaid
  dairymaid's
    (of the dairymaid)
  dairymaids'
    (of the dairymaids)
dais (platform)
  daises (*pl.*)
daisy
  daisies (*pl.*)
dale (valley)
dally (to dawdle)
  dalliance
  dallied
  dallies
  dallying

Dalmatian
dam (barrier)
  dammed
  damming
damage
  damageable
  damaging
damask
dame
damn
  (to condemn, curse)
  damnable
  damnably
  damnation
  damned
  damning
damp
  dampen
  dampened
  damper
  dampness
damsel
damson
dance
  dancer
  dancer's (of the dancer)
  dancers'
    (of the dancers)
  dancing
dandelion
dandle
  dandling
dandruff
dandy
  dandies (*pl.*)
  dandified
danger
  dangerous
  dangerously
dangle
  dangling
dank
  dankness
daphne (shrub)
dapper

dapple
dare
  daredevil
  daring
dark
  darken
  darker
  darkly
  darkness
darling
darn
dart
dash
  dashboard
dastardly
data (*from* datum)
date
  dating
date (fruit)
dative (*grammar*)
daub
  dauber
daughter
  daughter-in-law
  daughters-in-law (*pl.*)
  daughter-in-law's
   (of the daughter-in-law)
  daughters-in-law's
 (of the daughters-in-law)
  daughter's
      (of the daughter)
  daughters'
      (of the daughters)
daunt
  dauntless
  dauntlessly
Dauphin
davit
dawdle
  dawdler
  dawdling
dawn
day
  days (*pl.*)
  daily

daybreak
daylight
  day's (of the day)
  days' (of the days)
  day to day
daze
dazzle
  dazzling
deacon
  deaconess (*fem.*)
dead
  deaden
  deadened
  deadening
  dead heat
  deadlier
  deadline
  deadliness
  deadlock
  deadlocked
  deadly
deaf
  deafen
  deafened
  deafening
  deafeningly
  deafer
  deafness
deal
  dealer
  dealing
  dealt
dean
  deanery
  deaneries (*pl.*)
dear (expensive)
  dearer
  dearly
  dearness
dear (darling)
  dearest
dearth (scarcity)
death
  deathless
  deathlike

deathly
death-rate
débâcle
debar
  debarred
  debarring
debàrk
  debarkation
debase
  debasement
  debasing
debate
  debatable
  debatably
  debating
debauch (to pervert)
  debauchee
  debaucher
  debauchery
  debaucheries (*pl.*)
debenture
debilitate
  debilitating
  debilitation
  debility
debit
  debitable
  debited
  debiting
debonair
debouch (to emerge)
  debouchment
debrief
debris
debt
  debtor
  debtor's (of the debtor)
  debtors' (of the debtors)
debunk
debus
  debussed
  debussing
début
  débutant
  débutante (*fem.*)

decade

decadent

  decadence

decamp

decant

  decanter

decapitate

  decapitating

  decapitation

decarbonise

  decarbonize

  decarbonisation

  decarbonization

  decarbonising

  decarbonizing

decathlon

decay

decease (death)

  deceased

deceit

  deceitful

  deceitfully

deceive

  deceiver

  deceiving

decelerate

  decelerating

  deceleration

decent (respectable)

  decency

  decencies (*pl.*)

  decently

decentralise

  decentralize

  decentralisation

  decentralization

  decentralising

  decentralizing

deception

  deceptive

  deceptively

decibel

decide

  deciding

  decidedly

deciduous

decimal

  decimalisation

  decimalization

  decimalise

  decimalize

decimate (to kill)

  decimating

  decimation

decipher

  deciphered

  deciphering

  decipherment

decision

  decisive

  decisively

deck (to adorn)

  decked

  decking

deck (of ship)

declaim

  declamation

  declamatory

declare

  declaration

  declaring

declassify

  declassification

  declassified

decline (*grammar*)

  declension

  declinable

  declining

decline (slope down)

  declination

  declining

decline (to deteriorate)

  declining

decline (to refuse)

  declining

declivity

  declivities (*pl.*)

decoction

decode

  decoder

decoding

décolleté

  décolletage

decompose

  decomposable

  decomposing

  decomposition

decompress

  decompression

  decompressor

decongestant

decontaminate

  decontaminating

  decontamination

decontrol

  decontrolled

  decontrolling

décor

decorate

  decorating

  decoration

  decorative

  decorator

decorum

  decorous

  decorously

decoy

decrease

  decreasing

decree

  decreeing

decrement

decrepit

  decrepitude

decry

  decried

  decries

  decrying

dedicate

  dedicating

  dedication

  dedicatory

deduce (to infer)

  deducible

  deducing

deduction

deduct (to subtract)

  deductible

  deduction

deed

deem

deep

  deepen

  deepened

  deepening

  deeper

  deep-laid

  deeply

  deep-seated

deep-freeze

  deep-freezer

  deep-freezing

  deep-frozen

deep-fry

  deep-fried

  deep-frying

deer (animal)

de-escalate

  de-escalation

deface

  defacing

de facto

defame

  defamation

  defamatory

  defaming

default

  defaulter

defeat

  defeatism

  defeatist

defecate, defaecate

  defecating, defaecating

  defecation, defaecation

defect (failure)

  defective

defect (to desert)

  defection

  defector

defence

defense

defenceless

defenseless

defensibilty

defensible

defensibly

defensive

defend

  defendant

  defendant's

    (of the defendant)

  defendants'

    (of the defendants)

  defender

defer (to postpone)

  deferment

  deferred

  deferring

  defers

defer (to yield)

  deference

  deferential

  deferentially

  deferred

  deferring

  defers

defiant (*from* defy)

  defiantly

  defiance

deficient

  deficiency

  deficiencies (*pl.*)

deficit

defile

  defilement

  defiling

define

  definable

  defining

  definition

definite

  definitely

  definitive

  definitively

deflate

deflating

deflation

deflationary

deflect

deflection

deflector

deflower

  deflowered

  deflowering

defoliate

  defoliant

  defoliating

  defoliation

  defoliator

deform

  deformation

  deformity

  deformities (*pl.*)

defraud

defray

  defrayable

  defrayal

defreeze

  defreezing

defrost

deft (neat)

  deftly

  deftness

defunct

defuse

  defusing

defy

  defiance

  defiant

  defiantly

  defied

  defier

  defies

  defying

dégagé

degenerate

  degeneracy

  degenerating

  degeneration

  degenerative

degrade
  degradation
  degrading
degree
dehydrate
  dehydrating
  dehydration
de-ice
  deice
  de-icer
  deicer
  de-icing
  deicing
deify
  deifying
  deification
deign
deism
deity
  deities (*pl.*)
deject
  dejected
  dejection
de jure
delay
  delaying
delectable
delegate
  delegacy
  delegacies (*pl.*)
  delegating
  delegation
delete (to cross out)
  deleting
  deletion
deleterious (harmful)
deliberate (intentional)
  deliberately
deliberate (to consider)
  deliberating
  deliberation
delicate
  delicacy
  delicacies (*pl.*)
  delicately

delicatessen
delicious
  deliciously
delight
  delightful
  delightfully
delimit
  delimitation
delineate
  delineating
  delineation
  delineator
delinquent
  delinquency
  delinquencies (*pl.*)
deliquesce
  deliquescence
  deliquescent
delirium
  delirious
deliver
  deliverance
  delivered
  deliverer
  delivering
  delivery
  deliveries (*pl.*)
delouse
  delousing
delta
delude (to deceive)
  deluding
  delusion
  delusive
deluge (rain storm)
de luxe
delve
  delving
demagnetise
  demagnetize
  demagnetisation
  demagnetization
  demagnetising
  demagnetizing
demagogue

demagoguery
demagogic
demagogy
demand
demarcate
  demarcating
  demarcation
démarche
demean (to behave)
  demeanour (behaviour)
  demeanor
demented
dementia
demesne (estate)
demilitarise
  demilitarize
  demilitarising
  demilitarizing
demise (to bequeath)
  demising
demist
  demister
demitasse
demobilise
  demobilize
  demobilisation
  demobilization
  demobilising
  demobilizing
democracy
  democracies (*pl.*)
  democratic
  democratically
  democratisation
  democratization
  democratise
  democratize
  democratising
  democratizing
demolish
  demolition
demon
  demonic
  demon's (of the demon)

demons'
(of the demons)
demonstrate
demonstrable
demonstrating
demonstration
demonstrative
demonstrator
demoralise
demoralize
demoralisation
demoralization
demoralising
demoralizing
demote (to lower)
demoting
demotion
demount
demur (to object)
demurred
demurring
demurs
demurrage
(late delivery penalty)
demure (modest)
demurely
den
denationalise
denationalize
denationalisation
denationalization
denationalising
denationalizing
denaturalise
denaturalize
dengue (fever)
denial (*from* deny)
denier (thread thickness)
denigrate
denigrating
denigration
denigrator
denim (cloth)
denizen (inhabitant)
denominate

denominating
denomination
denominational
denominator
denote
denoting
dénouement
denouement
denounce
denouncement
denouncer
denouncing
de nouveau
de novo
dense
densely
denseness
denser
density
densities (*pl.*)
dent
dental
dentifrice
dentine
dentition
denture
dentist
dentistry
dentist's (of the dentist)
dentists'
(of the dentists)
denude
denudation
denuding
denunciate
denunciating
denunciation
denunciator
deny
denial
denied
denies
denying
deodorise
deodorize

deodorant
deodorisation
deodorization
deodorising
deodorizing
deo volente, D.V.
(God willing)
depart
departure
department
departmental
departmentalise
departmentalize
departmentally
depend
dependable
dependant (person)
dependent
dependence
dependency
dependencies (*pl.*)
dependent (relying)
depersonalise
depersonalize
depict
depiction
depilatory (hair remover)
depilatories (*pl.*)
deplete
depleting
depletion
deplore
deplorable
deplorably
deploring
deploy
deployment
depopulate
depopulating
depopulation
deport
deportation
deportee
deportment (behaviour)
depose

deposing
deposition
deposit
  deposited
  depositing
  depositor
  depository (store)
  depositories (*pl.*)
depot
deprave (to corrupt)
  depraved
  depraving
  depravity
deprecate (to disapprove)
  deprecating
  deprecation
  deprecator
  deprecatory
depreciate
  (to decrease in value)
  depreciating
  depreciation
depredation (plundering)
  depredator
depress
  depressant
  depressed
  depression
  depressive
depressurise
  depressurize
  depressurisation
  depressurization
  depressurising
  depressurizing
deprive (to take away)
  deprival
  deprivation
  depriving
depth
depute
  deputation
  deputing
  deputise
  deputize

deputising
deputizing
deputy
deputies (*pl.*)
deputy's (of the deputy)
deputies'
    (of the deputies)
derail
  derailment
derange
  derangement
  deranging
derelict
  dereliction
deride
  deriding
  derision
  derisive
  derisory
de rigueur
derive
  derivation
  derivative
  deriving
dermatitis
  dermatologist
  dermatology
derogate
  derogating
  derogation
  derogatory
  derogatorily
derrick
dervish
descant (melody)
descend (to go down)
  descendant (person)
  descent
  (going down, inheritance)
describe
  describable
  describing
  description
  descriptive
desecrate (to profane)

desecrating
desecration
desecrator
desecrater
desegregate
  desegregating
  desegregation
desensitise
  desensitize
desert (to abandon)
  deserter
  desertion
desert (barren region)
deserts (rewards)
deserve
  deservedly
  deserving
déshabillé, dishabille
desiccate (to dry)
  desiccating
  desiccation
  desiccator
desideratum
  desiderata (*pl.*)
design
  designer
  designer's
    (of the designer)
  designers'
    (of the designers)
designate
  designating
  designation
desire
  desirability
  desirable
  desirably
  desiring
  desirous
desist
desk
desolate
  desolation
despair
despatch, dispatch

dispatch
desperado
  desperadoes (*pl.*)
desperate (in despair)
  desperately
  desperation
despicable (*from* despise)
  despicably
despise
  despising
despite (notwithstanding)
despoil
  despoiler
  despoliation
despond
  despondency
  despondent
  despondently
despot
  despotic
  despotically
  despotism
dessert (fruit or sweet)
destination
destine
  destiny
  destinies (*pl.*)
destitute
  destitution
destroy
  destroyer
  destruction
  destructive
  destructively
  destructiveness
  destructor
desultory
  desultorily
  desultoriness
detach
  detachable
  detachment
detail
detain
detect

detectable
detection
detective
detective's
      (of the detective)
detectives'
      (of the detectives)
detector
détente
detention (*from* detain)
deter
  deterred
  deterrent
  deterring
  deters
detergent
deteriorate
  deteriorating
  deterioration
determine
  determinable
  determinant
  determination
  determining
  determinism
detest
  detestable
  detestation
dethrone
  dethroning
  dethronement
detonate
  detonating
  detonation
  detonator
detour
detract
  detraction
  detractor
detriment
  detrimental
  detrimentally
deuce (devil)
deuce (in tennis)
devalue

devaluation
devaluing
devastate
devastating
devastation
devastator
develop
developer
development
developmental
deviate
deviant
deviating
deviation
device (contrivance)
devil
devilment
devilish
devilishly
devilled
deviled
devilry
devious
deviously
deviousness
devise (to plan)
devising
devise (to bequeath)
devising
devoid
devolve
devolution
devolving
devote
devotee
devoting
devotion
devour
devoured
devout
devoutly
devoutness
dew
dewy
dexterity

dextrous
dexterous
dextrously
dexterously
dextrose (kind of glucose)
diabetes
  diabetic
diabolic
  diabolical
  diabolically
diadem
diaeresis
diagnose
  diagnosing
  diagnosis
  diagnoses (*pl.*)
  diagnostic
  diagnostician
diagonal
  diagonally
diagram
  diagrammatic
  diagrammatically
dial
  dialled
  dialed
  dialler
  dialer
  dialling
  dialing
  dials
dialect
dialectic
dialogue
diameter
  diametric
  diametrical
  diametrically
diamond
diapason
diaper
diaphanous
diaphragm
diarchy
  diarchies (*pl.*)

diarrhoea
  diarrhea
diary
  diaries (*pl.*)
  diarist
diastole (heart function)
  diastolic
diathermy
diatom (alga)
diatomic
    (having two atoms)
diatribe (fierce criticism)
dibble
  dibber
dice
  dicing
dicey (risky)
dichotomy
    (division in two)
dicker (to haggle)
  dickered
dicky (shaky)
  dickey
dicotyledon (botany)
dictaphone
dictate
  dictating
  dictation
  dictator
  dictatorial
  dictatorially
  dictator's
    (of the dictator)
  dictators'
    (of the dictators)
diction
dictionary
  dictionaries (*pl.*)
didactic
  didactically
  didacticism
diddle
  diddling
didn't (did not)
die (to end life)

died
die-hard
dying
die (game)
dice (*pl.*)
die (tool)
dies (*pl.*)
dielectric
diesel
diet
dietary
dieted
dietetics
dietician, dietitian
dieting
diets
differ
  differed
  difference
  different
  differential
  differentially
  differentiate
  differentiating
  differentiation
  differing
difficult
  difficulty
  difficulties (*pl.*)
diffident
  diffidently
  diffidence
diffract
  diffraction
diffuse
  diffuser
  diffusing
  diffusion
  diffusive
dig
  digger
  digging
  digs
  dug
digest

digestibility
digestible
digestion
digestive
digit
  digital
digitalin (poison)
  digitalis (drug)
dignify
  dignified (stately)
dignity
  dignitary (official)
  dignitaries (*pl.*)
digress
  digressed
  digresses
  digression
  digressive
dike, dyke
dilapidate
  dilapidating
  dilapidation
dilate
  dilatability
  dilatable
  dilatation
  dilating
  dilation
  dilator
dilatory (delaying)
  dilatorily
  dilatoriness
dilemma
dilettante
  dilettanti,
      dilettantes(*pl.*)
diligent
  diligently
  diligence
dill (herb)
dilly-dally
  dilly-dallied
  dilly-dallies
  dilly-dallying
dilute

diluent
diluting
dilution
diluvial
dim
  dimly
  dimmed
  dimmer
  dimming
dime (coin)
dimension
  dimensional
diminish
  diminution
  diminutive
diminuendo
dimity (fabric)
dimple
  dimpling
din
dinar (Yugoslav money)
dine
  dined
  diner (person)
  dining
  dinner (meal)
dinghy (boat)
  dinghies (*pl.*)
dingy (dark)
  dingier
  dingily
  dinginess
dinner
dinosaur
dint
diocese
  dioceses (*pl.*)
  diocesan
diode
diorama
dioxide
dip
  dipped
  dipper
  dipping

dips
diphtheria
diphthong
diploma
  diplomas (*pl.*)
diplomacy
  diplomacies (*pl.*)
diplomat
diplomatic
diplomatically
diplomatist
diplomat's
     (of the diplomat)
diplomats'
     (of the diplomats)
dipsomania
  dipsomaniac
dire
  direr
  direful
direct
  directing
  direction
  directional
  directive
  director
  directorate
  directory
  directories (*pl.*)
dirge (sad song)
dirigible (airship)
dirndl
dirt
  dirtied
  dirtier
  dirtily
  dirtiness
  dirty
  dirtying
disable
  disabled
  disability
  disabilities (*pl.*)
  disablement
  disabling

disabuse
  disabusing
disadvantage
  disadvantageous
disaffected
  disaffection
disagree
  disagreeable
  disagreeably
  disagreeing
  disagreement
disallow
disappear
  disappearance
  disappeared
  disappearing
disappoint
  disappointment
disapprove
  disapproval
  disapproving
disarm
  disarmament
disarrange
  disarrangement
  disarranging
disarray
disassociate
  disassociating
  disassociation
disaster
  disastrous
  disastrously
disband
  disbandment
disbar
  disbarred
  disbarring
disbelieve
  disbelief
  disbeliever
  disbelieving
disburden
  disburdened
disburse

disbursement
  disbursing
disc
  disk (computer)
  disk
  disc-brake
  disc-jockey
discard
discern
  discernible
  discernment
discharge
  discharging
disciple
  disciple's
      (of the disciple)
  disciples'
      (of the disciples)
discipline
  disciplinarian
  disciplinary
  disciplining
disclaim
  disclaimer
disclose
  disclosing
  disclosure
discolour
  discolor
  discoloration
  discoloured
  discolored
discomfit (to disconcert)
  discomfited
  discomfiting
  discomfiture
discomfort
      (lack of comfort)
discompose
  discomposing
  discomposure
disconcert (to fluster)
disconnect
  disconnection
disconsolate

disconsolately
discontent
discontinue
  discontinuance
  discontinuing
  discontinuity
  discontinuities (*pl.*)
  discontinuous
discord
  discordance
  discordant
discothèque, discotheque
discount
discourage
  discouragement
  discouraging
discourse
  discoursing
discourteous
  discourteously
  discourtesy
  discourtesies (*pl.*)
discover
  discovered
  discoverer
  discovering
  discovery
  discoveries (*pl.*)
discredit
  discredited
  discrediting
discreet (prudent)
  discreetly
  discretion
discrepance, discrepancy
  discrepancies (*pl.*)
  discrepant
discrete (separate)
  discretely
discriminate
  discriminating
  discrimination
  discriminatory
discursive
discus (heavy disc)

discuses, disci (*pl.*)
discuss (to talk over)
  discussion
disdain
  disdainful
  disdainfully
disease
disembark
  disembarkation
disembody
  disembodied
  disembodiment
disembowel
disenchant
  disenchantment
disengage
  disengagement
  disengaging
disentangle
  disentanglement
  disentangling
disestablish
  disestablishment
disfavour
  disfavor
  disfavoured
  disfavored
disfigure
  disfigured
  disfigurement
  disfiguring
disgorge
  disgorging
disgrace
  disgraceful
  disgracefully
  disgracing
disgruntled
disguise
  disguising
disgust
dish
  dishes (*pl.*)
dishabille, déshabillé
dishearten

disheartened
dishevelled
  disheveled
dishonest
  dishonestly
  dishonesty
dishonour
  dishonor
  dishonourable
  dishonorable
  dishonourably
  dishonorably
  dishonoured
  dishonored
disillusion
disincentive
disinclination
  disinclined
disinfect
  disinfectant
  disinfection
disinherit
  disinheritance
  disinherited
  disinheriting
disintegrate
  disintegrating
  disintegration
  disintegrator
disinter
  disinterment
  disinterred
  disinterring
disinterested
disjointed
dislike
  dislikable
dislocate
  dislocating
  dislocation
dislodge
  dislodgement
  dislodgment
  dislodging
disloyal

disloyally
disloyalty
dismal
  dismally
dismantle
  dismantling
dismay
  dismayed
dismember
  dismembered
  dismembering
  dismemberment
dismiss
  dismissal
dismount
disobedient
  disobedience
  disobediently
disobey
  disobeyed
disoblige
  disobliging
disorder
  disordered
  disordering
  disorderliness
  disorderly
disorganise
  disorganize
  disorganisation
  disorganization
  disorganising
  disorganizing
disorientate
  disorientation
disown
disparage
  disparaging
  disparagement
disparate (different)
  disparity
  disparities (*pl.*)
dispassionate
  dispassionately
dispatch, despatch

71

dispatcher
dispel
  dispels
  dispelled
  dispelling
dispense
  dispensary
  dispensaries (*pl.*)
  dispensation
  dispenser
  dispenser's
      (of the dispenser)
  dispensers'
      (of the dispensers)
  dispensing
disperse
  dispersal
  dispersing
  dispersion
dispirit
  dispirited
displace
  displacement
  displacing
display
displease
  displeasing
  displeasure
disport
dispose
  disposable
  disposal
  disposing
disposition
dispossess
  dispossession
      (taking away)
disproportion
  disproportionate
  disproportionately
disprove
  disproving
dispute
  disputable
  disputably

disputant
disputing
disqualify
  disqualification
  disqualified
  disqualifying
disquiet
  disquieten
  disquietened
  disquieted
  disquietening
  disquieting
  disquietude
disquisition
disregard
disrepair
disreputable
  disreputably
  disrepute
disrespect
  disrespectful
  disrespectfully
disrobe
  disrobing
disrupt
  disruption
  disruptive
dissatisfy
  dissatisfaction
  dissatisfied
  dissatisfies
dissect
  dissection
  dissector
dissemble
  dissembler
  dissembling
disseminate
  disseminating
  dissemination
  disseminator
dissent
  dissenter
  dissension
  dissertation

disservice
dissidence (disagreement)
  dissident
  dissident's
      (of the dissident)
  dissidents'
      (of the dissidents)
dissimilar
  dissimilarity
  dissimilarities (*pl.*)
dissimulate (to deceive)
  dissimulating
  dissimulation
  dissimulator
dissipate
  dissipating
  dissipation
dissociate
  dissociating
  dissociation
dissolute
  dissolutely
  dissoluteness
dissolve
  dissoluble
  dissolution
  dissolvent
  dissolving
dissonance
  dissonant
dissuade
  dissuading
  dissuasion
  dissuasive
distaff
  distaffs (*pl.*)
distance
  distant
  distantly
distaste
  distasteful
  distastefully
distemper
  distempered
  distempering

distend
  distensible
  distension
distil
  distill
  distillation
  distilled
  distiller
  distillery
  distilleries (*pl.*)
  distilling
  distils
distinct
  distinction
  distinctive
  distinctly
distingué
distinguish
  distinguishable
distort
  distortion
  distortionless
distract
  distraction
distrain (to seize goods)
  distraint
    (seizure of goods)
distrait
distraught
distress
distribute
  distributing
  distribution
  distributive
  distributor
district
  district nurse
distrust
  distrustful
disturb
  disturbance
  disturber
disunite
  disunion
  disuniting

disunity
disuse
  disusing
ditch
  ditches (*pl.*)
  ditcher
dither
  dithered
  dithering
  dithery
ditto
ditty
  ditties (*pl.*)
diuresis
  diuretic
diurnal (in a day)
  diurnally
diva (prima donna)
divagate
  divagating
  divagation
divan
dive
  diver
  diver's (of the diver)
  divers' (of the divers)
  diving
diverge
  divergence
  divergent
  diverging
divers (various)
diverse (different)
  diversely
  diversity
diversify
  diversification
  diversified
  diversifies
  diversifying
diversion (amusement)
divert (to turn aside)
  diversion
    (alternative route)
divertissement

divest
divide
  dividend
  divider
  dividing
divine (God-like)
  divinely
  divinity
  divinities (*pl.*)
divine (to discover)
  divination
  diviner
  divining
division
  divisible
  divisional
  divisive
  (causing disagreement)
  divisively
  divisor
divorce
  divorcee
  divorcing
divot
divulge
  divulging
dizzy
  dizzier
  dizzily
  dizziness
do
  doer
  does
  doesn't (does not)
  doing
  done
  don't (do not)
docile
  docilely
  docility
dock
  docker
  docker's (of the docker)
  dockers'
    (of the dockers)

dockyard
docket
  docketed
  docketing
doctor
  doctors (*pl.*)
  doctor's (of the doctor)
  doctors' (of the doctors)
  doctorate
  doctored
  doctoring
doctrine
  doctrinaire
  doctrinal
document
  documentary
  documentaries (*pl.*)
  documentation
dodder
  dodderer
  doddery
dodge
  dodging
  dodgy
doe (deer)
doff
dog
  doggie (diminutive)
  doggy (dog-like)
  dog's (of the dog)
  dogs' (of the dogs)
dog (to follow)
  dogs
  dogged
  dogging
dog-ear
  dog-eared
dogged (stubborn)
  doggedly
doggerel
dogma
  dogmas (*pl.*)
  dogmatic
  dogmatically
  dogmatise

dogmatize
dogmatising
dogmatizing
dogmatism
do-gooder
doing (*from* do)
doily
  doilies (*pl.*)
do-it-yourself, DIY
dolce far niente
doldrums
dole (to give out)
  doling
dole (payment)
doleful
  dolefully
doll
  dolled
  dolly
  dollies (*pl.*)
  doll's (of the doll)
  dolls' (of the dolls)
dollar (money)
dollop
dolour (sorrow)
  dolor
  dolorous
dolphin
dolt
domain
dome
Domesday-Book
domestic
  domestically
  domesticate
  domesticity
domicile
  domiciliary
dominate
  dominance
  dominant
  dominantly
  dominating
  domination
domineer

domineered
domineering
dominical
dominion
domino
  dominoes (*pl.*)
don
  donnish
don (to put on)
  donned
  donning
  dons
donate
  donating
  donation
done (*from* do)
donkey
  donkey's
     (of the donkey)
  donkeys'
     (of the donkeys)
donor (giver)
  donor's (of the donor)
  donors' (of the donors)
don't (do not)
doodle
    (to draw aimlessly)
  doodler
  doodling
doodle (*to cheat*)
doom
  doomed
door
dope
  dopey
  doping
dormant
  dormancy
dormer (window)
dormitory
  dormitories (*pl.*)
  dormitory's
    (of the dormitory)
  dormitories'
    (of the dormitories)

dormouse
  dormice (*pl.*)
dorsal
  dorsally
dory (fish)
  dories (*pl.*)
dose
  dosage
  dosing
  dosimeter
doss
  doss-house
dossier
dot
  dotted
  dottier
  dottiest
  dottily
  dotting
  dotty (crazy)
dot (dowry)
dote
  dotage
  dotard
  doting
double
  double-barrelled
  double-breasted
  doubling
  doubly
double entendre
doubt
  doubter
  doubtful
  doubtfully
  doubtfulness
  doubtless
douche
  douching
dough
  doughnut
doughty
  doughtier
  doughtily
  doughtiness

dour (grim)
  dourly
  dourness
douse
  (to drench, extinguish)
  dousing
dove
  dovecot
  dovecote
  dovetail
  dovetailed
dowager
  dowager's
      (of the dowager)
  dowagers'
      (of the dowagers)
dowdy
  dowdier
  dowdily
  dowdiness
dowel
dower
  dower-house
down
  downcast
  downfall
  downfallen
  downhearted
  downpour
  downright
  downstairs
  downtrodden
  downward
down (feathers or fluff)
  downy
Downs
dowry
  dowries (*pl.*)
dowse (for water)
  dowser
  dowsing
doyen
doze
  dozing
dozen

drab
drachma (Greek money)
Draconian (very severe)
draft
  (detachment of men)
draft (of money)
draft (rough copy)
drag
  dragged
  dragging
  drags
dragoman
  dragomans, dragomen
         (*pl.*)
dragon
  dragonfly
  dragonflies (*pl.*)
  dragon's
      (of the dragon)
  dragons'
      (of the dragons)
dragoon
  dragooned
drain
  drainage
drama
  dramatic
  dramatically
  dramatisation
  dramatization
  dramatise
  dramatize
  dramatising
  dramatizing
  dramatis personae
  dramatist
drank (*from* drink)
drape
  draper
  draper's (of the draper)
  drapers' (of the drapers)
  drapery
  draperies (*pl.*)
  draping
drastic

75

drastically

draught (of air)
 draft
 draughtier
 draftier
 draughty
 drafty
draught (drink)
 draft
draughts (game)
 checkers
draughtsman
 draftsman
 draughtsmen (*pl.*)
 draftsmen (pl.)
draw
 drawn
 drew
drawback
drawer
drawing-room
drawl
dread
 dreadful
 dreadfully
 dreadfulness
 dreadnought
dream
 dreamed
 dreamer
 dreamier
 dreamily
 dreamless
 dreamt
 dreamy
dreary
 drearier
 drearily
 dreariness
dredge
 dredger
 dredging
dregs
drench
 drenching

dress
 dresses (*pl.*)
 dressed
 dresser
 dresses
 dressmaker
 dressy
dressage
dribble
 dribbler
 dribbling
driblet
dried (*from* dry)
 drier (more dry)
drier, dryer
   (drying machine)
drift
 drifter
drill (military)
drill (dentist's)
drily (*from* dry)
 dryly
drink
 drank
 drinkable
 drinker
 drunk
 drunkard
drip
 drip-dried
 drip-dry
 drip-drying
 dripped
 dripping
 drips
drive
 driven
 driver
 driver's (of the driver)
 drivers' (of the drivers)
 driving
 drove
drivel
 drivelled
 driveled

driveller
driveler
drivelling
driveling
drivels
drizzle
drizzling
drizzly
drogue (buoy)
droll
drollery
drolleries (*pl.*)
drollness
drolly
dromedary
 dromedaries (*pl.*)
drone
 droning
droop
drop
 droplet
 drop-out
 drop-outs (*pl.*)
 dropped
 dropper
 dropping
 drops
dropsy
 dropsical
dross
drought
drove (*from* drive)
drove (herd)
 drover
drown
 drowned
drowse
 drowsier
 drowsily
 drowsiness
 drowsing
 drowsy
drudge
 drudgery
 drudging

drug
  drugged
  drugging
  druggist
  drugstore
drugget (fabric)
druid
drum
  drum-major
  drummed
  drummer
  drumming
  drums
drunk (*from* drink)
  drunkard
  drunken
  drunkenly
  drunkenness
dry
  dried
  drier, dryer
      (drying machine)
  drier (more dry)
  dries
  drily
  dryly
  dry-clean
  dry-cleaned
  dry-cleaning
  drying
  dryness
dual (double)
  dualism
  dual-purpose
dub
  dubbed
  dubbing
  dubs
dubbin, dubbing (grease)
dubious
  dubiously
ducal (*from* duke)
ducat (money)
duchess
  duchesses (*pl.*)

duchess's
      (of the duchess)
duchesses'
      (of the duchesses)
drugstore
duchy
  duchies (*pl.*)
duck
  duckling
  duck's (of the duck)
  ducks' (of the ducks)
duck
  (to dive or immerse)
duct
  ductless
  ductile
  ductility
dud
dudgeon
due
  duly
duel (fight)
  duelled
  dueled
  duelling
  dueling
  duellist
duenna
  duennas (*pl.*)
  duenna's
      (of the duenna)
  duennas'
      (of the duennas)
duet
duffel, duffle (cloth, coat)
duffer
dug (*from* dig)
  dug-out
  dug-outs (*pl.*)
duke
  dukery
  dukeries (*pl.*)
dulcet
dull
  dullard

duller
dullness
dully
duly (*from* due)
dumb
  dumb-bell
  dumbly
  dumbness
  dumbfound
  dumfound
dummy
  dummies (*pl.*)
  dummy's
      (of the dummy)
  dummies'
      (of the dummies)
dump
  dumpling
  dumpy
  dumpiness
dun
  duns
  dunned
  dunning
dun (dull brown)
dunce
  dunce's (of the dunce)
  dunces' (of the dunces)
dune
dung
  dunghill
  dungaree
  dungarees (*pl.*)
dungeon
duodecimal
  duodecimo
      (size of book)
duodenum
  duodenal
duologue
dupe
  duping
  dupery
duplex
duplicate

duplicating
duplication
duplicator
duplicity
durable
durability
durably
durance
duration
duress
during
dusk
dust
duster
dustiness
dusty
duty
duties (*pl.*)
dutiable
dutiful
dutifully
duty-free
dwarf
dwarfs (*pl.*)
dwarf's (of the dwarf)
dwarfs' (of the dwarfs)
dwell
dweller
dwelling
dwelt
dwindle
dwindling
dye (to colour)
dyed
dyeing
dyer
dying (*from* die)
dyke, dike
dynamic
dynamically
dynamite
dynamiting
dynamo
dynamos (*pl.*)
dynamometer

dynasty
dynasties (*pl.*)
dyne (unit)
dys- (bad)
dysentery
dyslexia
dyslexic
dyspepsia
dyspeptic

E

each
eager
eagerly
eagerness
eagle
eagle-eyed
eaglet
ear
earache
earful
earphone
ear-ring
earl
earldom
earl's (of the earl)
earls' (of the earls)
early
earlier
earliness
earmark
earn
earner
earnest
earnestly
earnestness
earth
earthed
earthenware
earthly
earthquake

earwig
earwig's (of the earwig)
earwigs'
(of the earwigs)
ease
easier
easily
easiness
easing
easy
easygoing
easel
east
easterly
eastern
eastward
eastwards
Easter
easy (*see* ease)
eat
ate
eatable
eaten
eater
eating
eats
eaves
eavesdrop
eavesdropped
eavesdropper
eavesdropping
eavesdrops
ebb
ebb-tide
ebony
ebonite
ebullient
ebullience
ebulliently
eccentric
eccentrically
eccentricity
eccentricities (*pl.*)
ecclesiastic
ecclesiastical

ecclesiastically
echelon
echo
echoes (*pl.*)
echoed
echoes
echoing
éclair
éclat
eclectic
eclecticism
eclipse
eclipsing
ecliptic
eclogue
ecology
ecological
ecologically
ecologist
economy
economies (*pl.*)
economic
economical
economically
economise
economize
economising
economizing
economist
ecstasy
ecstasies (*pl.*)
ecstatic
ecstatically
ecumenical
eczema
eddy
eddies (*pl.*)
eddied
eddying
edelweiss
edge
edgeways
edgily
edginess
edging

edgy
edible
edibility
edict
edifice (building)
edify (to instruct)
edification
edified
edit
edited
edition
editor
editorial
editorially
editor's (of the editor)
editors' (of the editors)
educate
educable
educatability
educability
educatable
educating
education
educational
educationalist
educationally
educationist
educative
educator
educe (to develop, infer)
educible
educing
eduction
eel
eel's (of the eel)
eels' (of the eels)
elver (young eel)
eerie (creepy)
eerier
eerily
eeriness
efface
effaceable
effacement
effacing

effect (to accomplish)
effective (useful)
effectively
effectiveness
effectual (actual)
effeminate
effeminacy
effeminately
effervesce
effervescence
effervescent
effervescing
effete
efficacious
efficaciously
efficacy
efficient
efficiency
efficiently
effigy
effigies (*pl.*)
efflorescence
efflorescent
effluent (liquid discharge)
effluvium (bad smell)
efflux
effort
effortless
effortlessly
effrontery
effronteries (*pl.*)
effusive (emotional)
effusively
effusiveness
effusion
egalitarian
egg (to urge)
egged
egg (bird's)
eggy
ego
egocentric
egocentricity
egoism (selfishness)
egoist

egoistic

egoistically

egotism (conceit)

egotist

egotistic

egotistical

egotistically

egregious

      (absurd, shocking)

egregiously

egregiousness

egress (exit)

eiderdown

Eiffel (tower)

eight

eighteen

eighteenth

eighth

eighthly

eightieth

eighty

eighties (*pl.*)

Eire

Eisteddfod

either (.... or)

ejaculate

ejaculating

ejaculation

ejaculatory

eject

ejection

ejector

eke (out)

eking

elaborate (complicated)

elaborately

elaborateness

elaborate (to work out)

elaborating

elaboration

elapse

elapsing

elastic

elastically

elasticity

elate

elating

elation

elbow

elbowed

elder (older)

elderly

eldest

elder (tree)

elect

election

electioneering

elective

elector

electoral

electorate

electric

electrical

electrically

electrician

electricity

electrification

electrified

electrify

electrifying

electrocardiogram (E.C.G.)

electrocardiograph

electrocardiography

electrocute

electrocuting

electrocution

electrode

electrodynamic

electrodynamically

electrolysis

electrolyte

electrolytic

electromagnet

electromagnetic

electrometer

electrometric

electromotive

electromotive force

      (E.M.F.)

electron

electronic

electronically

electroplate

electroplating

electrostatic

electrotechnical

eleemosynary (charitable)

elegant

elegance

elegantly

elegy

elegies (*pl.*)

elegiac

element

elemental

elementarily

elementary

elephant

elephantine

elephant's

      (of the elephant)

elephants'

      (of the elephants)

elevate

elevating

elevation

elevator

eleven

eleventh

elf

elves (*pl.*)

elfin

elfish

elicit (to get information)

elicited

eliciting

elide (to leave out)

eliding

elision

eligible (suitable)

eligibility

eliminate

eliminating

elimination

eliminator

élite
  élitism
  élitist
elixir
Elizabethan
ellipse
  elliptic
  elliptical
  elliptically
elm
elocution
  elocutionist
elongate
  elongating
  elongation
elope
  elopement
  eloping
eloquence
  eloquent
  eloquently
else
  elsewhere
elucidate
  elucidating
  elucidation
elude (to escape)
  eluding
  elusion
  elusive
  elusiveness
elver (young eel)
elves (*from* elf)
Elysian
emaciate
  emaciating
  emaciation
emanate
  emanating
  emanation
emancipate
  emancipating
  emancipation
  emancipator
emasculate

emasculating
emasculation
embalm
  embalmer
  embalmment
embankment
embargo
  embargoes (*pl.*)
  embargoed
  embargoes
  embargoing
embark
  embarkation
embarras de richesse
embarrass
  embarrassed
  embarrasses
  embarrassment
embassy
  embassies (*pl.*)
  embassy's
        (of the embassy)
  embassies'
        (of the embassies)
embattle
  embattling
embed
  embedded
  embedding
embellish
  embellishment
ember
embezzle
  embezzlement
  embezzler
  embezzling
embitter
  embittered
  embittering
  embitterment
emblazon
emblem
  emblematic
  emblematically
embody

embodied
embodies
embodiment
embodying
embolism
embonpoint (plumpness)
emboss
  embossment
embrace
  embracing
embrasure
embrocation
embroider
  embroidered
  embroidery
  embroideries (*pl.*)
embroil
  embroilment
embryo
  embryos (*pl.*)
  embryologist
  embryology
  embryonic
emend (to remove error)
  emendation
emerald
emerge (to appear)
  emergence
  emergent
  emerging
  emersion (reappearance)
emergency
  emergencies (*pl.*)
  emergently
emeritus
emery
emetic
emigrate
        (to leave country)
  emigrant
  emigrating
  emigration
  émigré
eminent (distinguished)
  eminently

eminence
emissary
emissaries (*pl.*)
emit
emission
emits
emitted
emitter
emitting
emollient (softening)
emolument (pay)
emotion
emotional
emotionally
emotive
empathy
emperor
emperor's
(of the emperor)
emperors'
(of the emperors)
emphasise
emphasize
emphasis
emphases (*pl.*)
emphasising
emphasizing
emphatic
emphatically
emphysema (lung disease)
empire
empirical (experimental)
empirically
emplacement
employ
employability
employable
employe
employee (worker)
employee's
(of the employee)
employees'
(of the employees)
employer (boss)

employer's
(of the employer)
employers'
(of the employers)
employment
emporium
empower
empowered
empowering
empress
empresses (*pl.*)
empress's
(of the empress)
empresses'
(of the empresses)
empty
empties (*pl.*)
emptied
emptier
empties
emptily
emptiness
emptying
emu
emulate (to imitate)
emulating
emulation
emulative
emulator
emulsion
emulsification
emulsified
emulsifier
emulsify
enable
enablement
enabling
enact
enactment
enamel
enamelled
enameled
enameller
enameler
enamelling

enameling
enamour
enamor
enamoured
enamored
en bloc
encampment
encase
encasing
enceinte (pregnant)
encephalitis
enchant
enchanter
enchantment
enchantress (*fem.*)
encircle
encirclement
encircling
enclave
enclose
enclosing
enclosure
encode
encoding
encomium (praise)
encompass
encore
encored
encoring
encounter
encountered
encountering
encounters
encourage
encouragement
encouraging
encroach
encroachment
encumber
encumbered
encumbering
encumbrance
encyclical
encyclopedia,
encyclopaedia

encyclopedic,
    encyclopaedic
end
  endless
  endlessly
endanger
  endangered
  endangering
endear
  endeared
  endearing
  endearment
endeavour
  endeavor
  endeavoured
  endeavored
  endeavouring
  endeavoring
endemic
  endemically
endive
endocrine (gland)
endorse, indorse
  endorsement,
    indorsement
  endorser, indorser
  endorsing, indorsing
endow
  endowment
endure
  endurable
  endurance
  enduring
enema
  enemas (*pl.*)
enemy
  enemies (*pl.*)
energise
  energize
  energiser
  energizer
  energising
  energizing
energy
  energies (*pl.*)

energetic
energetically
enervate (to weaken)
  enervating
  enervation
en famille
enfeeble
  enfeeblement
  enfeebling
enforce
  enforceability
  enforceable
  enforcement
  enforcing
enfranchise
  enfranchisement
  enfranchising
engage
  engagement
  engaging
engender
  engendered
  engendering
engine
  engineer
  engineered
  engineering
  engineer's
    (of the engineer)
  engineers'
    (of the engineers)
engorge
  engorged
engrained
engrave
  engraver
  engraving
engross
  engrossment
engulf
enhance
  enhancement
  enhancing
enigma
  enigmatic

enigmatically
enjoin (to command)
enjoy
  enjoyable
  enjoyably
  enjoyment
enlarge
  enlargeable
  enlargement
  enlarger
  enlarging
enlighten
  enlightened
  enlightenment
enlist
  enlistment
enliven
  enlivened
  enlivenment
en masse
enmity
  enmities (*pl.*)
ennoble
  ennoblement
  ennobling
ennui (boredom)
  ennuyé (bored)
  ennuyée (*fem.*)
en passant
enormous
  enormity
  enormities (*pl.*)
  enormously
enough
enquire, inquire
  inquire
  enquiring, inquiring
  inquiring
  enquiry, inquiry
  inquiry
  enquiries, inquiries (*pl.*)
  inquiries
enrage
  enraging
enrapture

enraptured
enrich
enrichment
enrol
enroll
enrolled
enrolling
enrolment
enrollment
enrols
en route
ensconce
ensconcing
ensemble
enshrine
enshrining
ensign
ensign's (of the ensign)
ensigns' (of the ensigns)
enslave
enslavement
enslaving
ensue (to follow)
ensuing
ensure (to make sure)
ensuring
entail
entailment
entangle
entanglement
entangling
entente
enter
entered
entering
enteric
enteritis
enterprise
enterprising
entertain
entertainer
entertainment
enthrall, enthral
enthralled
enthralling

enthralment
enthrallment
enthrone
enthronement
enthroning
enthuse
enthusiasm
enthusiast
enthusiastic
enthusiastically
enthusing
entice
enticement
enticing
entire
entirely
entirety
entitle
entitlement
entitling
entity
entities (*pl.*)
entomb
entombment
entomology
entomological
entomologist
entourage
entr'acte
entrails
entrance (to delight)
entranced
entrancement
entrancing
entrance (way in)
entrant
entrap
entrapped
entrapping
entraps
entreat
entreaty
entreaties (*pl.*)
entrée
entrench

entrenchment
entrepôt
entrepreneur
entrepreneurial
entropy
entrust
entry
entries (*pl.*)
entwine
entwining
enumerate
enumerating
enumeration
enumerator
enunciate
enunciating
enunciation
enunciator
envelop (to cover)
enveloped
enveloping
envelopment
envelope (covering)
envenom
environ
environment
environmental
environmentally
envisage
envisaging
envoy
envoys (*pl.*)
envoy's (of the envoy)
envoys' (of the envoys)
envy
enviable
envied
envies
envious
enviously
envying
enwrap
enwrapped
enwrapping
enwraps

enzyme
eolith (ancient flint)
epaulette
  epaulet
ephemera, ephemeron (fly)
  ephemeras, ephemerae,
        ephemerons(*pl.*)
ephemeral (short-lived)
  ephemerally
epic
  epical
  epically
epicene (both sexes)
epicentre
  epicenter
epicure
  epicurean
  epicureanism
epicycle
  epicyclic
epidemic
epidermis
  epidermal
epidiascope
epigastrium
  epigastric
epiglottis
epigram (clever saying)
  epigrammatic
epigraph (inscription)
epilepsy
  epileptic
epilogue
Epiphany
episcopal
  episcopacy
  episcopalian
  episcopate
episode
  episodic
epistle
  epistolary
epitaph
    (inscription on tomb)
epithet (adjective)

epitome
epitomise
  epitomize
  epitomising
  epitomizing
epoch
  epochal
eponym
  eponymous
epsilon
equable
  equability
  equably
equal
  equality
  equalities (*pl.*)
  equalled
  equaled
  equally
  equals
equalise
  equalize
  equaliser
  equalizer
  equalising
  equalizing
equanimity
equate
  equating
  equation
equator
  equatorial
equerry
  equerries (*pl.*)
equestrian
  equestrianism
equidistant
equilateral
equilibrate
  equilibrating
  equilibration
equilibrium
equine
equinox
  equinoctial

equip
  equipage
  equipment
  equipped
  equipping
equipoise
equitable
  equitably
  equity
  equities (*pl.*)
equivalent
  equivalence
equivocal
  equivocally
  equivocate
  equivocating
  equivocation
  equivocator
era
  eras (*pl.*)
eradicate
  eradicable
  eradicating
  eradication
erase
  erasable
  eraser
  erasing
  erasure
ere (before)
erect
  erection
  erector
erg (unit)
ergo (therefore)
ergonomics
ergotism (disease)
ermine
erode
  eroding
  erosion
  erosive
erogenous
erotic
  erotica

85

erotically
eroticism
erotism
err
erred
erring
errs
errand (short journey)
errant (wandering)
errancy
errantry
errata (mistakes)
erratic
erratically
error
erroneous
erroneously
ersatz
erstwhile
eructate (to belch)
eructating
eructation
erudite (learned)
eruditely
erudition
erupt (of a volcano)
eruption
eruptive
eruptively
erysipelas
escalade (to climb over)
escalading
escalate (to increase)
escalating
escalation
escalator (moving stairs)
escallop, scallop (shellfish)
escalope (slice of veal)
escapade
escape
escaper
escaping
escapism
escapologist
escapement (of a clock)

escargot (snail)
escarpment (of a hill)
eschatology
eschatological
eschew
escort
Eskimo
Eskimos, Eskimo (pl.)
Eskimo's
(of the Eskimo)
Eskimos'
(of the Eskimos)
esoteric
esoterical
esoterically
esotericism
espalier
especial
especially
Esperanto
espionage
esplanade
espouse
espousal
espousing
espresso
esprit de corps
espy
espied
espies
espying
Esquire
Esq.
essay
essays (pl.)
essayist
essence
essential
essentially
establish
establishable
establishment
estate
esteem
estimable

estimate
estimating
estimation
estimator
estrange
estrangement
estuary
estuaries (pl.)
et cetera, etc.
etch
etcher
etching
eternal
eternally
eternity
eternities (pl.)
ether (drug)
ether (of space)
ethereal
ethereally
ethic
ethical
ethically
ethics (morals)
ethnic (about nations)
ethnically
ethnological
ethnology
ethos (custom, belief)
ethyl
ethylene
etiolate (to make pale)
etiolation
etiquette
étude (music)
etymology
etymological
etymologically
etymologist
eucalyptus
eucalyptuses (pl.)
eucalypti (pl.)
Eucharist
Euclid
Euclidean

eugenic
eugenically
eugenics
eulogy
eulogies (*pl.*)
eulogise
eulogize
eulogising
eulogizing
eulogistic
eulogistically
eunuch
euphemism
euphemistic
euphemistically
euphony (pleasant sound)
euphonious
euphoria (feeling happy)
euphoric
euphuism
(affected style of speech)
euphuistic
Eurasian
eureka
eurhythmics
Eurocrat
Eurodollar
Europe
European
eustachian (tube in ear)
euthanasia
evacuate
evacuating
evacuation
evacuee
evade
evading
evasion
evaluate
evaluating
evaluation
evanesce (to disappear)
evanescent
evangelical
evangelism

evangelist
evaporate
evaporating
evaporation
evaporator
evasion
evasive
evasively
evasiveness
eve
evening
eventide
even
evenly
evenness
event
eventful
eventfully
eventual
eventuality
eventualities (*pl.*)
eventually
eventuate
eventuating
ever
everlasting
evermore
every
everybody
everybody's
(of everybody)
everyone
everywhere
evict
eviction
evidence
evident
evidently
evil
evilly
evince
evincing
eviscerate (to degut)
eviscerating
evisceration

evoke
evocation
evocative
evoking
evolve
evolution
evolutionary
evolutionism
evolutionist
evolving
ewe (sheep)
ewer (jug)
exacerbate
exacerbating
exacerbation
exact
exactitude
exactly
exactness
exaggerate
exaggerating
exaggeration
exaggerator
exalt
exaltation
examine
examination
examiner
examiner's
(of the examiner)
examiners'
(of the examiners)
examining
example
exasperate
exasperating
exasperation
excavate
excavating
excavation
excavator
exceed
exceedingly
excel
excelled

excellence
excellent
excellently
excelling
excels
Excellency
  Excellencies (*pl.*)
  Excellency's
    (of His Excellency)
  Excellencies'
  (of Their Excellencies)
except
  exception
  exceptional
  exceptionally
excerpt (extract)
excess
  excesses (*pl.*)
  excessive
  excessively
exchange
  exchangeable
  exchanger
  exchanging
exchequer
excise (to cut away)
  excisable
  excising
  excision
excise (tax)
excite
  excitability
  excitable
  excitation
  excitement
  exciter
  exciting
exclaim
  exclamation
  exclamatory
exclude
  excluding
  exclusion
  exclusive
  exclusively

exclusiveness
exclusivity
excommunicate
  excommunicating
  excommunication
excrescence
excrete
  excrement
  excreta
  excreting
  excretion
excruciate
  excruciating
  excruciatingly
exculpate (to pardon)
  exculpating
  exculpation
excursion
excuse
  excusable
  excusably
  excusing
execrate
  execrable
  execrably
  execration
executant (performer)
execute
  executing
  execution
  executioner
  executioner's
    (of the executioner)
  executioners'
    (of the executioners)
executive (manager)
  executive's
    (of the executive)
  executives'
    (of the executives)
executor (of a Will)
  executrix (*fem.*)
  executrices (*pl.*)
exemplary
  exemplarily

exemplify
  exemplification
  exemplified
  exemplifies
exempt
  exemption
exercise
  exercising
exert
  exertion
exhale
  exhaling
  exhalation
exhaust
  exhausted
  exhaustible
  exhaustion
  exhaustive
  exhaustively
exhibit
  exhibited
  exhibition
  exhibitionism
  exhibitionist
  exhibitor
exhibition (scholarship)
  exhibitioner
exhilarate
  exhilarant
  exhilarating
  exhilaration
exhort
  exhortation
exhume
  exhumation
  exhuming
exigency
  exigencies (*pl.*)
  exigent
  exigently
exiguous (scanty)
  exiguity
exile
  exiling
exist

existence
existent
existential
existentialism
exit (way out)
exit (he, she goes out)
exeunt (they go out)
exodus
ex officio
exonerate
exonerating
exoneration
exorbitant
exorbitance
exorbitantly
exorcise
     (to free from evil)
exorcize
exorcising
exorcizing
exorcism
exorcist
exotic
exotica
exotically
expand
expandable
expanse
expansible
expansion
expansive
expansively
expatiate
     (to talk at length)
expatiating
expatriate
expatriating
expatriation
expect
expectancy
expectant
expectation
expectorate (to spit)
expectorant
expectorating

expectoration
expedient
expediency
expediencies (*pl.*)
expedite (to hasten)
expediting
expedition
expeditionary
expeditious
expeditiously
expel
expelled
expelling
expels
expulsion
expend
expendability
expendable
expenditure
expense
expensive
experience
experiencing
experiment
experimental
experimentally
experimentation
experimenter
expert
expertise (skill)
expertly
expertness
expert's (of the expert)
experts' (of the experts)
expiate
expiating
expiation
expire (to breathe out)
expiration
expiratory
expiring
expire (to die, finish)
expiring
expiry
explain

explainable
explanation
explanatory
expletive
explicable
explicate (to explain)
explicating
explicit (definite)
explicitly
explicitness
explode
exploding
explosion
explosive
explosively
exploit
exploitation
exploiter
explore
exploration
exploratory
explorer
explorer's
     (of the explorer)
explorers'
     (of the explorers)
exploring
exponent
exponential
export
exportable
exportation
exporter
exporter's
     (of the exporter)
exporters'
     (of the exporters)
exposé
expose
     (detailed description)
exposing
exposition
exposure
expostulate
expostulating

expostulation
expound (to explain)
express
  expressible
  expression
  expressionless
  expressive
  expressively
  expressly
expropriate
  expropriating
  expropriation
  expropriator
expulsion (*from* expel)
expunge
  expunction
  expunging
expurgate
  expurgating
  expurgation
  expurgatory
exquisite
  exquisitely
ex-Service
extant (existing)
extempore
  extemporaneous
  extemporaneously
  extemporisation
  extemporization
  extemporise
  extemporize
  extemporising
  extemporizing
extend
  extendible
  extensible
  extension
  extensive
  extensively
extent (scope)
extenuate (to weaken)
  extenuating
  extenuation
exterior

exterminate (to destroy)
  exterminating
  extermination
  exterminator
external
  externally
extinct
  extinction
extinguish
  extinguisher
extirpate (to root out)
  extirpating
  extirpation
  extirpator
extol
  extolled
  extolling
  extols
extort
  extortion
  extortionate
  extortioner
extra
extract
  extractable
  extraction
  extractive
  extractor
extra-curricular
extradite
  extraditable
  extraditing
  extradition
extra-marital
extramural
extraneous
  extraneously
extraordinary
  extraordinarily
extrapolate
  extrapolating
  extrapolation
extra-sensory
extra-systole (heart-beat)
  extra-systolic

extra-territorial
  extra-territoriality
extravagant
  extravagance
  extravagantly
  extravaganza
extreme
  extremely
  extremist
  extremity
  extremities (*pl.*)
extricate
  extricable
  extricating
  extrication
extrinsic
  extrinsically
extrovert
  extroversion
extrude (to squeeze out)
  extruder
  extruding
  extrusion
exuberant
  exuberance
  exuberantly
exude
  exudation
  exuding
exult
  exultant
  exultation
eye
  eyeball
  eyebrow
  eyed
  eyeful
  eyeing
  eying
  eyelash
  eyelashes (*pl.*)
  eyelid
  eye-opener
  eyepiece
  eyesight

eyesore
eyewash
eyewitness
eyrie (eagle's nest)

F

fable
fabric
fabricate
  fabricating
  fabrication
  fabricator
fabulous
  fabulously
façade
face
  faceless
  facial
  facially
  facing
facet (side or aspect)
  faceted
facetious (humorous)
  facetiously
  facetiousness
facia, fascia (panel)
facial (*from* face)
facile (easy)
  facility
  facilities (*pl.*)
facilitate
  facilitating
  facilitation
facsimile
fact
  factual
  factually
faction
factitious (artificial)
factious (seditious)
factor

factorial
factorially
factorisation
factorization
factorise
factorize
factorising
factorizing
factory
  factories (*pl.*)
  factory's
      (of the factory)
  factories'
      (of the factories)
factotum
  factotums (*pl.*)
facultative (optional)
faculty
  faculties (*pl.*)
fad
  faddish
  faddy
fade
  fadeless
  fading
faeces
  feces
  faecal
  fecal
fag
  fag-end
  fagged
  fagging
faggot
  fagot
Fahrenheit
faience (porcelain)
fail
  failure
fain (willing)
faint
  fainter
  faint-hearted
  faintly
  faintness

fair (light-coloured)
  fairer
  fair-haired
fair
  (outdoor entertainment)
fair (satisfactory)
  fairer
  fairly
  fairness
fair (clear)
  fairway
fairy
  fairies (*pl.*)
  fairy's (of the fairy)
  fairies' (of the fairies)
  fairy tale
fait accompli
faith
  faithful
  faithfully
  faithfulness
  faithless
  faithlessly
  faithlessness
fake
  faker
  faking
fakir (Indian holy man)
falcon
  falconer
  falconry
fall
  fallen
  fell
fallacy
  fallacies (*pl.*)
  fallacious
fallible
  fallibility
fallow
false
  falsehood
  falsely
  falseness
  falsity

falsetto
  falsettos (*pl.*)
falsify
  falsification
  falsified
  falsifies
falter
  faltered
  faltering
fame
  famous
  famously
familiar
  familiarisation
  familiarization
  familiarise
  familiarize
  familiarising
  familiarizing
  familiarity
  familiarly
family
  families (*pl.*)
  family's (of the family)
  families'
      (of the families)
famine
famish
famous
fan
  fanned
  fanning
  fans
fanatic
  fanatically
  fanaticism
fancy
  fancies (*pl.*)
  fancies
  fancied
  fancier
  fanciful
  fancifully
  fancy-free
fanfare

fantasise
  fantasize
  fantasising
  fantasizing
fantasy
  fantasies (*pl.*)
  fantastic
  fantastically
far
  far-fetched
  far-reached
  far-reaching
  far-seeing
  far-sighted
  farther (more distant)
farad (electrical unit)
farce
  farceur
  farcical
  farcically
fare (to travel)
  farewell
  faring
fare (journey money)
farinaceous
      (made of cereal)
farm
  farmer
  farmer's (of the farmer)
  farmers'
      (of the farmers)
  farmhouse
  farmyard
farrier
  farriery
farther, further
  farthest, furthest
farthing
fascia, facia (panel)
fascicle (part of book)
fascinate
  fascinating
  fascination
  fascinator
Fascism

Fascist
fashion
  fashionable
  fashionably
fast (to go without food)
fast (quick)
  faster
fasten
  fastened
  fastener
  fastening
fastidious
  fastidiously
  fastidiousness
fat
  fat-head
  fatness
  fatter
  fattest
fatal
  fatalism
  fatalist
  fatalistic
  fatalistically
  fatality
  fatalities (*pl.*)
  fatally
fate
  fateful
  fatefully
father
  fathered
  fathering
  father-in-law
  fathers-in-law (*pl.*)
  father-in-law's
      (of the father-in-law)
  fathers-in-law's
      (of the fathers-in-law)
  fatherland
  fatherless
  fatherly
  father's (of the father)
  fathers' (of the fathers)
fathom

fatigue
  fatiguing
fatten
  fattened
  fattening
fatuous
  fatuity
  fatuously
faucet (tap)
fault
  faultfinding
  faultier
  faultily
  faultless
  faulty
faun (deity)
fauna (animals)
fauteuil
faux pas
favour
  favor
  favourable
  favorable
  favourably
  favorably
  favoured
  favored
  favouring
  favoring
  favourite
  favorite
  favouritism
  favoritism
fawn (colour)
fawn (deer)
fawn (to flatter or caress)
fay (fairy)
fealty (allegiance)
fear
  fearful
  fearfully
  fearing
  fearless
  fearlessness
  fearsome

feasible
  feasibility
  feasibly
feast
feat (achievement)
feather
  featherbed
  featherbedding
  feathered
  feathering
  featherweight
  feathery
feature
  featureless
  featuring
febrile (feverish)
February
feckless
fecund (fertile)
  fecundity
fed
  fed-up
federal
  federalisation
  federalization
  federalise
  federalize
  federalising
  federalizing
  federalism
  federalist
  federally
federate
  federating
  federation
fee
feeble
  feebler
  feebly
feed
  fed
  fed-up
  feedback
feel
  feeler

feeling
feelingly
felt
feet (*pl.* of foot)
feign (to pretend)
feint (pretence)
felicitate (to congratulate)
  felicitating
  felicitation
felicity (happiness)
  felicitous
  felicitously
feline (catlike)
  felinity
fellow
  fellow's (of the fellow)
  fellows' (of the fellows)
  fellowship
felon (criminal)
  felonious
  felony
  felonies (*pl.*)
felt (cloth)
felt (*from* feel)
female
  female's (of the female)
  females' (of the females
feminine
  femininity
  feminism
  feminist
femme de chambre
  femmes de chambre
                    (*pl.*)
femme fatale
  femmes fatales (*pl.*)
femur (thigh-bone)
  femoral
fence (sword-play)
  fencer
  fencing
fence (hedge)
fend
  fender
fennel

ferment
  fermentation
fern
  fernery
ferocious
  ferociously
  ferociousness
  ferocity
ferret
  ferreted
  ferreting
ferric
  ferrite
  ferrous
ferrule
ferry
  ferries (*pl.*)
  ferried
  ferrying
fertile
  fertilisation
  fertilization
  fertilise
  fertilize
  fertiliser
  fertilizer
  fertilising
  fertilizing
  fertility
fervent
  fervency
  fervently
  fervid
  fervour
  fervor
festal
fester
  festered
  festering
festive
  festival
  festively
  festivity
  festivities (*pl.*)
festoon

fetch
fête
fetid, foetid (smelly)
fetish
  fetishism
fetlock
fetter
  fettered
fettle
feud
feudal
  feudalism
fever
  fevered
  feverish
  feverishly
few
  fewer
fey
fez
  fezzes (*pl.*)
fiancé (male)
  fiancée (female)
  fiancé's (of the fiancé)
  fiancés' (of the fiancés)
  fiancée's (of the fiancée)
  fiancées'
      (of the fiancées)
fiasco
  fiascos (*pl.*)
fiat (order or decree)
fib
  fibbed
  fibber
  fibbing
fibre
  fiber
  fibroid
  fibrositis
  fibrous
fickle
  fickleness
  fickly
fiction
  fictional

fictitious (imaginary)
  fictitiously
fiddle (to cheat)
  fiddler
  fiddling
fiddle (violin)
  fiddler
fidelity
fidget
  fidgeted
  fidgets
  fidgety
fiduciary (trustee)
field
  field marshal
fiend
  fiendish
  fiendishly
fierce
  fiercely
  fierceness
  fiercer
fiery
  fierier
  fierily
  fieriness
fife (flute)
fifteen
  fifteenth
fifth
  fifthly
fifty
  fifties
  fiftieth
fig
  fig-leaf
fight
  fighter
  fought
figment
figurative
  figuratively
figure
  figurehead
  figurine

figuring
filament
filbert
filch (to steal)
  filched
  filches
file
  filing
filial
  filially
filibuster
  filibustered
  filibustering
filigree
fill
  filled
  filler
fillet
  filleted
  filleting
  fillets
fillip (stimulus)
filly (young horse)
  fillies (*pl.*)
film
filter
  filtered
  filtering
  filtrate
  filtration
filth
  filthier
  filthiest
  filthily
  filthiness
  filthy
fin
  finned
  finny
final
  finale (end in music)
  finalise
  finalize
  finalising
  finalizing

finalist
finality
finally
finance
  financial
  financially
  financier
  financier's
        (of the financier)
  financiers'
        (of the financiers)
  financing
finch
  finches (*pl.*)
find
  finder
  found
fine
  finely
  fineness
  finer
  finery
fine (to penalise)
  fined
  fining
finesse (subtlety)
  finessing
finger
  finger-board
  fingered
  fingering
  fingerprint
  fingers
finical
  finically
  finicky
finis (end)
finish
finite
  finitely
fiord, fjord
fir (tree)
fire
  fierily
  fieriness

fiery
fire brigade
fire engine
fire extinguisher
firefly
fireflies (*pl.*)
fireplace
firework
firing
firm (business company)
firm
  firmer
  firmly
  firmness
firmament
first
  first aid
  firstly
  first-rate
firth (estuary)
fiscal
  fiscally
fish
  fish (*pl.*)
  fishes (*pl.*)
  fished
  fisher
  fishery
  fisheries (*pl.*)
  fishes' (of the fishes)
  fishily
  fishmonger
  fish's (of the fish)
  fishy
fission
  fissionable
  fissile
  fissure
fist
  fisticuff
fit
  fits
  fitted
  fitter
  fitting

fit (healthy)
  fitter
  fitness
fit (sudden illness)
fitful
  fitfully
five
  fivefold
  fivepence
  fiver
  fives (game)
fix
  fixation
  fixative
  fixes
  fixed
  fixedly
  fixture
fizz
  fizzle
  fizziness
  fizzling
  fizzy
fjord, fiord
flabbergast
  flabbergasted
flabby
  flabbier
  flabbily
  flabbiness
flaccid
  flaccidity
  flaccidly
flag (to become tired)
  flagged
  flagging
flag (national)
flagellate (to flog)
  flagellating
  flagellation
flageolet (bean)
flageolet (flute)
flagon
flagrant (outrageous)
  flagrancy

flagrantly
flail (to beat)
flail (stick for threshing)
flair (aptitude)
flake
  flaking
  flaky
flambé
flamboyant
  flamboyance
  flamboyantly
flame
  flaming
flamenco
  flamencos (*pl.*)
flamingo
  flamingos (*pl.*)
flammable (inflammable)
flâneur (idler)
flange
flank
flannel
  flannelette
  flannelled
  flanneled
  flannelling
  flanneling
flap
  flapped
  flapper (girl)
  flapping
  flaps
flare (blaze)
  flaring
flash
  flashes (*pl.*)
  flashy
flask
flat
  flatly
  flatter
flatten
  flattened
  flattening
flatter

flattered
flatterer
flattery
flatulent
  flatulence
flaunt
flautist (flute-player)
flavour
  flavor
flavoured
  flavored
flavouring
  flavoring
flavourless
  flavorless
flaw (blemish)
  flawless
  flawlessly
flax
  flaxen
flay
flea (insect)
  flea's (of the flea)
  fleas' (of the fleas)
fledgling (young bird)
flee (to run away)
  fled
  fleeing
fleece (sheep's wool)
  fleecy
fleece (to plunder)
  fleecing
fleet (fast)
  fleeting (passing quickly)
fleet (of ships, cars, etc.)
flesh
  fleshiness
  fleshy
flew (*from* fly)
flex (electric wire)
flex (to bend)
  flexed
  flexibility
  flexible
flick

flicker
  flickered
  flickering
  flickers
flier, flyer
flight
flighty (fickle)
  flightiness
flimsy
  flimsier
  flimsily
  flimsiness
flinch
  flinched
  flinches
fling
  flung
flint
flippant
  flippantly
  flippancy
flipper
flirt
  flirtation
  flirtatious
  flirt's (of the flirt)
  flirts' (of the flirts)
flit
  flitted
  flitting
float
  floated
  floating
  flotation, floatation
flock
floe (floating ice)
flog
  flogged
  flogging
  flogs
flood
  floodgate
  floodlight
  floodlighting
  floodlit

floodlighted
floor (to baffle)
  floored
floor (of a room)
  flooring
flop
  flopped
  floppy
flora (flowers)
  floral
  florist
  florist's (of the florist)
  florists' (of the florists)
florid
floss
  flossy
flotation, floatation
flotilla
  flotillas (*pl.*)
flotsam
flounce
  flouncing
flounder
  floundered
  floundering
flounder (fish)
flour (for bread)
  floury
flourish
flout (to scoff at)
flow
flower (of a plant)
  flowered
  flowering
  flowers
  flowery
flown (*from* fly)
flu (influenza)
fluctuate
  fluctuating
  fluctuation
flue (chimney)
fluent
  fluency
  fluently

fluff
  fluffiness
  fluffy
fluid
  fluidity
fluke (fish)
fluke (lucky chance)
flummox
  flummoxed
flung (*from* fling)
flunkey
  flunky
  flunkeys (*pl.*)
  flunkies (*pl.*)
  flunkey's
    (of the flunkey)
  flunkeys'
    (of the flunkeys)
fluoresce
  fluorescence
  fluorescent
fluoride
  fluoridation
fluorine
flurry
  flurries (*pl.*)
flush
fluster
  flustered
flute
  flautist
  flutist
flutter
  fluttered
  fluttering
fluvial (of a river)
flux
fly
  flew
  flier
  flown
  fly-by-night
  flyer
  flying
  flyleaf

flyleaves (*pl.*)
flywheel
fly (insect)
  flies (*pl.*)
  flies' (of the flies)
  fly's (of the fly)
  flyweight
foal
foam
fob
  fobbed
  fobbing
focal
fo'c's'le, forecastle
focus
  foci, focuses (*pl.*)
  focuses (*pl.*)
  focused
  focuses
  focusing
fodder
foe
  foes (*pl.*)
foetid, fetid (smelly)
foetus, fetus
  foetuses, fetuses (*pl.*)
  foetal, fetal
fog
  fogbound
  fogged
  foggier
  foggily
  fogginess
  fogging
  foggy
  foghorn
fogey, fogy
  (old-fashioned person)
  fogeys, fogies (*pl.*)
foible
foil (to prevent)
  foiled
foil (thin metal)
foist
fold

foldaway
folder
foliage
folio
  folios (*pl.*)
folk
  folklore
follicle
  follicular
follow
  follower
  followthrough
folly
  follies (*pl.*)
foment
  fomentation
fond
  fonder
  fondly
  fondness
fondant (sweetmeat)
fondle
  fondling
fondue
font
food
  foodstuff
fool
  fooled
  foolery
  foolhardiness
  foolhardy
  foolish
  foolishly
  foolproof
  fool's (of the fool)
  fools' (of the fools)
  foolscap
foot
  feet (*pl.*)
  footage
  football
  footsore
  footlight
  footnote

footstool
footwear
footling (silly)
fop
  foppish
forage
  forager
  foraging
foray
  forays (*pl.*)
forbear (to abstain)
  forbearance
  forbearing
  forbears
  forbore
  forborne
forebear, forbear
      (ancestor)
forbid
  forbade, forbad
  forbidden
  forbidding
force
  forceful
  forcefully
  forcefulness
  forcible
  forcibly
  forcing
force majeure
forceps
  forceps (*pl.*)
ford
fore (before, in front of)
forearm
forebode
  foreboding
forecast
  forecaster
forecastle, fo'c's'le
foreclose
  foreclosing
  foreclosure
forecourt
forefather

forefinger
forefront
forego (to go before)
  foregoing
  foregone
  forwent
foreground
forehead
foreign
  foreigner
  foreigner's
     (of the foreigner)
  foreigners'
    (of the foreigners)
  foreignness
foreknowledge
forelock
foreman
  foremen (*pl.*)
  foreman's
     (of the foreman)
  foremen's
     (of the foremen)
foremost
forenoon
forensic
forerunner
foresee
  foresaw
  foreseeable
  foreseeing
  foreseen
foreshadow
foreshore
foreshorten
  foreshortened
  foreshortening
foresight
foreskin
forest
  forester
  forestry
forestall
  forestalled
  forestalling

foretaste
foretell
  foretold
forethought
forever
forewarn
forewoman
  forewomen (*pl.*)
  forewoman's
     (of the forewoman)
  forewomen's
     (of the forewomen)
foreword
forfeit
  forfeited
  forfeiture
forgather
  forgathered
  forgathering
forge
  forger
  forgery
  forgeries (*pl.*)
  forging
forget
  forgetful
  forgetfulness
  forgettable
  forgetting
  forgot
  forgotten
  forgot
forget-me-not
forgive
  forgave
  forgivable
  forgiven
  forgiveness
  forgiving
forgo (to do without)
  forgoes
  forgoing
  forgone
  forwent
fork

fork-lift
forlorn
  forlornly
form
  formation
  formative
  formed
formal
  formalisation
  formalization
  formalise
  formalize
  formalising
  formalizing
  formality
  formalities (*pl.*)
  formally (properly)
format (shape)
  formatted
  formatting
former
  formerly (before)
Formica
formidable
  formidably
formula
  formulae, formulas (*pl.*)
  formulas (pl.)
formulate
  formulating
  formulation
fornicate
  fornicating
  fornication
  fornicator
forsake
  forsaken
  forsaking
  forsook
forsooth
forsythia
fort
  fortress
  fortresses (*pl.*)
forte (loud)

fortissimo (very loud)
forte (special skill)
forth (forward)
  forthcoming
  forthright
  forthwith
fortify
  fortification
  fortified
  fortifies
  fortifying
fortitude
fortress
  fortresses (*pl.*)
  fortress's
     (of the fortress)
  fortresses'
     (of the fortresses)
fortuitous (by chance)
  fortuitously
  fortuity
fortune
  fortunate
  fortunately
  fortune-teller
  fortune-telling
forty
  forties (*pl.*)
  fortieth
forum
  forums, fora (*pl.*)
forward
  forwards
fossil
  fossilisation
  fossilization
  fossilise
  fossilize
foster
  fostered
  fostering
fought (*from* fight)
foul (filthy)
  foully
  fouler

foul-mouthed
foulness
foul (unfair)
foul (unfairness)
found (to establish)
  foundation
  founder
found (*from* find)
  foundling
  foundry
  foundries (*pl.*)
fount
fountain
four
  fourfold
  four score
  foursome
  fourth
  fourthly
fourteen
  fourteenth
fowl (bird)
fox
  foxhound
foyer
fracas (disturbance)
fraction
  fractional
  fractionally
fractious (quarrelsome)
fracture
  fracturing
fragile
  fragilely
  fragility
fragment
  fragmentary
  fragmentation
fragrant (sweet-smelling)
  fragrantly
  fragrance
frail
  frailer
  frailty
  frailties (*pl.*)

frame
  frame-up
  framework
  framing
franc (money)
Frances (*fem.* name)
franchise
Francis (*male* name)
frank (open-hearted)
  frankly
  frankness
frankfurter
frankincense
frantic
  frantically
frater- (brother)
fraternal
  fraternally
  fraternisation
  fraternization
  fraternise
  fraternize
  fraternising
  fraternizing
  fraternity
  fraternities (*pl.*)
Frau
  Fräulein
fraud
  fraudulence
  fraudulent
  fraudulently
fraught
fray
  frayed (torn)
fray (brawl)
freak
  freakish
freckle
free
  freed
  freedom
  freeing
  freely
  freer

freest
free-for-all
freehold
  freeholder
freelance
  freelancing
freemason
  freemasonry
free trade
  free trader
free-wheel
  free-wheeled
  free-wheeling
freeze
  freezer
  freezing
  froze
  frozen
freight (cargo)
  freightage
  freighter
French fries
frenetic, phrenetic
frenzy
  frenzies (*pl.*)
  frenzied
frequency
  frequencies (*pl.*)
frequent (often)
  frequently
frequent (to visit often)
fresco
  frescoes, frescos (*pl.*)
  frescos (pl.)
fresh
  fresher
  freshly
  freshman
  freshness
freshen
  freshened
  freshening
fret
  fretful
  fretted

frets
fretting
fretsaw
fretwork
Freudian
friable (crumbly)
  friability
friar (monk)
  friary
  friaries (*pl.*)
  friar's (of the friar)
  friars' (of the friars)
fricassee
friction
  frictional
Friday
fried (*from* fry)
friend
  friendlier
  friendliness
  friendly
  friend's (of the friend)
  friends' (of the friends)
  friendship
frieze (decoration)
frigate
fright
  frightful
  frightfully
  frightfulness
frighten
  frightened
  frightening
frigid
  frigidity
  frigidly
frill
fringe
  fringe benefit
  fringing
frippery
  fripperies (*pl.*)
Frisbee
frisk (to search)
frisky (lively)

friskiness
fritter
  frittered
  frittering
fritter (fried food)
frivol
  frivolity
  frivolities (*pl.*)
  frivolled
  frivoled
  frivolling
  frivoling
  frivolous
  frivolously
frizzle
frock
frog
  frogman
  frogmen (*pl.*)
  frog's (of the frog)
  frogs' (of the frogs)
frolic
  frolicked
  frolicking
  frolics
  frolicsome
front
  frontage
  frontal
  frontally
  frontier
  frontispiece
frost
  frostbite
  frostbitten
  frostily
  frosty
froth
  frothy
frown
froward (unreasonable)
  frowardness
frowzy
  frowziness
frozen

frugal
  frugality
  frugally
fruit
  fruitarian
  fruiterer
  fruitful
  fruitfully
  fruitfulness
  fruitiness
  fruitless
  fruitlessly
  fruity
fruition
frump
  frumpish
frustrate
  frustation
  frustrating
fry
  fried
  frier
  fries
  fryer
  frying
fry (young fish)
fuchsia (flower)
  fuchsias (*pl.*)
fuddle
  fuddled
fudge
  fudging
fuel
  fuelled
  fueled
  fuelling
  fueling
  fuels
fugal (*from* fugue)
fugitive
fugue (music)
  fugal
fulcrum
fulfil
  fulfill

fulfilled
fulfilling
fulfils
fulfilment
  fulfillment
full
  full-blooded
  fully
fulminate
  fulminating
  fulmination
fulsome
  fulsomely
  fulsomeness
fumble
  fumbling
fume
  fuming
fumigate
  fumigating
  fumigation
  fumigator
fun
  funnier
  funnily
  funny
function
  functional
  functionally
  functionary
  functionaries (*pl.*)
fund
fundamental
  fundamentally
funeral
  funereal (gloomy)
  funerary
fungus
  fungi, funguses (*pl.*)
  fungicidal
  fungicide (fungus killer)
  fungoid (like a fungus)
funicular
funk
  funky

funnel
  funnelled
  funneled
  funnelling
  funneling
fur
  furred (roughened)
  furrier
  furry
furbelow (trimmings)
furbish
  furbished
  furbishes
furious
  furiously
furl
  furled
furlong (eighth of a mile)
furlough (military leave)
furnace
furnish
  furnisher
  furniture
furore
  furor
furrier
furrow
further, farther
  furtherance
  furthered
  furthering
  furthermore
  furthermost
  furthest, farthest
furtive
  furtively
  furtiveness
fury
  furies (*pl.*)
  furious
  furiously
furze
fuse
  fusibility
  fusible

fusing
fusion
fuselage
fusilier
fusillade
fuss
fussed
fusses
fussier
fussily
fussiness
fussy
fusty
futile
futilely
futility
future
futurism
futurist
futuristic
futurologist
futurology
fuzz
fuzzily
fuzziness
fuzzy

G

gabardine (cloth)
gabble (to chatter)
gabbler
gabbling
gable
gad
gadabout
gadded
gadding
gads
gadfly
gadflies (*pl.*)
gadget

gadgetry
Gaelic
gaffe (mistake)
gag
gagged
gagging
gags
gage (pledge)
gaggle (of geese)
gaiety (*from* gay)
gaily
gain
gainer
gainful
gainfully
gainsay
gainsaid
gainsays
gainsaying
gait (style of walking)
gaiter
gaitered
gala
galactic
galantine
galanty show
galaxy
galaxies (*pl.*)
gale
gall (bile)
gall-bladder
galling
gallstone
gallant
gallantry
galleon (ancient ship)
gallery
galleries (*pl.*)
galley
galley-slave
gallivant
gallon
gallop
galloped
galloper

galloping
gallows
gallows (*pl.*)
gallowses (*pl.*)
galore
galosh, golosh
galoshes, goloshes (*pl.*)
galumph
galumphing ·
galvanic
galvanisation
galvanization
galvanised
galvanized
galvanising
galvanizing
galvanism
galvanometer
gambit
gamble (to speculate)
gambler
gambling
gamboge (yellow resin)
gambol (to jump about)
gambolled
gamboled
gambolling
gamboling
gambols
game
gamekeeper
game (ready, willing)
gamely
game, gammy (lame)
game (football, etc.)
game (to gamble)
gaming room
gamin (urchin)
gamine (*fem.*)
gamma
gamma radiation
gamma rays
gammon
gammy (lame)
gamp (umbrella)

103

gamut
gamy
gander
gang
  gangster
  gangsterism
gangling (loose-limbed)
ganglion
    (swelling on nerve)
  ganglia, ganglions (*pl.*)
gangrene
  gangrenous
gangway
gannet
  gannetry
gantry
  gantries (*pl.*)
gaol, jail (prison)
  jail
  gaoled, jailed
  jailed
  gaoler, jailer, jailor
  jailer
gap
gape
  gaping
garage
  garaging
garb (costume)
garbage (rubbish)
garble
  garbled
garçon (waiter)
garden
  gardened
  gardener
  gardener's
    (of the gardener)
  gardeners'
    (of the gardeners)
  gardening
  gardens
gardenia
gargantuan (enormous)
gargle

gargling
gargoyle
garish
garland
garlic
  garlicky
garment
garner (to collect)
  garnered
  garnering
garnet (gem)
garnish
  garnished
garret (attic room)
garrison
  garrisoned
garrotte (to strangle)
  garrote
garrulous
  garrulity
  garrulously
garter
  gartered
  gartering
gas
  gases (*pl.*)
  gaseous
  gaslight
  gassed
  gasses
  gassiness
  gassing
  gassy
gash
  gashed
gasify
  gasified
  gasification
  gasifying
gasket
gasoline
  gasolene
gasometer (gas holder)
gasp
gastric

gastritis
gastronome
  gastronomic
  gastronomical
  gastronomy
gastropod (snail, etc.)
  gastropoda (*pl.*)
gate (entrance)
  gateway
gâteau
  gâteaus, gâteaux (*pl.*)
gather
  gathered
  gathering
gauche (awkward)
  gaucherie
  gaucheness
gaudy
  gaudily
  gaudiness
gauge (measure)
  gauging
gaunt
gauntlet
gauss (unit of magnetism)
gauze
  gauzy
gave (*from* give)
gavel (hammer)
gavotte
gawky (clumsy)
  gawkiness
gay
  gaiety
  gaily
gaze
  gazing
gazebo
  gazebos, gazeboes (*pl.*)
gazelle
gazette (newspaper)
  gazetteer
  gazetting (map index)
gazette
    (official publication)

gazetted

gazetting

gazette (newspaper)

gazetteer

    (geographical index)

gear

  gearbox

  gearing

  gearless

geese (*pl.* of goose)

geezer (old man)

Geiger counter

geisha

gel (to become jelly)

  gelled

  gelling

  gels

gelatine

  gelatin

  gelatinous

geld

  (to castrate an animal)

  gelding

gelid (very cold)

gelignite

gem

gendarme

    (French policeman)

  gendarmerie,

        gendarmery

gender

gene

genealogy

  genealogical

  genealogically

  genealogist

genera (*pl.* of genus)

general (soldier)

  generalissimo

  generalissimos (*pl.*)

  general's

    (of the general)

  generals'

    (of the generals)

general (usual)

generality

generalities (*pl.*)

generally

generalise

generalize

generalisation

generalization

generalising

generalizing

generate

  generating

  generation

  generative

  generator

generic

  generically

generous

  generously

  generosity

Genesis

genetic

  genetically

genial

  geniality

  genially

genie, jinnee (goblin)

  genies, genii, jinn (*pl.*)

  genies (*pl.*)

genital

genitive (*grammar*)

  genitival

genius

  geniuses (*pl.*)

genocide

genre (style)

genteel (well-bred)

  genteelism

  genteelly

  gentility

gentian (plant)

gentile (non-Jew)

gentle (mild or kind)

  gentleness

  gently

gentleman

gentlemen (*pl.*)

gentlemanly

gentleman's

  (of the gentleman)

gentlemen's

  (of the gentlemen)

gentlewoman

gentlewomen (*pl.*)

gentlewoman's

  (of the gentlewoman)

gentlewomen's

  (of the gentlewomen)

gentry

genuflect

  (to bend the knee)

  genuflexion

  genuflection

genuine

  genuinely

  genuineness

genus (biological family)

  genera (*pl.*)

Geoffrey

geo- (earth)

geography

  geographer

  geographic

  geographical

  geographically

geology

  geological

  geologically

  geologist

geometry

  geometric

  geometrical

  geometrically

  geometrician

geophysics

  geophysical

  geophysicist

geranium

  geraniums (*pl.*)

gerbil, jerbil

geriatrics

geriatrician

germ
  germicidal
  germicide
germane (relevant)
germinate
  germinating
  germination
geron- (old man)
  gerontocracy
      (rule by old men)
  gerontocracies (pl.)
  gerontology
      (study of old age)
gerrymander
gerund
  gerundive
gestate
  gestating
  gestation
gesticulate
  gesticulating
  gesticulation
gesture
  gesturing
get
  getting
  gets
  got
gewgaw
geyser (hot spring)
geyser (water-heater)
ghastly
  ghastlier
  ghastliness
gherkin
ghetto
  ghettos (pl.)
ghost
  ghostly
ghoul
  ghoulish
giant
  giant's (of the giant)
  giants' (of the giants)

giantess (fem.)
giantesses (pl.)
giantess's
      (of the giantess)
giantesses'
      (of the giantesses)
gibber
  gibbered
  gibbering
  gibberish
  gibbers
gibbet (gallows)
gibbon (ape)
gibbous (convex)
gibe (to mock)
  gibing
giblets
giddy
  giddier
  giddily
  giddiness
gift
  gift-wrap
  gift-wrapping
gig (small boat)
gig (small carriage)
gigantic
  gigantically
giggle
  giggler
  giggling
gigolo
  gigolos (pl.)
gild (to paint with gold)
  gilded
  gilt
gill (of a fish)
  gilled (having gills)
gill (quarter pint)
gillie, ghillie
      (sportsman's attendant)
gillyflower
gilt-edged
gimcrack
gimlet

gimmick
  gimmickry
  gimmicky
gin (trap)
gin (drink)
ginger
  gingerbeer
  gingerbread
  gingerly
gingham
gingival
  gingivitis
      (disease of gums)
gipsy, gypsy
  gipsies, gypsies (pl.)
giraffe
gird
  girded
  girt
girder
girdle
girl
  girlish
  girlishly
  girlishness
  girl's (of the girl)
  girls' (of the girls)
giro
girth
gist
give
  gave
  given
  giver
  giving
gizzard
glacial
  glaciation
glacé
glacier
glad
  gladden
  gladdened
  gladdening
  gladder

gladly
gladsome
glade
gladiator
gladiolus
  gladioli, gladioluses (*pl.*)
glamour
  glamorisation
  glamorization
  glamorise
  glamorize
  glamorising
  glamorizing
  glamorous
  glamorously
glance
  glancing
gland
  glandular
glare
  glaring
glass
  glasses (*pl.*)
  glassily
  glassware
  glassy
glaucoma (eye-disease)
  glaucous (greyish)
glaze
  glazier
  glazing
gleam
glean (to collect)
  gleaner
glebe
glee
  gleeful
  gleefully
glen
glengarry
glib
  glibber
  glibly
  glibness
glide

glider
gliding
glimmer
  glimmered
  glimmering
glimpse
  glimpsing
glint
glisten
  glistened
  glistening
glitter
  glittered
  glittering
gloaming
gloat
globe
  global
  globally
  globe-trotter
  globe-trotting
  globule
  globular
gloom
  gloomier
  gloomily
  gloominess
  gloomy
glorify
  glorification
  glorified
  glorifies
  glorifying
glory
  glories (*pl.*)
  gloried
  glories
  glorious
  gloriously
gloss
  glossier
  glossiness
  glossy
glossary
  glossaries (*pl.*)

glottis
  glottal
glove
  glover
glow
  glow-worm
glower (to frown)
  glowered
  glowering
glucose
glue
  gluey
  gluing
glum
  glumly
  glummer
  glumness
glut
  glutted
gluten (of flour)
  glutinous (gluey)
  glutenous
     (having gluten)
glutton (greedy person)
  gluttonous
  glutton's
    (of the glutton)
  gluttons'
    (of the gluttons)
  gluttony
glycerine
  glycerin
gnarled
gnash
gnat
  gnat's (of the gnat)
  gnats' (of the gnats)
gnaw
  gnawed
gnocchi
gnome
gnu (antelope)
go
  go-between
  goer

goes
going
gone
went
goad
goal
goalkeeper
goalless
goat
goatee (beard)
gobble
gobbling
gobbledegook
gobbledygook
goblet
goblin
god
goddess (*fem.*)
goddesses (*pl.*)
goddess's
(of the goddess)
goddesses'
(of the goddesses)
God-fearing
God-forsaken
godliness
godly
goggle
goggling
goitre
goiter
goitrous
gold
golden
goldfinch
goldilocks
goldsmith
golf
golf-course
golfer
golf-links
Goliath
golliwog
golosh, galosh
goloshes, galoshes (*pl.*)

gondola
gondolas (*pl.*)
gondolier
gone (*from* go)
goner
gong
gonorrhoea
gonorrhea
goo
gooey (sticky)
good
goodbye
good-humoured
good-humored
good-looking
goodly
goodness
goodness' sake
goodnight
goodwill
goody
goodies (*pl.*)
goon
goose
geese (*pl.*)
gooseflesh
gosling
gooseberry
gooseberries (*pl.*)
gore (blood)
gory
gore (to pierce)
goring
gorge (to eat greedily)
gorging
gorge (deep valley)
gorgeous
gorgeously
Gorgonzola
gorilla
gorillas (*pl.*)
gorilla's (of the gorilla)
gorillas' (of the gorillas)
gorse
gosling (*from* goose)

gospel
gospeller
gospeler
gossamer
gossip
gossiper
gossiping
got (*from* get)
gotten
gouache
gouge
gouging
goulash
gourd
gourmand (greedy person)
gourmandism
gourmet
(connoisseur of food)
gout
gouty
govern
governable
governance
governess
governesses (*pl.*)
governess's
(of the governess)
governesses'
(of the governesses)
governor
governor's
(of the governor)
governors'
(of the governors)
government
governmental
gown
grab
grabbed
grabbing
grabs
grace
graceful
gracefully
gracing

gracious
graciously
graciousness
gradation
grade
gradient
grading
gradual
gradualism
gradually
graduate
graduating
graduation
graduator
graffiti
graft
grail
grain
gram, gramme
grammar
grammarian
grammatical
grammatically
gramophone
granary
granaries (*pl.*)
grand
grandchild
grandchildren (*pl.*)
grandchild's
(of the grandchild)
grandchildren's
(of the grandchildren)
granddaughter
grandee
grandeur
grandfather
grandma
grandmama
grandmother
grandpa
grandpapa
grandson
grandson's
(of the grandson)

grandsons'
(of the grandsons)
grandiloquence
grandiloquent
grandiloquently
Grand Prix
grandiose
grandiosely
grandiosity
grange
granite
granny, grannie
grannies (*pl.*)
granny's (of granny)
grannies' (of grannies)
grant
granulate
granulating
granulation
granule
granular
granularity
grape
grapefruit
graph
graphic
graphical
graphically
graphite
graphology
graphologist
grapnel
grapple
grappling
grasp
grass
grassy
grasshopper
grate (to scrape)
grater (scraper)
grating
grate (of fireplace)
grateful
gratefully
graticule

gratify
gratification
gratified
gratifies
gratifying
gratin
gratis
gratitude
gratuitous (free)
gratuitously
gratuity (grant of money)
gratuities (*pl.*)
grave (serious)
gravely
grave (tomb)
graveyard
gravel
gravelled
graveled
gravelly
gravitate
gravitating
gravitation
gravitational
gravity
gravy
gray
grey, gray
grayling (fish)
graze
grazing
grease
greaser
greasier
greasily
greasiness
greasing
greasy
great
greater
greatly
greatness
greed
greedier
greedily

greediness
greedy
green
greenback
greener
greenery
greengage
greengrocer
greengrocer's
(of the greengrocer)
greengrocers'
(of the greengrocers)
greenness
greet
greeting
gregarious
gregariousness
gremlin
grenade
grenadier
grew (*from* grow)
grey
gray
greyer
grayer
greying
graying
greyhound
grayhound
greyish
grayish
greyness
grayness
grid
gridded
gridiron
griddle
grief
grieve
grievance
grieving
grievous
grievously
griffin, griffon, gryphon
(fabulous beast)

griffon (dog)
griffon (vulture)
grill (to cook)
grilled
grill-room
grille (grating)
grim
grimly
grimmer
grimness
grimace
grimacing
grime
grimier
griminess
grimy
grin
grinned
grinning
grins
grind
grinder
ground
grip
gripped
gripping
grips
gripe
gripes (colic)
griping (pain)
grippe (influenza)
grisly (terrifying)
grist
gristle
gristly (tough)
grit
gritted
grits
gritting
gritty
grizzle
grizzled (grey)
grizzle (to whimper)
grizzling
grizzly (grey)

grizzly bear
groan
groats (oats)
grocer
grocery
groceries (*pl.*)
grocer's (of the grocer)
grocers' (of the grocers)
grog (alcoholic drink)
groggy (unwell)
groggier
grogginess
groin
grommet, grummet
(washer)
groom
groom's (of the groom)
grooms' (of the grooms)
groove
groovy
grope
groping
gross (coarse)
grosser (coarser)
grossly
grossness
gross (to make a profit)
gross (twelve dozen)
grotesque
grotesquely
grotesqueness
grotto
grottoes, grottos (*pl.*)
grouchy
ground
groundless
groundlessly
ground (*from* grind)
group
group's (of the group)
groups' (of the groups)
grouse (to grumble)
grouser
grousing
grouse (bird)

grout

grove

grovel

  grovelled

  groveled

  groveller

  groveler

  grovelling

  groveling

  grovels

grow

  grew

  grower

  growing

  grown

  grown-up

  growth

growl

  growler

groyne (breakwater)

grub

  grubbed

  grubbier

  grubbiness

  grubbily

  grubby

grudge

  grudging

  grudgingly

gruelling

  grueling

gruel (porridge)

gruesome

  gruesomely

  gruesomeness

gruff

  gruffer

  gruffly

  gruffness

grumble

  grumbler

  grumbling

grummet, grommet

        (washer)

grumpy

grumpily

grumpiness

grunt

gruyère (cheese)

gryphon, griffin, griffon

        (fabulous beast)

guano

guarantee

  guarantees (*pl.*)

  guaranteed

  guaranteeing

  guarantees

  guarantor

  guaranty

guard

  guard-room

  guard's (of the guard)

  guards' (of the guards)

  guardsman

  guardsmen (*pl.*)

guardian

  guardianship

guava

gubernatorial

Guernsey

guerrilla, guerilla

guess

  guessed

  guesswork

guest (visitor)

guffaw

  guffawing

guide

  guidance

  guide's (of the guide)

  guides' (of the guides)

  guiding

guild (society)

  Guildhall

guilder (Dutch money)

guile (cunning)

  guileless

guillotine

  guillotining

guilt

guiltier

guiltily

guiltiness

guilty

guinea

  guinea-pig

guise

guitar

  guitarist

gulf

  Gulf Stream

gull

  gulled

  gullibility

  gullible

gull (bird)

gullet

gully (water channel)

  gullies (*pl.*)

gulp

gum (sticky substance)

  gummed

  gumminess

  gumming

  gummy

gum (in mouth)

  gumboil

gumption

gun

  gunned

  gunner

  gunnery

  gunning

  gunpowder

gunnel, gunwale

gurgle

  gurgling

Gurkha

guru (Hindu teacher)

gush

gusset

gust

  gusty

gusto

gut (bowel)

gut (to remove gut)
  gutted
  gutting
gut (to destroy by fire)
  gutted
guts (determination)
gutta-percha
gutter
  guttering
guttersnipe
guttural
  gutturally
guy
  Guy Fawkes
guzzle
  guzzler
  guzzling
gybe (in sailing)
  jibe
  gybing
  jibing
gymkhana
gymnasium, gym
  gymnasiums, gymnasia
          (*pl.*)
  gymnast
  gymnastic
gyne- (woman)
gynaecology
  gynecology
  gynaecological
  gynecological
  gynaecologist
  gynecologist
gypsum
gypsy, gipsy
  gypsies, gipsies (*pl.*)
gyrate
  gyrating
  gyration
  gyratory
gyroscope
  gyroscopic

H

habeas corpus
haberdasher
  haberdashery
habit
  habit-forming
habit (clothes)
  habited (clothed)
habitable
habitat
habitation
habitual (usual)
  habitually
  habituate
  habituated (accustomed)
  habituating
  habituation
  habitude
habitué (frequent visitor)
hack
  hacksaw
  hackle
  hackney
  hackneyed
had
  hadn't (had not)
  haddock
hades
haema-, haemo- (blood)
  hema-, hemo-
  haematologist
  hematologist
  haematology
  hematology
  haematoma
  hematoma
  haemoglobin
  hemoglobin
  haemophilia
  hemophilia

  haemophiliac
  hemophiliac
  haemorrhage
  hemorrhage
  haemorrhoids
  hemorrhoids
hag
  haggard
  haggis
  haggle
  haggler
  haggling
haiku (Japanese poem)
  haiku (*pl.*)
hail (frozen rain)
hail (to greet)
  hailer
hair
  hairbreadth
  hair's breadth
  hairier
  hairiness
  hairless
  hairy
hake (fish)
halcyon
hale (robust)
half
  halves (*pl.*)
  half-caste
  half-hearted
  half holiday
  halfway
  halved
  halving
halibut
halitosis (bad breath)
hall
hallelujah, halleluiah,
          alleluia
hallmark
  hallmarked
hallo, hello, hullo
hallow (make sacred)
  hallowed

Hallowe'en
Halloween
hallucinate
hallucinating
hallucination
hallucinatory
hallucinogen
halo (circle of light)
haloes (*pl.*)
halos (*pl.*)
halt
haltingly
halter
halve (*from* half)
halving
halyard, halliard
ham
hamburger
hamlet
hammer
hammered
hammering
hammers
hammock
hamper (food basket)
hamper (to hinder)
hampered
hampering
hamster
hamstring
hamstrung
hand
handful
handfuls (*pl.*)
hand-made
(made by hand)
handmaid (girl)
hand-me-down
handcuff
handcuffed
handcuffing
handcuffs
handicap
handicapped
handicapping

handicraft
handiwork
handkerchief
handkerchiefs (*pl.*)
handle
handlebar
handler
handling
handsome (good-looking)
handsomely
handsomeness
handwriting
handwritten
handy
handyman
handymen (*pl.*)
handyman's
(of the handyman)
handymen's
(of the handymen)
handier
handily
handiness
hang
hanged
hanger
hangman
hung (picture, etc.)
hangar (for aircraft)
hanger-on
hangover
hang-up
hank (of cotton, etc.)
hanker (to long for)
hankered
hankering
hanky-panky
hansom (cab)
haphazard
hapless (unlucky)
happen
happened
happening
happy
happier

happily
happiness
happy-go-lucky
harangue
haranguing
harass
harassed
harasses
harassment
harbinger
harbour
harbor
harbourage
harborage
harboured
harbored
harbouring
harboring
harbours
harbors
hard
harder
hard-hearted
hard-headed
hardly
hardness
hardship
harden
hardened
hardener
hardening
hardware
hardy
hardier
hardily (boldly)
hare (animal)
harebell
hare-brained
harelip
hare's (of the hare)
hares' (of the hares)
harem
haricot
hark
harlequin

harlequinade
harlot
harlotry
harm
harmful
harmfully
harmless
harmlessly
harmlessness
harmonic
harmonically
harmonica (mouth-organ)
harmonious
harmoniously
harmonise
harmonize
harmonisation
harmonization
harmonising
harmonizing
harmonium
harmony
harmonies (*pl.*)
harness
harp
harpist
harpoon
harpooned
harpooner
harpsichord
harpy (monster)
harpies (*pl.*)
harrier
harrow (to distress)
harrow (mobile rake)
harry (to harass)
harried
harries
harrying
harsh
harshly
harshness
hart (deer)
hartebeest (antelope)
harum-scarum

harvest
harvester
has
has-been
hasn't (has not)
hash
hashish, hasheesh
hasp
hassle
hassock
haste
hastily
hasty
hasten
hastened
hastening
hat
hatter
hatch (egg)
hatchery
hatcheries (*pl.*)
hatch (opening)
hatchway
hatchet
hate
hateful
hating
hatred
haughty
haughtier
haughtily
haughtiness
haul
haulage
hauled
haulier
haunch
haunt
haunted
hausfrau
hauteur
Havana
have
haven't (have not)
having

haven (refuge)
haver (to hesitate)
havered
havering
haversack
havoc
hawk
hawkish
hawser (rope)
hawthorn
hay
hay fever
haymaker
hayrick
haystack
hazard
hazardous
hazardously
haze
hazier
hazily
haziness
hazy
hazel
head
headache
headachy
header
headless
headline
headlong
headmaster
headmaster's
(of the headmaster)
headmasters'
(of the headmasters)
headmistress
headmistresses (*pl.*)
headmistress's
(of the headmistress)
headmistresses'
(of the headmistresses)
headquarters
headstrong
headway

heal (to çure)
  healer
  healing
health
  healthier
  healthily
  healthy
heap
  heaped
hear
  heard
  hearer
  hearing
  hearsay
hearken
  harken
  hearkened
hearse
heart
  heartbreaking
  heartbroken
  heartbrokenly
  heart disease
  heart failure
  heartfelt
  heartless
  heartlessly
  heart-rending
hearten
  heartened
  heartening
hearth
hearty
  heartier
  heartily
  heartiness
heat
  heater
heath
heathen
  heathenism
heather
heave
  heaved
  heaving

hove (nautical use)
heaven
  heavenly
heavy
  heavier
  heavily
  heaviness
  heavyweight
hebdomadal (weekly)
Hebrew
  Hebraic
hecatomb
heckle
  heckler
  heckling
hectare (measure of area)
hectic
  hectically
hecto- (hundred)
  hectogram
  hectolitre
  hectoliter
hector (to bully)
  hectored
  hectoring
hedge
  hedgehog
  hedgehop
  hedgehopped
  hedgehopping
  hedgehops
  hedger
  hedgerow
  hedging
hedonism
    (theory of pleasure)
  hedonist
heed
  heedful
  heedless
heel (to lean over)
heel (of foot)
hefty
  heftier
  heftily

heftiness
hegemony (leadership)
heifer
height (*from* high)
heighten
  heightened
  heightening
heinous (atrocious)
heir (inheritor)
  heir apparent
  heiress (*fem.*)
  heiresses (*pl.*)
  heiress's (of the heiress)
  heiresses'
    (of the heiresses)
  heirloom
  heir's (of the heir)
  heirs' (of the heirs)
held (*from* hold)
hele, heal, heel
  (to put plant in earth)
helicopter
helio- (sun)
  heliotrope
  heliograph
heliport
helium
helix
  helices (*pl.*)
  helical
hell
  hellish
  hellishly
  hell's (of hell)
hello, hallo, hullo
helm
  helmsman
helmet
helot (serf)
  helotry
help
  helper
  helpful
  helpfully
  helpfulness

helpless
helplessly
helplessness
helpmate
helter-skelter
hem
  hemmed
  hemming
  hemstitch
hemi- (half)
  hemiplegia
  hemiplegic
  hemisphere
  hemispherical
hemlock
hemp
  hempen
hen
  hen-coop
  henpecked
hence
  henceforth
henchman
henna
  hennaed
hepatitis (liver disease)
hepta- (seven)
  heptagon
  heptarchy
her
  hers
  herself
herald
  heraldic
  heraldry
  herald's (of the herald)
  heralds' (of the heralds)
herb
  herbaceous
  herbage
  herbal
  herbalist
  herbicide (plant killer)
  herbivore
    (plant-, grass-eater)

herbivorous
herd
  herdsman
here
  hereabout
  hereafter
  hereby
  herein
  hereof
  hereto
  heretofore
  hereunder
  herewith
heredity
  hereditary
  hereditarily
  hereditament
heresy
  heresies (*pl.*)
  heretic
heritance
  heritable
  heritage
  heritor
hermaphrodite
  hermaphroditic
hermetic
  hermetically
hermit
  hermitage
hernia
hero
  heroes (*pl.*)
  heroes' (of the heroes)
  heroic
  heroically
  heroine (brave woman)
  heroism
  hero's (of the hero)
heroin (drug)
heron (bird)
  heronry
herpes
herring
  herring-bone

herring roe
hesitate
  hesitancy
  hesitant
  hesitantly
  hesitating
  hesitation
hessian
hetero- (other)
  heterodox
  heterodoxy
  heterodyne
  heterogeneous
  heterogenous
  heterogeneity
  heterosexual
heuristic
    (by trial and error)
hew (to cut down)
  hewed
  hewer
  hewn
hexa- (six)
  hexagon
  hexagonal
heyday
hiatus
  hiatuses (*pl.*)
hibernate
  hibernating
  hibernation
  hibernator
hiccup, hiccough
  hiccuped
  hiccuping
  hiccups
hide
  hid
  hidden
  hideaway
  hide-out
  hiding
hidebound
hideous
  hideosity

hideously
hier- (sacred)
  hierarch
  hierarchy
  hierarchies (*pl.*)
  hieroglyph
  hieroglyphic
hi-fi
higgledy-piggledy
high
  height
  higher
  highlight
  Highness
  highly
highfalutin,
            highfaluting
highland
  highlander
highway
  highwayman
  highwaymen (*pl.*)
hijack
  hijacked
  hijacker
hike
  hiker
  hiking
hilarious
  hilarity
hill
  hillier
  hillock
  hilly
hilt
him
  himself
hind
  hindmost, hindermost
  hindsight
hinder
  hindered
  hindering
  hindrance
hinge

hinging
hint
hinterland
hip
  hipped
hip (of rose bush)
hippo- (horse)
  hippodrome
  hippopotamus
  hippopotamuses (*pl.*)
hippy, hippie
  hippies (*pl.*)
hire
  hireling
  hire purchase
  hiring
hirsute (hairy)
his
hiss
  hisses (*pl.*)
  hissed
  hisses
  hissing
histology
        (science of tissues)
history
  histories (*pl.*)
  historian
  historic
  historical
  historically
histrionic (theatrical)
  histrionically
hit
  hits
  hitter
  hitting
hitch
  hitch-hike
  hitch-hiker
  hitch-hiking
hitch (fault)
hither
  hitherto
hive

hiving
hoar (grey)
  hoariness
  hoary
hoard (to store)
  hoarder
  hoarding (wooden boards)
hoarse (husky)
  hoarsely
  hoarseness
  hoarser
hoax
  hoaxes (*pl.*)
  hoaxer
hobble
  hobbling
hobbledehoy
hobby
  hobby-horse
  hobbies (*pl.*)
hobgoblin
hobnob
  hobnobbed
  hobnobbing
  hobnobs (he, she)
hobo
  hobos, hoboes (*pl.*)
hock (of horse)
hock (wine)
hockey
hocus (to hoax)
  hocussed
  hocused
  hocussing
  hocusing
hocus-pocus
hod
hodgepodge (mixture)
hoe
  hoed
  hoeing
hog
  hogged
  hoggish
  hog's (of the hog)

117

hogs' (of the hogs)
hogshead
hog-wash
hogmanay
hoi polloi
    (ordinary people)
hoist
hold
  held
  holdall
  holder
  holdup
hole
  holey (full of holes)
holiday
  holidayer
hollandaise
hollow
holly (tree)
hollyhock
holo- (whole)
  holocaust
  hologram
  holograph
holster
holy (sacred)
  Holy Ghost
  holier
  holiness
homage
home
  home-coming
  homeless
  home-made
  homesick
  homesickness
  homespun
  homestead
  homeward
  homewards
  homework
  homing
homely
  homelier
  homeliness

homicide
homicidal
homily (sermon)
  homilies (*pl.*)
homo- (same)
  homoeopath
  homoeopathy
  homoeopathic
  homogeneous
  homogeneity
  homogenise
  homogenize
  homogenous
        (same kind)
  homologous
    (same relative value)
  homonym
  homonymic
  homophone
  homosexual
  homosexuality
homo sapiens
hone
  honing
honest
  honestly
  honesty
honey
  honeycomb
  honeydew
  honeyed
honeymoon
  honeymooner
honeysuckle
honorarium
  honorariums,
        honoraria(*pl.*)
honorary
honorific
honour
  honor
  honourable
  honorable
  honourably
  honorably

honoured
honored
honouring
honoring
hood
hoodlum
hoodwink
  hoodwinked
hoof
  hooves, hoofs (*pl.*)
hook
hookah, hooka (pipe)
hookey, hooky (truancy)
  hooky
hooligan
  hooliganism
  hooligan's
    (of the hooligan)
  hooligans'
    (of the hooligans)
hoop
hoop-la
hoot
  hooter
hop
  hopped
  hopper
  hopping
  hops
hope
  hopeful
  hopefully
  hopeless
  hopelessly
  hopelessness
  hoping
hopscotch
horde (crowd)
horizon
  horizontal
  horizontally
hormone
horn
  horned
  hornless

hornpipe

hornet

  hornet's (of the hornet)

  hornets' (of the hornets)

horoscope

horrendous

horrible

  horribly

horrid

horrific

  horrifically

horrify

  horrified

  horrifies

  horrifying

horror

hors d'oeuvre

horse (animal)

  horseback

  horsehair

  horsepower

  horse-radish

  horseshoe

  horsewhip

  horsewhipped

  horsewhipping

  horsewhips

  horsy

horticulture

  horticultural

  horticulturist

hosanna

hose (pipe)

  hosing

hose (stocking)

  hosier

  hosiery

hospice

hospitable (welcoming)

  hospitably

  hospitality

hospital

  hospitalisation

  hospitalization

  hospitalise

hospitalize

host

  hostess (*fem.*)

  hostesses (*pl.*)

  hostess's

      (of the hostess)

  hostesses'

      (of the hostesses)

  host's (of the host)

  hosts' (of the hosts)

hostage

hostel

hostelry

  hostelries (*pl.*)

hostile

  hostilely

  hostility

  hostilities (*pl.*)

hot

  hotheaded

  hotly

  hotter

hotchpot (legal)

  hotchpot, hotchpotch

      (cookery)

hotel

  hotelier

hound (dog)

hound (to chase)

hour

  hourly

houri

  houris (*pl.*)

house

  housebreaker

  houseful

  household

  householder

  housekeeper

  housekeeping

  housemaster

  housemaster's

    (of the housemaster)

  housemasters'

    (of the housemasters)

housewife

housewives (*pl.*)

housewife's

    (of the housewife)

housewives'

    (of the housewives)

housework

housing

hovel

hover

  hovercraft

  hovered

  hovering

how

  however

  howsoever

howitzer

howl

  howler (bad mistake)

hoyden

hub

hubbub

huddle

  huddling

hue (colour)

hue (outcry)

huff

  huffily

  huffy

hug

  hugged

  hugging

  hugs

huge

  hugely

  huger

Huguenot

hulk

  hulking

hull

hullabaloo

hullo, hallo, hello

hum

  hummed

  humming

humming-bird
hums
human
  humanly
humane (kind)
  humanely
  humaneness
humanist
  humanism
  humanistic
humanitarian
  humanitarianism
humanity
  humanities (*pl.*)
humble
  humbleness
  humbly
humbug
  humbugged
  humbugging
humdrum
humerus (arm-bone)
  humeral
humid
  humidified
  humidifier
  humidifies
  humidify
  humidifying
  humidity
humiliate
  humiliated
  humiliating
  humiliation
humility
hummock (mound)
humoresque
humour
  humor
  humorist
  humorous
  humorously
  humoured
  humored
  humouring

humoring
hump
  humpback
humus (of soil)
hunch (lump)
  hunchback
hunch (sudden idea)
hundred
  hundredfold
  hundredth
  hundredweight
hung (*from* hang)
hunger
  hungrier
  hungrily
  hungry
hunk
hunt
  hunter
  hunter's (of the hunter)
  hunters' (of the hunters)
  huntress (*fem.*)
  huntsman
  huntsmen (*pl.*)
hurdle
  hurdling
hurdy-gurdy
hurl (to throw)
hurly-burly
hurrah, hurray
hurricane
hurry
  hurried
  hurriedly
  hurries
  hurrying
hurt
hurtle
  hurtling
husband
  husbandry
  husband's
    (of the husband)
  husbands'
    (of the husbands)

hush
husk (shell)
husky (dog)
  huskies (*pl.*)
husky (hoarse)
  huskily
  huskiness
hussar
hussy
  hussies (*pl.*)
hustings
hustle
  hustler
  hustling
hut
  hutment
  hutted
  hutting
hutch
  hutches (*pl.*)
hyacinth
hybrid
hydr- (water)
hydra (water-snake)
hydrangea
hydrant
hydrate
  hydrating
  hydration
hydraulic
  hydraulically
hydrocarbon
hydrocephalus
  hydrocephalic
  hydrocephalous
hydrochloric
hydrodynamic
hydro-electric
hydrofoil
hydrogen
hydrology
hydrolysis
  hydrolytic
hydrometer
  hydrometric

hydrometry
hydropath
  hydropathic
hydrophobia
hydroplane
hydrostatic
hydrotherapy
  hydrotherapeutic
hydroxide
hyena, hyaena
hygiene
  hygienic
  hygienically
hygro- (wet)
  hygrometer
  hygrometric
  hygroscope
  hygroscopic
hymen (membrane)
  hymeneal
hymn
  hymnal
hyper- (over, beyond)
  hyperbola (curve)
  hyperbole (exaggeration)
  hyperbolic
  hyperbolical
  hypermarket
  hypersensitive
  hypertension
  hypertensive
  hyperthyroidism
hyphen
  hyphenated
hypno- (sleep)
  hypnosis
  hypnotic
  hypnotise
  hypnotize
  hypnotising
  hypnotizing
  hypnotism
  hypnotist
hypo- (under)
hypochondria

hypochondriac
hypocrisy
  hypocrite
  hypocritical
  hypocritically
hypodermis
  hypodermic
  hypodermically
hypotenuse
hypothermia
hypothesis
  hypotheses (*pl.*)
  hypothetical
  hypothetically
hysteria
  hysterical
  hysterically
  hysterics
hysteresis (in magnetism)
hysterectomy

I

I'd (I had, would)
I'll (I shall, will)
I'm (I am)
I've (I have)
ice
  iceberg
  icebreaker
  icecap
  icecream
  ice-hockey
  icicle
  icily
  icing
  icy
ichthyo- (fish)
  ichthyology
  ichthyologist
icon

iconoclasm
iconoclast
idea
ideal
  ideally
idealise
  idealize
  idealisation
  idealization
  idealising
  idealizing
  idealism
  idealist
idée fixe
identical
  identically
identify
  identifiable
  identification
  identified
  identifies
  identifying
identity
  identities (*pl.*)
  identikit
ideology
  ideologies (*pl.*)
  ideological
  ideologically
idiom
  idiomatic
  idiomatically
idiosyncrasy
  idiosyncrasies (*pl.*)
  idiosyncratic
  idiosyncratically
idiot
  idiocy
  idiotic
  idiotically
  idiot's (of the idiot)
  idiots' (of the idiots)
idle (lazy)
  idleness
  idler (lazy person)

idler (more idle)
idling
idly
idol (image)
idolater
idolatrous
idolatry
idolise
idolize
idolisation
idolization
idolising
idolizing
idyll
(rural poem or prose)
idyllic
igloo
igneous
ignite
ignitable
igniter
igniting
ignition
ignoble
ignobly
ignominy
ignominies (*pl.*)
ignominious
ignominiously
ignoramus
ignoramuses (*pl.*)
ignorance
ignorant
ignorantly
ignore
ignoring
ilk
ill
illness
illnesses (*pl.*)
I'll (I will)
illegal
illegality
illegalities (*pl.*)
illegally

illegible (unreadable)
illegibility
illegibly
illegitimate
illegitimacy
illegitimately
illicit (unlawful)
illicitly
illimitable (without limit)
illiterate (can't read)
illiteracy
illogical
illogicality
illogicalities (*pl.*)
illogically
illuminate
illuminating
illumination
illusion (misleading idea)
illusionist
illusive (deceptive)
illusory
illustrate
illustrating
illustration
illustrative
illustrator
illustrious
illustriously
illustriousness
I'm (I am)
image
imagery
imagine
imaginable
imaginary
imagination
imaginative
imaginatively
imagining
imbalance
imbecile
imbecility
imbibe
imbibing

imbroglio
imbroglios (*pl.*)
imbue
imbued
imbuing
imitate
imitating
imitation
imitative
imitator
immaculate
immaculacy
immaculately
immanent (inherent)
immanence
immanency
immaterial
immaterially
immature
immaturely
immaturity
immeasurable
immeasurably
immediacy
immediate
immediately
immemorial (very ancient)
immense
immensely
immensity
immerse
immersing
immersion
immigrate
(to come as settler)
immigrant
immigrant's
(of the immigrant)
immigrants'
(of the immigrants)
immigrating
immigration
imminent
(happening soon)
imminently

imminence
immiscible (not mixable)
immobile
  immobilisation
  immobilization
  immobilise
  immobilize
  immobilising
  immobilizing
  immobility
immoderate
  immoderately
immodest
  immodestly
  immodesty
immoral
  immorality
  immorally
immortal
  immortality
  immortally
immortalise
  immortalize
  immortalisation
  immortalization
  immortalising
  immortalizing
immovable
  immovably
immune
  immunity
immunise
  immunize
  immunisation
  immunization
  immunising
  immunizing
  immunology
immure
  immuring
immutable
  immutability
  immutably
imp
  impish

impishly
impishness
imp's (of the imp)
imps' (of the imps)
impact
  impaction
impair
  impaired
  impairing
  impairment
impale
  impalement
  impaling
impalpable
  impalpably
impart
impartial
  impartiality
  impartially
impassable
impasse
impassioned
impassive
  impassively
  impassiveness
  impassivity
impatience
  impatient
  impatiently
impeach
  impeachable
  impeachment
impeccable
  impeccability
  impeccably
impecunious
  impecuniosity
impede
  impedance (*electr.*)
  impeding
impediment
  impedimenta
    (army luggage)
impel
  impelled

impeller
impelling
impels
impend
  impending
impenetrable
  impenetrability
impenitence
  impenitent
  impenitently
imperative
  imperatively
imperceptible
  imperceptibly
imperfect
  imperfection
  imperfectly
imperial
  imperialism
  imperialist
  imperialistic
  imperially
imperil
  imperilled
  imperiled
  imperilling
  imperiling
  imperilment
  imperils
imperious
  imperiously
  imperiousness
imperishable
  imperishably
impermissible
impermeable
  impermeability
impersonal
  impersonally
impersonate
  impersonating
  impersonation
  impersonator
impertinence
  impertinent

impertinently
imperturbable
  imperturbability
  imperturbably
impervious
  imperviousness
impetigo
impetuous
  impetuosity
  impetuously
impetus
  impetuses (*pl.*)
impinge
  impingement
  impinging
impious
  impiety
implacable
  implacability
  implacably
implant
  implantation
implausible
  implausibility
  implausibly
implement
  implementation
implicate
  implicating
  implication
implicit
  implicitly
implied (*from* imply)
implode
    (to burst inwards)
  imploding
  implosion
  implosive
implore
  imploring
imply
  implication
  implied
  implies
  implying

impolite
  impolitely
  impoliteness
impolitic (not prudent)
  impoliticly
imponderable
  imponderability
import
  importation
  importer
importance
  important
  importantly
importunate
    (very persistent)
  importunately
  importunity
importune
    (to ask persistently)
  importuning
impose
  imposing
  imposition
impossible
  impossibility
  impossibly
impost (tax)
impostor (deceiver)
imposture (fraud)
impotence (helplessness)
  impotent
  impotently
impound
impoverish
  impoverishment
impracticable
  impracticability
  impracticably
impractical
imprecate (to curse)
  imprecation
imprecise
  imprecisely
  imprecision
impregnable

impregnability
impregnably
impregnate
  impregnating
  impregnation
impresario
  impresarios (*pl.*)
  impresario's
    (of the impresario)
  impresarios'
    (of the impresarios)
impress
  impressed
  impressible
impression
  impressionable
  impressionism
impressive
  impressively
  impressiveness
imprest (money advanced)
  imprest account
imprimatur
  (permission to print)
imprint (publisher's name)
imprint
  (to impress or stamp)
imprison
  imprisonment
improbable
  improbability
  improbably
impromptu
improper
  improperly
  impropriety
  improprieties (*pl.*)
improve
  improvable
  improvement
  improver
  improving
improvidence
    (carelessness)
  improvident

improvidently
improvise
improvisation
improviser
improvising
imprudence (indiscretion)
imprudent
imprudently
impudence (rudeness)
impudent
impudently
impugn (to discredit)
impugned
impugning
impulse
impulsive
impulsively
impunity
(without punishment)
impure
impurity
impurities (*pl.*)
impute (to blame)
imputable
imputation
imputing
inability
inaccessible
inaccessibility
inaccuracy
inaccuracies (*pl.*)
inaccurate
inaccurately
inaction
inactive
inactively
inactivity
inadequacy
inadequacies (*pl.*)
inadequate
inadequately
inadmissible
inadmissibility
inadmissibly
inadvertence

inadvertent
inadvertently
inadvisable
inadvisability
inadvisably
inalienable
(not transferable)
inalienability
inamorato (lover)
inamorata (*fem.*)
inane
inanely
inanity
inanities (*pl.*)
inanimate
inapplicable
inapplicably
inappreciable (very small)
inappreciably
inappropriate
inappropiateness
inappropriately
inapt (unsuitable)
inaptly
inaptness
inaptitude
inarticulate
inarticulately
inarticulateness
inartistic
inartistically
inasmuch
inattention
inattentive
inattentively
inaudible
inaudibility
inaudibly
inaugurate
inaugural
inaugurating
inauguration
inaugurator
inauguratory
inauspicious (unlucky)

inauspiciously
inborn
inbreed
inbred
inbreeding
incalculable
incalculability
incalculably
incandescence
incandescent
incantation
incapable
incapability
incapably
incapacitate
incapacitating
incapacitation
incapacity
incarcerate (to imprison)
incarcerating
incarceration
incarnate
incarnation
incautious
incautiously
incendiary
incendiaries (*pl.*)
incendiarism
incense (to make angry)
incensing
incense (perfumed smoke)
incentive
inception
incertitude
incessant
incessantly
incest
incestuous
incestuously
inch
inches (*pl.*)
incidence
incident
incidents (*pl.*)
incidental

125

incidentally
incinerate
  incinerating
  incineration
  incinerator
incipient
incise
  incision
  incisive
  incisively
  incisor (tooth)
incite (to urge)
  incitation
  incitement
  inciter
  inciting
incivility
  incivilities (*pl.*)
inclement
  inclemency
  inclemently
incline
  inclination
  inclining
include
  including
  inclusion
  inclusive
  inclusively
incognito
incoherence
  incoherent
  incoherently
incombustible
  incombustibility
income
  income tax
incomer
  incoming
incommensurable
    (not comparable)
incommensurate
    (not adequate)
incommode
  incommoded

incommoding
incommodious
incommunicado
incomparable
  incomparably
incompatible
  incompatibility
incompetence
  incompetent
  incompetently
incomplete
  incompletely
  incompleteness
incomprehensible
  incomprehensibility
  incomprehensibly
incompressible
  incompressibility
inconceivable
  inconceivably
inconclusive
  inconclusively
incongruous
  incongruously
  incongruity
  incongruities (*pl.*)
inconsequent
  inconsequential
  inconsequently
inconsiderable
    (very small)
  inconsiderably
inconsiderate
  inconsiderately
inconsistency
  inconsistencies (*pl.*)
  inconsistent
  inconsistently
inconsolable
inconspicuous
  inconspicuously
  inconspicuousness
inconstant
  inconstancy
incontestable

incontestably
incontinence
incontinent
incontrovertible
  incontrovertibly
inconvenience
  inconvenient
  inconveniently
inconvertible
  inconvertibility
incorporate
  incorporating
  incorporation
incorrect
  incorrectly
  incorrectness
incorrigible
  incorrigibility
  incorrigibly
incorruptible
  incorruptibility
increase
  increasing
  increasingly
incredible (unbelievable)
  incredibility
  incredibly
incredulous (unbelieving)
  incredulity
increment
incriminate
  incriminating
  incrimination
  incriminatory
incrustation
incubate
  incubating
  incubation
  incubator
incubus
  incubuses (*pl.*)
  incubi (*pl.*)
inculcate
    (to suggest strongly)
  inculcating

inculcation
inculpate (to accuse)
  inculpating
  inculpation
incumbency
  incumbencies (*pl.*)
  incumbent
incur
  incurred
  incurring
  incurs
incurable
  incurability
  incurably
incurious
incursion
  incursive
indebted
  indebtedness
indecency
  indecencies (*pl.*)
  indecent
  indecently
indecipherable
indecision
  indecisive
  indecisively
indeclinable (*grammar*)
indecorous
  indecorously
  indecorousness
  indecorum
indeed
indefatigable
  indefatigability
  indefatigably
indefensible
  indefensibly
indefinable
indefinite
  indefinitely
indelible
  indelibly
indelicate
  indelicacy

indelicacies (*pl.*)
indelicately
indemnify
  indemnification
  indemnified
  indemnifies
  indemnifying
indemnity
  indemnities (*pl.*)
indent
  indentation
  indented
indenture
independent
  independence
  independently
indescribable
  indescribably
indestructible
  indestructibility
  indestructibly
indeterminable
    (can't be settled)
indeterminate (doubtful)
  indeterminately
index
  indexes (*pl.*)
  indices (*pl.*)
  indexation
indicate
  indicating
  indication
  indicative
  indicatively
  indicator
indict (to accuse)
  indictable
  indictment
indifference
  indifferent
  indifferently
indigenous (native)
indigent (poor)
  indigence (poverty)
indigestion

indigestibility
indigestible
indignant (angry)
  indignantly
  indignation
indignity
  indignities (*pl.*)
indigo
indirect
  indirectly
indiscernible
indiscipline
indiscreet
  indiscretion
  indiscreetly
indiscriminate
  indiscriminately
indispensable
  indispensability
  indispensably
indisposed
  indisposition
indisputable
  indisputably
indistinct
indistinguishable
indite (to write)
  inditing
individual
  individualism
  individualist
  individualistic
  individuality
  individually
individualise
  individualize
  individualisation
  individualization
  individualising
  individualizing
indivisible
  indivisibility
  indivisibly
indoctrinate
  indoctrination

indoctrinating
indolence
  indolent
  indolently
indomitable
  indomitably
indoor
  indoors
indubitable
  indubitably
induce
  inducement
  inducing
induct (to introduce)
  induction
inductance (*electr.*)
  induction
  inductive
  inductively
indulge
  indulgence
  indulgent
  indulgently
  indulging
industrial
  industrialisation
  industrialization
  industrialise
  industrialize
  industrialising
  industrializing
  industrialism
  industrialist
  industrialist's
    (of the industrialist)
  industrialists'
    (of the industrialists)
  industrially
industry
  industries (*pl.*)
  industrious
  industriously
inebriate
  inebriating
  inebriation

inebriety
inedible (uneatable)
  inedibility
ineducable
ineffable (indescribable)
  ineffably
ineffaceable
  ineffaceably
ineffective (not efficient)
  ineffectively
  ineffectiveness
ineffectual (useless)
  ineffectually
inefficient
  inefficiency
  inefficiencies (*pl.*)
  inefficiently
inelastic
  inelastically
  inelasticity
inelegant
  inelegancy
  inelegantly
ineligible (unsuitable)
  ineligibilty
ineluctable (unavoidable)
inept (silly)
  ineptitude (silliness)
  ineptly
inequality
  inequalities (*pl.*)
inequitable
  inequitably
ineradicable
  ineradicably
inert
  inertia
  inertly
  inertness
inescapable
  inescapably
inessential
inestimable
  inestimably
inevitable

inevitableness
inevitability
inevitably
inexact
  inexactitude
inexcusable
  inexcusably
inexhaustible
  inexhaustibly
inexorable
  inexorably
inexpedient
  inexpediency
  inexpediently
inexpensive
  inexpensively
inexperience
inexplicable
  inexplicably
inexpressible
  inexpressibly
inextinguishable
inextricable
  inextricably
infallible
  infallibility
  infallibly
infamous
  infamously
  infamy
infant
  infancy
  infanticide
  infantile
  infant's (of the infant)
  infants' (of the infants)
infantry
  infantryman
infatuate
  infatuation
infect
  infection
  infectious
  infectiousness
infelicity

infelicities (*pl.*)
infelicitous
infelicitously
infer
inference
inferential
inferred
inferring
infers
inferior
inferiority
infernal
infernally
inferno
infernos (*pl.*)
infertile
infertility
infest
infestation
infidel
infidelity
infidelities (*pl.*)
infiltrate
infiltrating
infiltration
infiltrator
infinite (very large)
infinitely
infinitude
infinity
infinitesimal (very small)
infinitesimally
infinitive (*grammar*)
infinitival
infirm
infirmary
infirmaries (*pl.*)
infirmity
infirmities (*pl.*)
inflame
inflaming
inflammable
inflammation
inflammatory
inflate

inflatable
inflating
inflation
inflationary
inflect
inflection
inflective
inflexion
inflexible
inflexibility
inflexibly
inflict
infliction
influence
influencing
influential
influentially
influenza
influx
inform
informant
information
informative
informer
informal
informality
informally
infraction
infra dig.
infra-red
infrastructure
infrequent
infrequency
infrequently
infringe
infringement
infringing
infuriate
infuriating
infuse
infuser
infusing
infusion
ingenious (clever)
ingeniously

ingenuity
ingénue
ingenuous (naïve)
ingenuously
ingenuousness
ingest
ingestion
inglorious
ingloriously
ingoing
ingot
ingrain
ingrained
ingratiate
ingratiating
ingratitude
ingredient
ingress
ingrowing
inhabit (to dwell in)
inhabitable
inhabitant
inhale
inhalant
inhalation
inhaling
inherent
inherence
inherently
inherit
inheritable
inheritance
inherited
inheritor
inhibit (to restrain)
inhibited
inhibition
inhibitory
inhospitable
inhospitably
inhuman (barbarous)
inhumanity
inhumanities (*pl.*)
inhumanly
inhumane (cruel)

inhumanely
inimical
inimitable
  inimitably
iniquitous
  iniquitously
  iniquity
  iniquities (*pl.*)
initial (at the beginning)
  initially
initial (to sign)
  initialled
  initialed
  initialling
  initialing
  initials
initiate
  initiating
  initiation
  initiative
  initiator
inject
  injection
injudicious
  injudiciously
injunction
injure
  injuring
  injurious
  injuriously
  injury
  injuries (*pl.*)
injustice
ink
  inky
inkling (hint)
inland
in-law
inlay
  inlaid
inlet
inmate
in memoriam
inmost
inn

innkeeper
innkeeper's
    (of the innkeeper)
innkeepers'
    (of the innkeepers)
innards
innate
  innately
inner
  innermost
innings
  innings (*pl.*)
innocence
  innocent
  innocently
innocuous (harmless)
  innocuously
innovate
  innovating
  innovation
  innovator
innuendo
  innuendoes, innuendos
         (*pl.*)
  innuendos (*pl.*)
innumerable
  innumerably
inoculate
  inoculating
  inoculation
inoffensive
  inoffensively
  inoffensiveness
inoperable
  (unfit for operation)
inoperative
  (not functioning)
  inoperativeness
inopportune
  inopportunely
inordinate
  inordinately
inorganic
input
  inputting

inquest
inquire (to investigate)
  enquire (to ask)
  inquiring
  inquiry
  inquiries (*pl.*)
inquisition
  inquisitor
  inquisitorial
inquisitive
  inquisitively
  inquisitiveness
inroad
inrush
insalubrious
  insalubrity
insane (mad)
  insanely
  insanity (madness)
insanitary (unhealthy)
  insanitariness
insatiable
  insatiably
inscribe
  inscribing
  inscription
inscrutable
  inscrutability
  inscrutably
insect
  insecticide
  insect's (of the insect)
  insects' (of the insects)
insecure
  insecurely
  insecurity
inseminate
  inseminating
  insemination
insensate (stupid)
insensible (unconscious)
  insensibility
  insensibly
insensitive (unfeeling)
  insensitively

insensitiveness
insensitivity
inseparable
inseparably
insert
insertion
inset
insetting
inshore
inside
insider
insidious
insidiously
insidiousness
insight
insignia
insignia (*pl.*)
insignificant
insignificance
insignificantly
insincere
insincerely
insincerity
insinuate
insinuating
insinuation
insinuator
insipid
insipidly
insipidness
insist
insistence
insistent
insistently
insobriety
insolent
insolence
insolently
insoluble
insolubility
insolubly
insolvent
insolvence
insomnia
insomniac

insouciant
insouciance
inspect
inspection
inspector
inspectorate
inspector's
(of the inspector)
inspectors'
(of the inspectors)
inspire
inspiration
inspiring
instability
install
installed
installing
installation
instalment
installment
instance
instancing
instant
instantaneous
instantaneously
instantly
instead
instep
instigate
instigating
instigation
instigator
instil
instill
instilled
instilling
instils
instills
instinct
instinctive
instinctively
institute
instituting
institution
institutional

institutionalise
institutionalize
institutionalising
institutionalizing
instruct
instruction
instructional
instructive
instructor
instructor's
(of the instructor)
instructors'
(of the instructors)
instrument
instrumental
instrumentalist
instrumentality
instrumentation
insubordinate
insubordinately
insubordination
insubstantial (unreal)
insufferable
insufferably
insufficient
insufficiency
insufficiently
insular
insularity
insulate
insulating
insulation
insulator
insulin
insult
insuperable
insuperably
insupportable
insure
insurability
insurable
insurance
insurer
insuring
insurgent

insurgence
insurgency
insurmountable
insurmountably
insurrection
insurrectionary
intact
intake
intangible
intangibly
integer
integral
integrally
integrate
integrating
integration
integrity
intellect
intellectual
intellectualise
intellectualize
intellectualising
intellectualizing
intellectualism
intellectually
intelligent (clever)
intelligence
intelligently
intelligentsia
intelligible
(understandable)
intelligibility
intelligibly
intemperate
intemperance
intemperately
intend
intention
intense
intensely
intensify
intensification
intensified
intensifies
intensifying

intensity
intensities (*pl.*)
intensive
intensively
intent (purpose)
intention
intentional
intentionally
intent (earnest)
intently
inter (to bury)
interment (burial)
interred
interring
inters
inter alia
interact
interaction
interbreed
interbred
intercalate (to insert)
intercalary
intercalating
intercalation
intercede
interceding
intercession
intercept
interception
interceptor
interchange
interchangeable
interchanging
intercommunicate
intercom.
intercommunicating
intercommunication
interconnect
interconnection
intercontinental
intercourse
interdenominational
interdepartmental
interdependence
interdependent

interdependently
interdict
interdiction
interdisciplinary
interest
interested
interface
interfere
interference
interfering
interim
interior
interiorly
interject
interjection
interlace
interlacing
interleave
interleaving
interline
interlining
interlock
interlope
interloper
interloping
interlude
intermarry
intermarriage
intermarried
intermarries
intermarrying
intermediary
intermediaries (*pl.*)
intermediate
intermediately
interment (burial)
intermezzo
intermezzos, intermezzi
(*pl.*)
intermezzi (pl.)
interminable
interminably
intermingle
intermingling
intermission

intermittent
intermittently
intern, interne (doctor)
intern (to confine)
internee
internment
internal
internally
international
internationalisation
internationalization
internationalise
internationalize
internationalised
internationalized
internationalism
internationally
internecine
interpellate
    (to ask questions)
interpellating
interpellation
interplanetary
Interpol
interpolate (to insert)
interpolating
interpolation
interpose
interposing
interposition
interpret
interpretation
interpreter
interracial
interregnum
interrelated
interrelating
interrelation
interrogate
interrogating
interrogation
interrogative
interrogator
interrupt
interrupter

interruption
interruptor
intersect
intersection
intersperse
interspersion
interspersing
interstellar
interstice
interstitial
interval
intervene
intervening
intervention
interview
interviewee
interviewer
interweave
interweaving
interwove
interwoven
intestate (without a Will)
intestacy
intestine
intestinal
intimate (to suggest)
intimating
intimation
intimate (friendly)
intimacy
intimately
intimidate (to frighten)
intimidating
intimidation
intolerable (unbearable)
intolerably
intolerance (impatience)
intolerant
intolerantly
intonation (pitch of voice)
intone (to chant)
intoning
intoxicate
intoxicant
intoxicated

intoxicating
intoxication
intractable
intractableness
intractably
intramuscular
intransigent
intransigence
intransigently
intransitive
intrauterine
intravenous
intrepid
intrepidity
intrepidly
intricate
intricacy
intricacies (*pl.*)
intricately
intrigue
intriguer
intriguing
intrinsic
intrinsically
introduce
introducing
introduction
introductory
introspection
introspective
introvert
introversion
intrude
intruder
intruding
intrusion
intrusive
intuition
intuitive
intuitively
inundate
inundating
inundation
inure
inured

invade
  invader
  invading
  invasion
invalid (ill person)
  invalidism
  invalid's (of the invalid)
  invalids'
      (of the invalids)
invalid (not valid)
  invalidate
  invalidating
  invalidation
invaluable (very valuable)
invariable
  invariably
invasion
invective
inveigh (to abuse)
  inveighed
inveigle (to entice)
  inveigling
invent
  invention
  inventive
  inventiveness
  inventor
  inventor's
      (of the inventor)
  inventors'
      (of the inventors)
inventory (list)
  inventories (*pl.*)
inverse
  inversely
  inversion
invert
  inverter
invertebrate
invest
  investment
  investor
  investor's
      (of the investor)

investors'
      (of the investors)
investigate
  investigating
  investigation
  investigator
investiture
inveterate
  inveteracy
  inveterately
invidious (causing offence)
  invidiously
invigilate
  invigilating
  invigilation
  invigilator
invigorate
  invigorating
  invigoration
invincible
  invincibility
  invincibly
inviolable (sacred)
inviolate (unbroken)
invisible
  invisibility
  invisibly
invite
  invitation
  inviting
invocation (*from* invoke)
invoice
  invoicing
invoke
  invocation
  invoking
involuntary
  involuntarily
involuted (complicated)
involve
  involvement
  involving
invulnerable
  invulnerability
inward

inwardly
inwardness
inwards
iodine
iodide
ion
ionic
ionisation
ionization
ionise
ionize
ionising
ionizing
ionosphere
iota
ipecacuanha
ipso facto
irascible
irascibility
irascibly
irate
irately
ire (anger)
ireful
iridescence
iridescent
iris
  irises (*pl.*)
irk
irksome
iron
ironmonger
ironmonger's
  (of the ironmonger)
ironmongers'
  (of the ironmongers)
ironmongery
iron ore
irony
  ironies (*pl.*)
ironic
ironical
ironically
irradiate
irradiating

irradiation
irrational
  irrationality
  irrationally
irreconcilable
  irreconcilability
  irreconcilableness
  irreconcilably
irrecoverable
  irrecoverably
irredeemable
  irredeemably
irreducible
  irreducibly
irrefutable
  irrefutably
irregular
  irregularity
  irregularities (*pl.*)
  irregularly
irrelevance
  irrelevant
     (not to the point)
  irrelevantly
irreligious
irremediable
  irremediably
irremissible
irremovable
  irremovably
irreparable
  irreparably
irreplaceable
irrepressible
  irrepressibly
irreproachable
  irreproachably
irresistible
  irresistibly
irresolute
  irresolutely
irrespective
  irrespectively
irresponsible
  irresponsibility

irresponsibly
irretrievable
  irretrievably
irreverent (not pious)
  irreverence
  irreverently
irreversible
  irreversibility
  irreversibly
irrevocable
  irrevocability
  irrevocably
irrigate
  irrigating
  irrigation
  irrigator
irritable
  irritability
  irritably
irritate
  irritant
  irritating
  irritation
irrupt (to break in)
  irruption
  irruptive
isinglass
island
  islander
  island's (of the island)
  islands' (of the islands)
  isle
  islet
isn't (is not)
isobar
isochronous
isolate
  isolating
  isolation
isometric
  isometrically
isosceles
isotherm
  isothermal
isotope

issue
  issuance
  issuing
isthmus
  isthmuses, isthmi (*pl.*)
italic
  italicise
  italicize
  italicising
  italicizing
itch
  itched
  itches
  itching
  itchy
item
  itemise
  itemize
  itemising
  itemizing
iterate (to repeat)
  iterating
  iteration
  iterative
itinerant
  itinerary
  itineraries (*pl.*)
it's (it is)
its (of it)
  itself
I've (I have)
ivory
  ivories (*pl.*)
ivy
  ivies (*pl.*)
  ivy's (of the ivy)
  ivies' (of the ivies)

J

jab
  jabbed

jabbing
jabs
jabber
jabbered
jabbering
jack
jackanapes
jack-knife
jack-knives (*pl.*)
jack-knifed
jack-knifing
jackal
jackass
jackasses (*pl.*)
jackdaw
jacket
Jacobean
(of James I's time)
Jacobin
(French revolutionary)
Jacobinic
Jacobinical
Jacobite
(loyal to James II)
jade
jaded
jag
jagged
jaguar
jail, gaol
jailer, gaoler, jailor
jam
jammed
jamming
jammy
jamb (of door)
jamboree
jangle
jangling
janitor
January
japan (to varnish)
japanned
japanning
japonica

jar
jarred
jarring
jardinière
jargon
jasmine, jasmin,
jessamine
jasper
jaundice
jaundiced
jaunt (short walk)
jaunty (sprightly)
jauntily
jauntiness
javelin
jaw
jawbone
jay
jazz
jazzy
jealous
jealously
jealousy
jeans
jeep
jeer
jeered
jeering
jejune (scanty)
jelly
jellies (*pl.*)
jellied
jellified
jellifies
jellifying
jemmy
jemmies (*pl.*)
jeopardy
jeopardise
jeopardize
jeopardising
jeopardizing
jeremiad (lamentation)
jeroboam (large bottle)
jerk

jerkily
jerkiness
jerky
jerkin (jacket)
jerry
jerry-builder
jerry-building
jerry-built
jersey
jerseys (*pl.*)
jessamine, jasmine
jest
jester
jet
jet-propelled
jetting
jetsam
jettison
jettisoned
jetty
jetties (*pl.*)
jewel
jewelled
jeweled
jeweller
jeweler
jeweller's
(of the jeweller)
jewellers'
(of the jewellers)
jewellery, jewelry
jewelry
jib
jibbed
jibbing
jibe (to agree, fit)
jibe (*see* gibe, gybe)
jiffy
jig
jiggered
jigsaw
jilt
jingle
jingling
jingo

jingoes (*pl.*)
jingoism
jinx
jitter
jittery
jiu-jitsu
   (Japanese wrestling)
      jiu-jutsu, ju-jitsu
jive
  jiving
job
  jobber
  jobbery
  jobless
jockey
  jockeys (*pl.*)
  jockey's (of the jockey)
  jockeys'
      (of the jockeys)
  jockeyed
jocose (playful)
  jocosely
  jocosity
jocular (humorous)
  jocularity
  jocularly
jocund (cheerful)
  jocundity
  jocundly
jodhpurs
jog
  jogged
  jogging
  jogs
joggle
  joggling
joie de vivre
join
  joiner
  joinery
  joiner work
joint
  jointer
  jointly
jointure (inheritance)

joist
joke
  joker
  joking
  jokingly
jolly
  jollier
  jolliest
  jollification
  jollify
  jollifying
  jollily
  jollity
jolt
jonquil
josser (fellow)
jostle
  jostling
jot
  jotted
  jotting
joule (unit of energy)
journal
  journalese
  journalism
  journalist
journey
  journeys (*pl.*)
  journeyed
  journeying
  journey's
      (of the journey)
  journeys'
      (of the journeys)
jovial
  joviality
  jovially
jowl
joy
  joyful
  joyfully
  joyless
  joyous
  joyously
  joy-ride

joy-riding
jubilant
  jubilantly
  jubilation
jubilee
judder
  juddered
  juddering
judge
  judgement
  judging
  judgment
judicature (jurisdiction)
judicial (lawful)
  judicially
judiciary
  (all judges in a country)
judicious (reasonable)
  judiciously
judo (ju-jitsu)
jug
  jugged
juggernaut
juggle
  juggler
  jugglery
  juggling
jugular (vein)
juice
  juicier
  juiciest
  juicily
  juiciness
  juicy
ju-jitsu
jujube
juke-box
julep
julienne
jumble
  jumble sale
  jumbling
jumbo
jump
  jumper

jumpily
jumpiness
jumpy
junction
juncture
jungle
junior
  juniority
juniper
junk
junket
  junketed
  junketing
junta
juridical (relating to law)
jurisconsult (legal expert)
jurisdiction (legal power)
  jurisdictional
jurisprudence
     (science of law)
  jurisprudent
jurist (legal expert)
juror
  juror's (of the juror)
  jurors' (of the jurors)
jury
  juries (*pl.*)
  juryman
  jurymen (*pl.*)
just
  justly
justice
justiciary
  (legal administrator)
  justiciaries (*pl.*)
justify
  justifiable
  justifiably
  justification
  justified
  justifying
jut
  jutted
  jutting
  juts

jute
juvenile
juxtapose
  juxtaposing
  juxtaposition

K

kale (cabbage)
kaleidoscope
  kaleidoscopic
kalends, calends
kamikaze
kangaroo
  kangaroos (*pl.*)
  kangaroo's
     (of the kangaroo)
  kangaroos'
     (of the kangaroos)
kaolin
kapok
karate
kata- (down)
  katabolism
kayak
kebab
kedgeree
keel
keen
  keener
  keenly
  keenness
keep
  keeper
  keepsake
  kept
keg
kelp
kempt
ken
kennel
  kennelled

  kenneled
  kennelling
  kenneling
kept (*from* keep)
kerb, curb (road edge)
  curb
  kerbstone
  curbstone
kerchief
  kerchiefs (*pl.*)
kernel (centre)
kerosine, kerosene
kestrel
ketch
ketchup
  catsup
kettle
  kettledrum
key
  keyboard
  keyhole
  keynote
khaki
khan (Oriental title)
kibbutz
  kibbutzim (*pl.*)
  kibbutznik
kibosh
kick
  kick-off
kid (to deceive)
  kidded
  kidding
  kids
kid (child)
  kid's (of the kid)
  kids' (of the kids)
kidnap
  kidnapped
  kidnaped
  kidnapper
  kidnaper
  kidnapping
  kidnaping
  kidnaps

kidney
  kidneys (*pl.*)
kill
  killer
kiln
kilo- (thousand)
  kilocycle
  kilogram, kilogramme
  kilohertz
  kilolitre
  kiloliter
  kilometre
  kilometer
  kiloton
  kilotonne (metric)
  kilowatt
kilt
kimono
  kimonos (*pl.*)
kin
  kindred
  kinsfolk
  kinship
  kinsman
  kinsmen (*pl.*)
  kinswoman
  kinswomen (*pl.*)
kind
  kinder
  kind-hearted
  kindliness
  kindly
  kindness
kindergarten
  kindergartens (*pl.*)
kindle
  kindling
kinetic
king
  kingdom
  king's (of the king)
  kings' (of the kings)
kink
  kinky
kiosk

kipper
  kippered
kirk
kiss
  kisses (*pl.*)
  kissed
  kisses
kit
kitchen
  kitchenette
kite
kith
kitten
  kittenish
kitty (fund of money)
klaxon
kleptomania
  kleptomaniac
knack
knacker
knapsack
knave
  knavery
  knavish
knead (to mix dough)
knee
  kneecap
kneel
  kneeled
  knelt
knell (sound of bell)
knew (*from* know)
knickers
  knickerbockers
knick-knack
knife
  knives (pl.)
knight
  knighted
  knight-errant
  knight-errantry
  knighthood
  knightly (chivalrous)
knit
  knits

knitted
knitter
knitting
knob
  knobby
knock
  knocker
  knock-kneed
  knock out (to disable)
  knock-out (disablement)
knoll (small hill)
knot
  knotted
  knotting
knout (to flog)
know
  knew
  know-how, knowhow
  known
knowledge
  knowledgeable
  knowledgeably
knuckle
  knuckling
koala
  koala bear
Kodak
kohlrabi
Koran
kosher
kowtow
krona (Swedish money)
  kronor (*pl.*)
krone (Danish, Norwegian)
  kroner (*pl.*)
kudos

L

laager (encampment)
label
  labelled

labeled
labelling
labeling
labels
labial (of the lips)
laboratory
laboratories (*pl.*)
laborious
laboriously
labour
labor
labourer
laborer
labourer's
    (of the labourer)
labourers'
    (of the labourers)
laburnum
laburnums (*pl.*)
labyrinth
labyrinthine
lace
lacing
lacerate (to tear)
lacerating
laceration
lachrymal
lachrymose (tearful)
lack
lackadaisical
lackadaisically
lackey
lackeys (*pl.*)
lack-lustre
laconic
laconically
lacquer (varnish)
lacquered
lacquering
lacrosse
lactation
lactic
lad
lad's (of the lad)
lads' (of the lads)

laddie (young fellow)
ladder
laden (loaded)
lading
ladle
ladling
lady
ladies (*pl.*)
ladies' (of the ladies)
ladylike
lady's (of the lady)
ladyship
lady's-maid
lag
lagged
lagging
lager (beer)
laggard
lagoon
laid (*see* Appendix)
lain (*see* Appendix)
lair (den)
laird
laird's (of the laird)
lairds' (of the lairds)
laissez-faire
laity
lake
lama (priest)
lamb
lamb's (of the lamb)
lambs' (of the lambs)
lambkin (baby lamb)
lambskin
lambda (Greek letter L)
lambent (softly radiant)
lambast, lambaste
        (to beat)
lame
lamely
lameness
lamé (fabric)
lament
lamentable
lamentably

lamentation
lamented
lamina
laminae (*pl.*)
laminated
lamination
lamp
lamplight
lampoon
lampooner
lampoonist
lamprey
lampreys (*pl.*)
lance
lancing
lancer (soldier)
lancers (dance)
lancet (knife)
land
landfall
landlady
landladies (*pl.*)
landlady's
    (of the landlady)
landladies'
    (of the landladies)
landlocked
landlord
landlord's
    (of the landlord)
landlords'
    (of the landlords)
landlubber
landlubberly
landmark
landowner
landscape
landscaping
landslide
lane
language
languid (slack)
languidly
languidness
languish (to fade)

languor (feebleness)
  languorous
lank
  lankiness
  lanky
lanolin
lantern
lanyard
lap
  (to drink with tongue)
  lapped
  lapping
  laps (it)
lap (of a person)
  lap-dog
lapel
  lapelled
lapidary
     (like stone, heavy)
lapis lazuli
lapse
  lapsing
lapsus linguae
    (slip of tongue)
larboard
larceny
  larcenies (*pl.*)
larch
lard
larder
large
  largely
  larger
  largish
largesse (gifts)
  largess
largo (very slow)
  larghetto (rather slow)
lark (joke)
lark (bird)
larva
  larvae (*pl.*)
  larval
larynx
  larynges (*pl.*)

laryngeal
laryngitis
lascivious
  lasciviously
  lasciviousness
laser
lase
  lasing
lash
lass
  lasses (*pl.*)
  lassie
lassitude
lasso
  lassos, lassoes (*pl.*)
  lassoed
  lassoing
last
  lastly
latch
  latches (*pl.*)
  latchkey
late
  lately
  later
latent
  latency
lateral
  laterally
lath (strip of wood)
lathe (machine)
lather
  lathered
  lathering
latitude
latrine
latter
  latter-day
  latterly
lattice
laud (to praise)
  laudable
  laudably
laudanum
laugh

laughable
laughed
laughing-stock
laughs
laughter
launch
  launches (*pl.*)
  launched
  launches
launder
  laundered
  launderette
  laundress (*fem.*)
  laundrette
  laundry
  laundries (*pl.*)
laureate
  Poet Laureate
laurel
  laurel wreath
lava (from volcano)
lavatory
  lavatories (*pl.*)
lavender
laver (kind of seaweed)
lavish
  lavishly
  lavishness
law
  law-abiding
  lawful
  lawfully
  lawfulness
  lawless
  lawlessly
  lawlessness
  lawsuit
  lawyer
  lawyer's (of the lawyer)
  lawyers'
    (of the lawyers)
lawn
  lawn-mower
lax
  laxity

laxly
laxative
lay (person)
  laity
  layman
lay (*see* Appendix)
  laid
  layer (of eggs)
layby
  lay-bys (*pl.*)
layer
  layered
layette
layoff
laze
  lazier
  lazily
  laziness
  lazy
leach (to filter)
lead
  leader
  leadership
  led
lead (metal)
  leaded
  leaden (very heavy)
leaf
  leaves (*pl.*)
  leafage
  leafiness
  leafless
  leafy
leaflet
league
leak (hole in pipe)
  leakage
  leaky
lean (to slope)
  leaned
  leant
lean (thin)
  leanness
leaning (aptitude)
lean-to

leap
  leaped
  leapt
  leap-year
learn
  learned
  learned (very clever)
  learner
  learnt
lease
  leasing
  leasehold
leash
least
  leastways
  leastwise
leather
  leatherette
  leathery
leave
  leaving
  left
leaven (to add yeast)
  leavened
leaves (*from* leaf)
lecher
  lecherous
  lechery
lectern
lecture
  lecturer
  lecturing
led (*from* to lead)
ledge
ledger
lee
  leeward
  leeway
leech (sucking worm)
leek (vegetable)
leer
  leered
  leering
leery (sly)
left

left-handed
leftward
left wing
left-winger
left (*from* leave)
leg
  legged
  legging
  leggy
  leg-pull
legacy
  legacies (*pl.*)
legal
  legalisation
  legalization
  legalise
  legalize
  legalising
  legalizing
  legality
  legally
legate (Papal envoy)
legation
  (diplomat's residence)
legato
  (in music, smoothly)
legend
  legendary
legerdemain
legible
  legibility
  legibly
legion
  legionary
  legionaries (*pl.*)
legislate
  legislating
  legislation
  legislator
  (maker of laws)
  legislature
  (legal assembly)
legitimate
  legitimacy
  legitimately

legitimation
legitimatise
legitimatize
legitimise
legitimize
legitimising
legitimizing
legume (vegetable)
leguminous
Leicester
leisure
leisurely
leitmotiv, leitmotif
lemming (animal)
lemon
lemonade
lend
lender
lent
length
lengthen
lengthily
lengthways
lengthwise
lengthy
lenience
leniency
lenient
leniently
lens
lent (*from* lend, lean)
Lent
Lenten
lentil
leonine (lion-like)
leopard
leopardess
leopard's
(of the leopard)
leopards'
(of the leopards)
leotard
leper
leprosy
leprous

leprechaun
lesbian
lèse-majesté
lesion
less
lessen (to make less)
lessened
lessening
lesser
lessee (tenant)
lessor (granter of lease)
lesson
let
lettable
letting
lethal
lethally
lethargy
lethargic
lethargically
let's (let us)
letter
lettering
lettuce
leucocyte
leukaemia
leukemia
level
level-headed
levelled
leveled
leveller
leveler
levelling
leveling
lever
leverage
leviathan
levis (jeans)
levitate
levitating
levitation
levity (humour)
levy (payment)
levies (*pl.*)

levied
levying
lewd
lewdly
lewdness
lexicographer
lexicography
lexicon
liable
liability
liabilities (*pl.*)
liaison
liaise
liaising
liar (*see* Appendix)
libation
libel
libelled
libeled
libeller
libeler
libelling
libeling
libellous
libelous
libels
liberal (generous)
liberality
liberally
Liberal (politics)
liberate
liberating
liberation
liberator
libertine
(licentious person)
liberty
liberties (*pl.*)
libido
libidinal
libidinous
library
libraries (*pl.*)
librarian
libretto (text of opera)

libretti, librettos (*pl.*)
librettos (*pl.*)
lice (*pl.* of louse)
licence (permission)
license
licence
(freedom from restraint)
license
license
(to grant permission)
licensed
licensee
(holder of licence)
licenser
(granter of licence)
licensing
licentiate (graduate)
licentious (lewd)
licentiousness
lichen
lick
licorice, liquorice
licorice
lid
lidded
lido
lidos (*pl.*)
lie
(recline, *see* Appendix)
lain
lay
lying
lie (to fib, *see* Appendix)
liar
lied
lying
lied (song)
lieder (*pl.*)
lien (right to property)
lieu (instead of)
lieutenant
lieutenancy
life
lives (*pl.*)
lifebuoy

life-guard
lifeless
lifelessly
lifelike
lifelong
life-size
life-sized
lift
lift-off
ligament (bone binding)
ligature (cord)
light
lighted
lighter
light-hearted
light-heartedly
lighthouse
lightly
lightness
light-weight
lit
lighten
lightened
lightening
(making lighter)
lighter (boat)
lighterage
lightning
(in thunderstorm)
lignite
like
likeable, likable
likable
likelihood
likely
likeness
likewise
liking
liken
lilac
lilliputian
lilt
lily
lilies (*pl.*)
lilies' (of the lilies)

lily-livered
lily's (of the lily)
limb
limbless
limber
limbered
limbering
limbo
limbos (*pl.*)
lime
limelight
limerick
limit
limitation
limited
limousine
limp
limpness
limpet
limpid
linage, lineage
(number of lines)
linchpin
line
lineage (ancestry)
lineal
linear
linearity
lining
lineament
linen
linen-draper
liner
linger
lingered
lingering
lingerie
lingo
lingoes (*pl.*)
lingua (tongue)
lingual
linguist
linguistic
lining
liniment

link
linkage
linked
links (Golf)
linnet
lino
  linocut
  linoleum
  linotype
linseed
lint
lintel (over door)
lion
  lion's (of the lion)
  lions' (of the lions)
  lioness
  lionesses (*pl.*)
  lion-hearted
  lionisation
  lionization
  lionise
  lionize
  lionising
  lionizing
lip
  lipped
  lip-read
  lip-reader
  lip-reading
  lipstick
liquefy
  liquefaction
  liquefiable
  liquefied
  liquefies
  liquefying
  liquescent
liqueur
  (strong, sweet alcohol)
liquid
  liquidate
  liquidating
  liquidation
  liquidator
  liquidity

liquor (liquid)
liquorice, licorice
  licorice
lira (Italian money)
  lire (*pl.*)
  liras (*pl.*)
lisle
lisp
lissom (agile)
  lissome
list
list (of a ship, to lean)
listen
  listened
  listener
  listening
listless
  listlessly
  listlessness
lit (*from* light)
litany
  litanies (*pl.*)
literal (exact)
  literally
literary (learned)
literate (able to read)
  literacy
literature (books etc.)
lithe
litho- (stone)
  lithograph
  lithography
litigate
  litigant
  litigating
  litigation
  litigious
litmus
  litmus-paper
litre (measure)
  liter
litter (rubbish)
  littered
little
littoral (near the sea)

liturgy
  liturgies (*pl.*)
  liturgical
live
  liveable
  livable
  livelihood
  living
lively
  livelier
  liveliness
liven (to cheer up)
  livened
  livening
liver
  liverish
livery (costume)
  liveries (*pl.*)
livestock
living (clergyman's)
livid
lizard
llama (kind of camel)
load
loaf (bread)
  loaves (*pl.*)
loaf (to be idle)
  loafer
loam
  loamy
loan
loath, loth (unwilling)
loathe (to hate)
  loathing
  loathsome
lob
  lobbed
  lobbing
  lobs
lobby
  lobbies (*pl.*)
  lobbied
  lobbies
  lobbying
lobe (of the ear)

lobster
local
  localisation
  localization
  localise
  localize
  localising
  localizing
  locally
locale (locality of events)
locality
  localities (*pl.*)
locate
  locating
  location
locative (*grammar*)
loch (lake)
lock
  locked out
  locker
  lockjaw
  lockout
  lockouts (*pl.*)
lock (of hair)
lock (on river or canal)
locket
locksmith
locomotion
  locomotive
locum
  locum tenens
      (substitute)
locus
  loci (*pl.*)
locust
lode (of metal ore)
lodge
  lodgement
  lodger
  lodging
  lodgment
loft
  loftier
  loftily
  loftiness

lofty
loft (attic)
log
  log-book
  logged
  logging
loganberry
  loganberries (*pl.*)
logarithm
  logarithmic
  logarithmically
loggerhead
loggerheads
loggia
logic
  logical
  logically
  logician
logistics
logotype, logo
      (business symbol)
loin
loiter
  loitered
  loiterer
  loitering
loll
  lolled
  lolling
lollipop
lone
  lonelier
  loneliness
  lonely
  lonesome
long (extensive)
  longer
  long-suffering
  longways
  longwise
long (to wish for)
  longing
  longevity
  longitude
  longitudinal

  longitudinally
loo (lavatory)
loofah
  loofa
look
  looker-on
  lookers-on (*pl.*)
loom (for weaving)
loom
  (to appear threatening)
loop
  loophole
loose
  loose-leaf
  loosely
  looseness
  looser
loosen
  loosened
  loosening
loot
  looter
lop
  lopped
  lopping
  lops
  lopsided
lope (to run)
  loping
loquacious
  loquaciously
  loquaciousness
  loquacity
lord
  lordly
  lord's (of the lord)
  lords' (of the lords)
  Lord Mayor
  lordship
lore (tradition)
lorgnette
lorry
  lorries (*pl.*)
lose
  loser

losing
lost
loss
lot
loth, loath (unwilling)
Lothario
lotion
lottery
  lotteries (*pl.*)
lotus
  lotuses (*pl.*)
loud
  louder
  loudly
  loud-mouthed
  loudness
  loud-speaker
lounge
  lounging
lour, lower (to frown)
  lower
  loured, lowered
  lowered
  louring, lowering
  lowering
lòuse
  lice (*pl.*)
  lousy
lout
  loutish
louvre
  louver
  louvred
  louvered
love
  lovable, loveable
  lover
  lovelorn
  loving
lovely
  lovelier
  loveliness
low
  lower
  lowliness

lowly
lowness
low (to moo)
lower
(to make lower, reduce)
  lowered
  lowering
loyal
  loyalism
  loyalist
  loyally
  loyalty
  loyalties (*pl.*)
lozenge
lubber
  lubberly
lubricate
  lubricant
  lubricating
  lubrication
lucid
  lucidity
  lucidly
  lucidness
luck
  luckier
  luckily
  lucky
lucre
  lucrative
  lucratively
ludicrous
  ludicrously
  ludicrousness
luff
lug (to drag)
  lugged
  lugging
  lugs
lug (projection)
luggage
lugger (small ship)
lugubrious
  lugubriously
lukewarm

lull
  lullaby
  lullabies (*pl.*:)
lumbago
lumbar (of the loin)
lumber (rubbish)
  lumber-room
lumberjack
lumen (unit of light)
luminary
  luminaries (*pl.*)
luminescence
  luminescent
luminous
  luminosity
lump
  lumpiness
  lumpy
luna- (moon)
lunar
lunacy
lunatic
lunch
  luncheon
lung
lunge (to thrust forward)
  lunging
lurch
lure
  luring
lurid
  luridly
lurk
luscious
  lusciousness
lush
lust
  lustful
lustre
  luster
  lustrous
lusty
  lustier
  lustily
  lustiness

lute
luxury
  luxuries (*pl.*)
  luxuriance
  luxuriant
  luxuriate
  luxuriating
  luxurious
  luxuriously
lying (see Appendix)
lymph
  lymphatic
lynch (to murder)
lynx (animal)
lyre (harp)
lyric
  lyrical
  lyrically
  lyricism

M

ma'am (madam)
macabre
macadam
  macadamise
  macadamize
  macadamised
  macadamized
macaroni
macaroon
macassar (hair-oil)
macaw
mace
  mace-bearer
macerate
  macerating
  maceration
Mach (speed ratio)
machiavellian
machination
machine

machinery
machining
machinist
mackerel
mackintosh
macramé
macro- (large)
  macrobiotic
  macrocosm
  macroscopic
macula (spot on skin)
  maculae (*pl.*)
mad
  madder
  madding
  madly
  madman
  madmen (*pl.*)
  madness
madam
Madame (French for Mrs)
  Mesdames (*pl.*)
madden
  maddening
madder
    (plant or red dye)
made (*from* make)
Madeira
Mademoiselle
  Mesdemoiselles (*pl.*)
madonna
madrigal
maelstrom
maestro
  maestros, maestri (*pl.*)
Mafia
magazine
magenta
maggot
  maggoty
magic
  magical
  magically
  magician

  magician's
    (of the magician)
  magicians'
    (of the magicians)
magisterial
  magisterially
magistrate
  magistrate's
    (of the magistrate)
  magistrates'
    (of the magistrates)
magistracy
  magistracies (*pl.*)
magistral
magistrature
magnanimous
  magnanimity
  magnanimously
magnate (great man)
magnesia
magnesium
magnet
  magnetic
  magnetically
  magnetisable
  magnetizable
  magnetisation
  magnetization
  magnetise
  magnetize
  magnetising
  magnetizing
  magnetism
magneto
  magnetos (*pl.*)
magnificent
  magnificence
  magnificently
magnify
  magnification
  magnified
  magnifier
magnitude
magnolia
magnum

magnum opus
  magna opera (*pl.*)
magpie
maharajah, maharaja
maharani, maharanee
mah-jong, mah-jongg
mahogany
Mahomet, Mohammed,
        Muhammad
  Mahometan,
      Mohammedan,
      Muhammadan
maid
  maiden
  maidenly
  maid's (of the maid)
  maids' (of the maids)
mail (letters or armour)
maim
  maimed
main
  mainly
maintain
  maintenance
maisonette, maisonnette
maître d'hôtel
maize (corn)
majestic
  majestically
  majesty
  majesties (*pl.*)
  Majesty's
    (of Her Majesty)
  Majesties'
    (of Their Majesties)
majolica
major
  majority
  majorities (*pl.*)
major-domo
make
  made
  maker
  makeshift
  make-up

makeweight
making
maladjusted
  maladjustment
maladminstration
maladroit
  maladroitness
malady
  maladies (*pl.*)
malaise
malapropos
  malapropism
malaria
malcontent
male (masculine)
malediction
malefactor
  malefaction
malevolence
  malevolent
malformation
malfunction
malice
  malice aforethought
  malicious
  maliciously
malign (to slander)
  maligned
  maligner
  maligning
  malignity
malignant (very bad)
  malignancy
malinger (to feign illness)
  malingerer
  malingering
mall (shady walk)
mallard
malleable
  malleability
mallet
mallow
malnutrition
malodorous
malpractice

malt
maltreat
  maltreatment
mamma, mama (mother)
mammal
  mammalian
  mammary
mammon
mammoth
man
  men (*pl.*)
  manful
  manfully
  manhole
  manliness
  manly
  manned
  manning
  man's (of the man)
  men's (of the men)
  mans (he, she)
  manslaughter
manacle
manage
  manageable
  managed
  management
  manager
  managerial
  manager's
    (of the manager)
  managers'
    (of the managers)
  managing
mandarin
mandate
  mandatary (person)
  mandatory (compulsory)
mandible (lower jaw)
mandolin, mandoline
  mandolin
mandrel (part of lathe)
mandrake (plant)
mandrill (baboon)
mane (of horse)

manège (horsemanship)
manganese
mange
  mangy
mangel-wurzel,
        mangold-wurzel
  mangel-wurzel
manger
mangle
  mangling
mango
  mangoes, mangos (*pl.*)
mangrove
manhandle
manhood
mania
  maniac
  maniacal
  maniac's
        (of the maniac)
  maniacs'
        (of the maniacs)
manicure
  manicuring
  manicurist
manifest
  manifestation
  manifesto
  manifestos,
        manifestoes(*pl.*)
manifold
manikin (little man)
manilla
  manila
manipulate
  manipulating
  manipulation
  manipulative
  manipulator
mankind
manna (miraculous food)
mannequin (model)
manner
  mannered
  mannerism

mannerly
manoeuvre
  maneuver
  manoeuvrability
  maneuverability
  manoeuvrable
  maneuverable
  manoeuvring
  maneuvering
manometer
        (pressure gauge)
manor (estate)
  manorial
manse
mansion
manslaughter
mantel
  mantelpiece
mantle (cloak)
manu- (hand)
  manual
  manually
manufacture
  manufacturer
  manufacturing
manuscript
manure
  manuring
many
map
  mapped
  mapping
maple
mar
  marred
  marring
marathon
maraud
  marauder
marble
march
  marcher
marchioness
        (*fem.* of marquess)
Marconi

Mardi Gras
        (Shrove Tuesday)
mare (horse)
margarine
margin
  marginal
  marginally
marguerite
marigold
marijuana, marihuana
marina (harbour)
marinade (pickle solution)
  marinading
marinate (to pickle)
  marinating
marine
  mariner
  mariner's
        (of the mariner)
  mariners'
        (of the mariners)
marionette
marital
maritime
marjoram
mark
  marked
  markedly
  marker
  marksman
market
  marketability
  marketable
  marketeer
  marketing
marl
marlinspike
  marline-spike
marmalade
marmoreal (of marble)
marmoset (monkey)
marmot (kind of squirrel)
maroon
  marooned
marquee (large tent)

marquetry, marqueterie
marquis, marquess
marrow
marry
  marriage
  marriageable
  married
  marries
  marrying
marsh
  marsh-mallow
marshal
  marshalled
  marshaled
  marshalling
  marshaling
  marshals
marsupial
mart (market place)
marten (weasel)
martial
  martial law
  martially
Martian
martin (bird)
martinet (tyrant)
martyr
  martyrs (*pl.*)
  martyrdom
  martyrise
  martyrize
  martyrising
  martyrizing
marvel
  marvelled
  marveled
  marvelling
  marveling
  marvellous
  marvelous
  marvellously
  marvelously
  marvels
Marylebone
Marx (Karl)

Marxism
  Marxist
marzipan
mascara
mascot
masculine
  masculinity
mash
mask (face cover)
masochism
    (pleasure from pain)
  masochist
mason
  masonic
  masonry
masque (entertainment)
masquerade
  masquerading
mass
massacre
  massacred
  massacring
massage
  massaging
  masseur
  masseuse (*fem.*)
massif (mountain tops)
massive (very large)
  massively
  massiveness
mast
  mast-head
master
  mastered
  masterful
  masterfully
  mastering
  masterpiece
  master's (of the master)
  masters'
      (of the masters)
  mastery
masticate
  masticating
  mastication

mastiff
  mastiffs (*pl.*)
mastoid
masturbate
  masturbating
  masturbation
mat
  matted
  matting
mat, matt (dull surface)
matador
match
  matchless
matchmaker
mate
  matey
  mating
mater- (mother)
  maternal
  maternally
  maternity
material
  materialism
  materialist
  materially
materialise
  materialize
  materialisation
  materialization
  materialising
  materializing
mathematics, maths
  mathematical
  mathematician
matinée
matins
matriarch
  matriarchal
  matriarchy
matriculate
  matriculating
  matriculation
matrimonial
  matrimony
matrix

matrices, matrixes (*pl.*)
matrixes (*pl.*)
matron
matt, mat (dull surface)
matter
  mattered
  matter-of-fact
mattock
mattress
mature
  maturely
  maturing
  maturity
matutinal
  (in the morning)
maudlin
maul (hammer)
maul (to treat roughly)
mausoleum
mauve
maverick
mawkish
  mawkishness
maxim
maximum
  maxima (*pl.*)
  maximums (*pl.*)
  maximal
  maximisation
  maximization
  maximise
  maximize
  maximising
  maximizing
may
  maybe
  mayn't (may not)
May (month)
may (tree)
mayhem
mayonnaise
mayor
  mayoral
  mayoralty
  mayor's (of the mayor)

mayors' (of the mayors)
maypole
maze (tangle of paths)
mazurka
mead
meadow
meagre
  meager
  meagrely
  meagreness
meal (grain)
  mealy
  mealy-mouthed
meal (repast)
  mealtime
mean
  meaning
  meaningful
  meaningfully
  meaningless
  meant
mean (mid-point)
  meantime
  meanwhile
mean (miserly)
  meaner
  meanly
  meanness
meander
  meandered
means (money, etc.)
  means test
measles
  measly
measure
  measurable
  measureless
  measurement
  measuring
meat (food)
  meatless
mechanic
  mechanical
  mechanically
  mechanician

mechanic's
  (of the mechanic)
mechanics'
  (of the mechanics)
mechanisation
mechanization
mechanise
mechanize
mechanising
mechanizing
mechanism
medal (for bravery, etc.)
  medalled
  medaled
  medallion
  medallist
  medalist
meddle (to interfere)
  meddler
  meddlesome
  meddling
media (newspapers, etc.)
mediaeval, medieval
median
  medial
  medially
mediate
  mediating
  mediation
  mediator
Medicaid
medical
  medically
Medicare
medicate
  medicament
  medicating
  medication
medicine
  medicinal
  medicinally
medieval, mediaeval
mediocre
  mediocrity
  mediocrities (*pl.*)

meditate
meditating
meditation
meditator
Mediterranean
medium (newspapers, etc.)
media (*pl.*)
medium (spiritualist)
mediums (*pl.*)
medlar (fruit)
medley (mixture)
meek
meekly
meekness
meet (to encounter)
meeting
met
meet (proper)
mega- (great)
megahertz
(million cycles)
megalith (large stone)
megalithic
megaphone
megatonne
(million tonnes)
megaton (million tons)
megavolt
megawatt
megohm (million ohms)
megalo- (great)
megalomania
megalomaniac
melancholy
melancholia
melancholic
mélange
mêlée
mellifluous
mellow
melodrama
melodramatic
melodramatically
melody
melodies (*pl.*)

melodic
melodically
melodious
melon
melt
melted
molten (melted state)
member
member's
(of the member)
members'
(of the members)
membership
membrane
membraneous
membranous
memento
mementoes, mementos
(*pl.*)
memo
memos (*pl.*)
memoir
memorabilia
memorable
memorably
memorandum
memoranda,
memorandums(*pl.*)
memorandums (*pl.*)
memorial
memory
memories (*pl.*)
memorise
(to learn by heart)
memorize
memorising
memorizing
memsahib
menace
menacing
ménage
menagerie
mend
mended
mendacious (lying)

mendaciously
mendacity
mendicant (beggar)
mendicity
menhir (prehistoric stone)
menial
menially
meningitis
menopause
menopausal
menstrual
menstruate
menstruating
menstruation
mensuration
mental
mentality
mentally
menthol
mention
mentor (adviser)
menu
menus (*pl.*)
mercantile
mercenary
mercenaries (*pl.*)
mercerise
mercerize
merchandise
merchant
merchant's
(of the merchant)
merchants'
(of the merchants)
mercury
mercurial
mercy
mercies (*pl.*)
merciful
mercifully
merciless
mercilessly
mere (only)
merely
merest

mere (lake)
meretricious (showy)
merge
  merger
  merging
meridian
  meridional (southern)
meringue
merit
  merited
  meritorious
  meritoriously
  meritocracy
mermaid
  mermaid's
      (of the mermaid)
  mermaids'
      (of the mermaids)
merry
  merrier
  merrily
  merriment
mésalliance
      (inferior marriage)
Mesdames
      (pl. of Madame)
  Mesdemoiselles
    (pl. of Mademoiselle)
mesh
mesmerism
  mesmerise
  mesmerize
  mesmerising
  mesmerizing
mess
  messier
  messily
  messiness
  messy
message
messenger
  messenger's
      (of the messenger)
  messengers'
      (of the messengers)

Messiah
  Messianic
  Messieurs
      (pl. of Monsieur)
  Messrs. (pl. of Mister)
messuage
      (house property)
met (from meet)
metabolism
  metabolic
metal
  metalled
  metaled
  metallic
  metallurgical
  metallurgist
  metallurgy
metamorphose
  metamorphosis
  metamorphoses (pl.)
metaphor
  metaphorical
  metaphorically
metaphysical
  metaphysically
  metaphysics
mete (to apportion)
  meting
meteor
  meteoric
  meteorically
  meteorite
  meteoroid
  meteorological
  meteorologist
  meteorology
meter (gas, etc.)
  metered
methane
method
  methodical
  methodically
  methodology
methyl
  methylated

meticulous
  meticulously
  meticulousness
métier
metre (measure of length)
  meter
  metric
metricate
  metricating
  metrication
  metricize
  metricizing
metronome
metropolis
  metropolitan
mettle (temperament)
mews (stabling)
mezzanine
mezza voce (softly)
mezzo- (half)
  mezzo-forte
  mezzo-soprano
  mezzotint
miaow, miaou
miasma
  miasmal
mica
mice (pl. of mouse)
mickle, muckle
      (large amount)
micro- (small)
microbe
  microbial
microbiology
  microbiologist
microcosm
microfarad
micrometer
microphone
  microphonic
microscope
  microscopic
  microscopical
  microscopy
microtome

microwave
micturition
midday
midden (dunghill)
middle
  middleman
  middlemen (*pl.*)
  middleweight
  middling
middy (midshipman)
  middies (*pl.*)
  middy's (of the middy)
  middies'
    (of the middies)
midge
midget
midinette
midnight
midriff
midshipman
  midshipmen (*pl.*)
midst
midsummer
midway
Midwest
  Midwesterner
midwife
  midwives (*pl.*)
  midwife's
    (of the midwife)
  midwives'
    (of the midwives)
  midwifery
mien (appearance)
miffed
might
  mightier
  mightily
  mightiness
  mighty
might (*from* may)
mignonette
migraine
migrant (migrator)

migrant's
  (of the migrant)
migrants'
  (of the migrants)
migrate
  migrating
  migration
  migrator
mikado
mike (to idle)
  miking
milch-cow
mild
  milder
  mildly
  mildness
mildew
  mildewy
mile
  mileage
milieu (surroundings)
  milieus (*pl.*)
  milieux (*pl.*)
militant (aggressive)
  militancy
military
  militarily
  militarisation
  militarization
  militarise
  militarize
  militarised
  militarized
  militarising
  militarizing
  militarism
  militarist
militate (to influence)
  militating
militia
milk
  milker
  milkiness
  milkmaid
  milksop

milky
mill
  miller
  miller's (of the miller)
  millers' (of the millers)
  millstone
mille- (thousand)
  mille-feuille
  millenium
    (thousand years)
  millepede, millipede
  millipede
millet
milli- (thousandth part)
  milliampere
  milliamp
  milligram
  millilitre
  milliliter
  millimetre
  millimeter
  millivolt
  milliwatt
milliard (thousand million)
milliner
  millinery
million
  millionaire
  millionaire's
    (of the millionaire)
  millionaires'
    (of the millionaires)
  millionth
mime
  miming
mimic
  mimicked
  mimicker
  mimicking
  mimicry
mimosa
minaret
minatory (threatening)
mince
  mincemeat

mincepie
mincer
mincing
mind
  minder
  mindful
  mindless
mine
  miner (for coal)
  mining
mine (*from* my)
mineral
  mineralogist
  mineralogy
minestrone
mingle
  mingling
mingy (stingy)
mini- (small)
  miniature
  minim
  minimal
  minimally
  minimum
  minima (*pl.*)
  minimums (*pl.*)
  miniskirt
minimise
  minimize
  minimised
  minimized
  minimising
  minimizing
minion
minister
  ministered
  ministerial
  ministerially
  ministering
  minister's
    (of the minister)
  ministers'
    (of the ministers)
  ministrant
  ministration

ministry
ministries (*pl.*)
mink
minnow
minor (smaller)
  minority
  minorities (*pl.*)
minster (church)
minstrel (singer)
mint
  mint sauce
minuet
minus
  minus sign
minuscule
minute (to make notes)
  minutes
    (notes of meeting)
  minuting
minute (of time)
minute (very small)
  minutely
  minuteness
  minutiae (small details)
minx
mirabile dictu
  (wonderful to relate)
miracle
  miraculous
  miraculously
mirage
mire
  miry (muddy)
mirror
  mirrored
  mirroring
mirth
  mirthful
misadventure
misalliance
misanthrope (man hater)
  misanthropic
  misanthropist
  misanthropy
misapply

misapplication
misapplied
misapplying
misapprehend
  misapprehension
misappropriate
  misappropriating
  misappropriation
misbehave
  misbehaving
  misbehaviour
  misbehavior
miscalculate
  miscalculating
  miscalculation
miscarry
  miscarriage
  miscarried
  miscarries
  miscarrying
miscast
miscegenation
miscellaneous
  miscellany
  miscellanies (*pl.*)
mischance
mischief
  mischievous
  mischievously
miscible (mixable)
misconceive
  misconceiving
  misconception
misconduct
misconstrue
  misconstruction
  misconstruing
miscount
miscreant
misdeed
misdemeanour
  misdemeanor
mise-en-scène
miser
  miserliness

miserly
miser's (of the miser)
misers' (of the misers)
miserable
miserably
misery
miseries (*pl.*)
misfire
misfiring
misfit
misfortune
misgiving
misgovern
misgovernment
misguide
misguidance
misguiding
mishandle
mishandling
mishap
mishmash
misinform
misinterpret
misinterpretation
misjudge
misjudgement
misjudging
misjudgment
mislay
mislaid
mislead
misleading
misled
mismanage
mismanagement
mismanaging
mismatch
misnomer
misogyny
misogynist
misplace
misplacement
misplacing
misprint
mispronounce

mispronouncing
mispronunciation
misquote
misquotation
misquoting
misread
misreading
misrepresent
misrepresentation
misrule
miss
missed
missing
Miss
Misses (*pl.*)
missal (book of prayer)
missel (thrush)
misshapen
missile
mission
missionary
missionaries (*pl.*)
missionary's
(of the missionary)
missionaries'
(of the missionaries)
Mississippi
missive
misspell
misspelling
misspelt
misspelled
misspend
misspent
misstate
misstatement
misstating
mist
mistier
mistily
mistiness
misty
mistake
mistaken
mistakenly

mistaking
mistook
Mister, Mr
Messrs. (*pl.*)
mistime
mistiming
mistletoe
mistral
mistranslate
mistranslating
mistranslation
mistress
mistresses (*pl.*)
mistress's
(of the mistress)
mistresses'
(of the mistresses)
mistrust
mistrustful
misunderstand
misunderstood
misuse
misusing
mite (small insect)
mitigate
mitigating
mitigation
mitre
miter
mitten
mix
mixed
mixer
mixture
mizen, mizzen (sail)
mnemonic
moan
moaner
moat (ditch)
moated
mob
mobbed
mobbing
mobile
mobility

157

mobilise
mobilize
mobilisation
mobilization
mobilising
mobilizing
moccasin
Mocha (coffee)
mock
mockery
mock-heroic
mode
modal
modish
model·
modelled
modeled
modelling
modeling
models
model's (of the model)
models' (of the models)
moderate
moderately
moderating
moderation
moderator
modern
modernisation
modernization
modernise
modernize
modernising
modernizing
modernism
modernity
modest
modestly
modesty
modicum
modicums (*pl.*)
modify
modifiable
modification
modified

modifies
modifying
modulate
modulating
modulation
modulator
module
(unit of measurement)
modular
modulus
moduli (*pl.*)
modus operandi
mogul
mohair
Mohammed
(*see* Mahomet)
moiety
moire, moiré (fabric)
moist
moisten
moistened
moistening
moistness
moisture
moisturise
moisturize
moisturising
moisturizing
molar
molasses
mole
molehill
moleskin
molecule
molecular
molest
molestation
mollify
mollified
mollifies
mollifying
mollusc
mollusk
mollycoddle
mollycoddling

molten (*from* melt)
molybdenum
moment
momentarily
momentary
momentous
momentum
monachal (like a monk)
monachism
monarch
(king or emperor)
monarchical
monarchy
monarchies (*pl.*)
monarch's
(of the monarch)
monarchs'
(of the monarchs)
monastery
monasteries (*pl.*)
monastic
monasticism
Monday
monetary
monetarism
monetarist
money
moneys, monies (*pl.*)
moneyless
Mongol
Mongolian
mongolism
mongoose
mongooses (*pl.*)
mongrel
monitor
monitored
monitoring
monk
monkey
monkeys (*pl.*)
monkey's
(of the monkey)
monkeys'
(of the monkeys)

mono- (single)
monochrome
      (single colour)
  monochromatic
monocle
monogamy
  monogamist
  monogamous
monogram
monograph
monolith
  monolithic
monologue
monomania
  monomaniac
monoplane
monopoly
  monopolies (*pl.*)
  monopolisation
  monopolization
  monopolise
  monopolize
  monopolising
  monopolizing
  monopolist
  monopolistic
monorail
monosyllable
  monosyllabic
monotheism
monotony
  monotonous
  monotonously
monotype
monoxide
Monseigneur
Monsieur
  Messieurs (*pl.*)
monsoon
monster
  monstrosity
  monstrosities (*pl.*)
  monstrous
montage
month

monthly
month's (of the month)
months' (of the months)
monument
  monumental
  monumentally
moo
  mooed
  mooing
  moos
mooch
mood
  moodily
  moodiness
  moody
moon
  moonless
  moonlight
  moonlighting
  moonlit
  moonshine
moon (to mope)
moor (a boat)
  moorage
  moored
moor (hill)
moose
moot (not yet decided)
  moot point
mop (to wipe)
  mopped
  mopping
  mops
mope (to feel sad)
  moping
moppet
moral
  morale (state of mind)
  morality
  morally
moralise
  moralize
  moralising
  moralizing
  morally

morass
moratorium
  moratoriums,
        moratoria(*pl.*)
  moratoria (*pl.*)
morbid
  morbidity
  morbidness
mordant
more
  moreover
morganatic
  morganatically
morgue
moribund
morn
  morning
Morocco
  Moroccan
moron
  moronic
morose
  morosely
  moroseness
Morpheus
    (god of dreams)
morphia
morphine
morphinism
morphology
  morphological
morris dance
morrow
Morse (code)
morsel
mortal
  mortality
  mortally
mortar
  mortar-board
mortgage
  mortgagee
  (receiver of mortgage)
  mortgaging

mortgagor
(giver of mortgage)
mortify
  mortification
  mortified
  mortifies
  mortifying
mortise, mortice
mortuary
  mortuaries (*pl.*)
mosaic
  Moslem, Muslim
mosque
mosquito
  mosquitoes (*pl.*)
moss
  mossy
most
  mostly
mote (speck)
motel
motet (hymn)
moth
  moth-eaten
  moth's (of the moth)
  moths' (of the moths)
mother
  mothered
  mother-in-law
  mothers-in-law (*pl.*)
  mother-in-law's
    (of the mother-in-law)
  mothers-in-law's
    (of the mothers-in-law)
  mothering
  motherless
  motherly
  mother's
      (of the mother)
  mothers'
      (of the mothers)
  mother tongue
motif
  motifs (*pl.*)
motion

motionless
motive
  motivate
  motivating
  motivation
motley
motor
  motorboat
  motored
  motoring
  motorise
  motorize
  motorist
  motorway
mottled
motto
  mottoes (*pl.*)
moujik, muzhik
          (Russian peasant)
  muzhik
mould (small fungi)
  mold
  moulder
  molder
  mouldered
  moldered
  mouldering
  moldering
  mouldiness
  moldiness
  mouldy
  moldy
mould (to shape)
  mold
  moulded
  molded
  moulding
  molding
mould (pattern)
  mold
mould (soil)
  mold
moult
  molt
mound

mount
mountain
  mountaineer
  mountainous
mountebank
mourn (to grieve)
  mourned
  mourner
  mournful
  mournfully
  mourning (for the dead)
mouse
  mice (*pl.*)
  mouser
  mousy
moussaka (Greek food)
mousse (fruit cream)
moustache
  mustache
mouth
  mouthed
  mouthful
  mouthfuls (*pl.*)
  mouthing
  mouthpiece
move
  movable
  moveable
  movement
  moving
movie
mow
  mowed
  mower
  mown
  mowed
Mr (mister)
Mrs (missis)
much
mucilage
  mucilaginous
muck
  mucky
muckle, mickle
          (large amount)

mucus (phlegm)
  mucous (slimy)
mud
  muddied
  muddier
  muddy
muddle
  muddle-headed
  muddler
  muddling
mudslinging
muff
muffin
muffle
  muffler
  muffling
mufti
mug
  mugged
  mugger
  mugging
  mugs
mug (large cup)
muggy
mugwump
mulatto
  mulattos, mulattoes (*pl.*)
  mulattoes (*pl.*)
mulberry
  mulberries (*pl.*)
mulch
mulct
mule
  muleteer
  mulish
mulligatawny
mullion (of a window)
  mullioned
multi- (many)
multifarious
multiform
multilateral
  multilaterally
multiple
multiplex

multiplicity
multiply
  multiplication
  multiplied
  multiplier
  multiplying
multiracial
multitude
  multitudinous
mum (silent)
mumble
  mumbling
mumbo-jumbo
mummery
mummy
  mummies (*pl.*)
  mummified
munch
mundane
municipal
  municipality
  municipalities (*pl.*)
munificence
  munificent
munition
mural
murder
  murdered
  murderer
  murderer's
    (of the murderer)
  murderers'
    (of the murderers)
  murderess (*fem.*)
  murdering
  murderous
  murderously
murk
  murkily
  murkiness
  murky
murmur
  murmured
  murmuring
  murmurs

murrain (cattle disease)
muscat
  muscatel
muscle
  muscular
muse (goddess)
muse (to meditate)
  musing
museum
  museums (*pl.*)
mush
  mushy
mushroom
music
  musical
  musically
  musician
  musician's
    (of the musician)
  musicians'
    (of the musicians)
musk
musket
  musketry
Muslim, Moslem
muslin (cotton cloth)
  musquash
mussel (mollusc)
must
  mustn't (must not)
mustang
mustard
muster
  mustered
  mustering
musty
  mustiness
mutable
  mutability
mutation
  mutant
mute
  mutely
mutilate
  mutilating

mutilation
mutilator
mutiny
  mutinies (*pl.*)
  mutineer
  mutinied
  mutinies
  mutinous
  mutinying
mutter
  muttered
  muttering
  mutters
mutton
mutual
  mutually
Muzak
muzzle
  muzzling
muzzy
  muzzily
  muzziness
my
  myself
mycelium
mycology
myelitis
myo- (muscle)
  myocarditis
  myocardium
     (heart muscle)
myo- (shut)
  myopia
  myopic (short-sighted)
myriad
myrmidon
myrrh
myrtle
myself
mystery
  mysteries (*pl.*)
  mysterious
  mysteriously
mystic
  mystical

mysticism
mystify
  mystification
  mystified
  mystifies
mystique
myth
  mythical
mythology
  mythologies (*pl.*)
  mythological
  mythologist
myxomatosis

N

nab
  nabbed
  nabbing
  nabs
nabob
nadir
nag (to scold)
  nagged
  nagger
  nagging
  nags
nag (horse)
naiad
naïve, naïf
  naïveté
nail
naked
  nakedly
  nakedness
namby-pamby
name
  nameable
  namable
  name-dropper
  nameless
  namesake

namely
naming
nanny
  nannies (*pl.*)
  nanny's (of the nanny)
  nannies'
     (of the nannies)
nap
  napping
nape (of neck)
naphtha
  naphthalene
napkin
nappy
  nappies (*pl.*)
narcissus
  narcissi, narcissuses (*pl.*)
  narcissus (*pl.*)
  narcissism
narcosis
  narcotic
narrate
  narrating
  narration
  narrative
  narrator
narrow
  narrower
  narrowly
  narrow-minded
  narrowness
nasal
  nasally
nascent
  nascency
nasturtium
  nasturtiums (*pl.*)
nasty
  nastier
  nastily
  nastiness
natal
  natality
natation (swimming)
nation

national
nationalisation
nationalization
nationalise
nationalize
nationalising
nationalizing
nationalism
nationalist
nationalistic
nationality
nationalities (*pl.*)
nationally
nation's (of the nation)
nations' (of the nations)
native
nativity
NATO, N.A.T.O.
natter
nattered
natterer
nattering
natters
natty (smart)
nattier
natural
naturalism
naturalist
naturalistic
naturally
naturalise
naturalize
naturalisation
naturalization
naturalising
naturalizing
nature
naught (nothing)
naughty
naughtier
naughtily
naughtiness
nausea
nauseate
nauseating

nauseous
nautical
nautilus
nautiluses, nautili (*pl.*)
naval
   (of ships, navy, etc.)
nave (of church)
navel (umbilicus)
navigate
navigability
navigable
navigating
navigation
navigator
navvy (labourer)
navvies (*pl.*)
navvying
navy (ships)
navies (*pl.*)
navy's (of the navy)
navies' (of the navies)
nay (no)
N.B. (nota bene)
near
nearly
nearby
nearer
nearness
near-sighted
neat
neater
neatness
neatly
nebula
   nebulae, nebulas (*pl.*)
nebulous (vague)
nebulosity
necessary
necessarily
necessitate
necessitating
necessitous
necessity
necessities (*pl.*)
neck

neckerchief
necklace
necktie
necros (corpse)
necromancy
necrosis
nectar
nectarine
né (born)
   née (*fem.*)
need
needful
needless
needlessly
needy
needle
needlework
needling
ne'er (never)
ne'er-do-well
nefarious
nefariously
negate
negating
negation
negative
negatively
neglect
neglectful
negligé, negligée
negligence
negligent
negligently
negligible
negligibly
negotiate
negotiable
negotiating
negotiation
negotiator
Negro
   Negroes (*pl.*)
   Negro's (of the Negro)
   Negroes'
      (of the Negroes)

Negress (*fem.*)
Negresses (*pl.*)
Negress's
    (of the Negress)
Negresses'
    (of the Negresses)
Negroid
neigh (horse's cry)
neighing
neighbour
neighbor
neighbourhood
neighborhood
neighbouring
neighboring
neighbourliness
neighborliness
neighbourly
neighborly
neighbour's
    (of the neighbour)
neighbours'
    (of the neighbours)
neither
Nemesis
neo- (new)
neoclassic
neolithic
neologism
neology
neon (gas)
neophyte (novice)
nephew
nephew's
    (of the nephew)
nephews'
    (of the nephews)
nephritis
nephritic
nepotism
nerve
nerve-racking
nerving
nervy
nervous

nervously
nervousness
nest
nestle
nestling
net
netting
net, nett (weight or price)
net
nether (lower)
nettle
nettlerash
network
neuro- (nerve)
neural
neuralgia
neurasthenia
neurasthenic
neuritis
neurological
neurologist
neurology
neurosis
neurotic
neuter
neutered
neutral
neutralisation
neutralization
neutralise
neutralize
neutralising
neutralizing
neutrality
neutron
never
nevermore
nevertheless
new
new-born
newcomer
newer
newfangled
new-laid
newly

newness
newel
news
newsagent
newspaper
newsworthy
newt
next
nib
nibble
nibbling
nice
nicely
niceness
nicer
nicety
niceties (*pl.*)
niche
nick
nickel
nickelled
nickeled
nickname
nicotine
niece
niece's (of the niece)
nieces' (of the nieces)
niggard
niggardly
niggle
niggling
nigh
night
nightdress
nightdresses (*pl.*)
nightfall
nightlight
nightly (every night)
night porter
night shift
night-time
night watchman
nightingale
nightmare
nightmarish

nihilism
  nihilistic
nil
nimble
  nimbler
  nimbly
nimbus
  nimbi, nimbuses (*pl.*)
nincompoop
nine
  nineteen
  nineteenth
  ninetieth
  ninety
  nineties (*pl.*)
  ninth
  ninthly
ninny
  ninnies (*pl.*)
nip
  nipped
  nipper
  nipping
  nips
nipple
nirvana
nisi (unless)
nit
  nit-picking
  nitwit
  nitwitted
nitre
  niter
nitrate
    (salt of nitric acid)
  nitric
nitrite
    (salt of nitrous acid)
nitrogen
  nitro-glycerine
  nitro-glycerin
  nitrous
nitty-gritty
nob
Nobel prize

noble
  nobility
  nobleman
  nobleman's
    (of the nobleman)
  noblemen's
    (of the noblemen)
  nobler
  nobly
noblesse oblige
nobody
  nobodies (*pl.*)
  nobody's (of nobody)
  nobodies' (of nobodies)
nocturnal
  nocturnally
  nocturne
nod
  nodded
  nodding
  nods
noddle (head)
node
  nodal
nodule (lump)
  nodular
Noel, Noël
noes (those saying no)
noggin (mug)
nogging (brickwork)
nohow (by no means)
noise
  noiseless
  noiselessly
  noisier
  noisily
  noisiness
  noisy
noisome (disgusting)
nomad
  nomadic
nom de plume
nomenclature
nominal
  nominally

nominate
  nominating
  nomination
  nominator
  nominee
  nominative (*grammar*)
nonage
nonagenarian
nonce
  nonce-word
nonchalance
nonchalant
nonchalantly
non-combatant
non-commissioned
non-committal
  non-committally
non compos mentis
non-conductor
nonconformist
non-contributory
non-cooperation
  non-cooperative
nondescript
none
none the less,
        nonetheless
  nonetheless
nonentity
  nonentities (*pl.*)
non-essential
non-existent
nonpareil
nonplussed
  nonplused
nonsense
  nonsensical
  nonsensically
non sequitur
nonsuch, nonesuch
  nonesuch
noodle
nook
noon
no one

noose
normal
  normalisation
  normalization
  normalise
  normalize
  normalising
  normalizing
  normality
  normally
north
  northerly
  northern
  northward
  northwards
nose
  nosey
  nosiness
  nosing
  nosy
nosegay
nostalgia (homesickness)
  nostalgic
nostril
nostrum
  nostrums (*pl.*)
notable
  notability
  notabilities (*pl.*)
  notably
notary
  notaries (*pl.*)
  notary's (of the notary)
  notaries'
     (of the notaries)
notation
notch
  notches (*pl.*)
  notched
  notching
note
  noteworthiness
  noteworthy
  noting
nothing

notice
  noticeable
  noticeably
  noticing
notify
  notifiable
  notification
  notified
  notifies
  notifying
notion
  notional
  notionally
notorious
  notoriety
  notoriously
notwithstanding
nougat
nought (zero)
noun
nourish
  nourishment
nouveau riche
  nouveaux riches (*pl.*)
novel
  novelette
  novelist
  novelist's
     (of the novelist)
  novelists'
     (of the novelists)
novelty
  novelties (*pl.*)
novice
noviciate, novitiate
  novitiate
now
  nowadays
  nowhere
  nowise
noxious
nozzle
nuance
nubile
  nubility

nucleus
  nuclei (*pl.*)
  nuclear
nude
  nudism
  nudist
  nudity
nudge
  nudging
nugatory
nugget
nuisance
null
  nullification
  nullified
  nullifies
  nullify
  nullifying
numb
  numbness
number
  numbered
  numbering
numeral
numerator
numerical
  numerically
numerous
numismatic
  numismatist
numskull
nun
  nunnery
  nunneries (*pl.*)
  nun's (of the nun)
  nuns' (of the nuns)
nuncio
  nuncios (*pl.*)
nuptial
nurse
  nurseling
  nursemaid
  nurse's (of the nurse)
  nurses' (of the nurses)
  nursery

nurseries (*pl.*)
nurseryman
nurserymen (*pl.*)
nursing
nursling
nurture
  nurturing
nut
  nutcracker
  nutty
nutmeg
nutrient
  nutriment
  nutrition
  nutritious
  nutritive
nuzzle
  nuzzling
nylon
nymph
nymphomania
  nymphomaniac

O

oaf
  oafs (*pl.*)
  oafish
oak
  oaken
oakum (fibre)
oar (of boat)
oasis
  oases (*pl.*)
oast
  oast-house
oat
  oatmeal
oath
  oaths (*pl.*)
obbligato
obdurate

obduracy
obdurately
obedient
  obedience
  obediently
obeisance (bowing)
obelisk
obese (fat)
  obesity
obey
  obeyed
obituary
  obituaries (*pl.*)
object
  objection
  objectionable
  objector
object (thing)
objective
  objectively
  objectivity
objet d'art
  objets d'art (*pl.*)
oblation
oblige
  obligation
  obligatory
  obliging
oblique
  obliquely
  obliquity
obliterate
  obliterating
  obliteration
oblivion
  oblivious
oblong
obloquy
  obloquies (*pl.*)
obnoxious
  obnoxiously
  obnoxiousness
oboe
  oboes (*pl.*)
  oboist

obscene
  obscenely
  obscenity
  obscenities (*pl.*)
obscure
  obscurely
  obscurity
  obscurities (*pl.*)
obsequious
    (over-respectful)
  obsequiously
  obsequiousness
obsequy (funeral)
  obsequies (*pl.*)
observatory
  observatories (*pl.*)
observe
  observable
  observance
  observant
  observation
  observer
  observer's
    (of the observer)
  observers'
    (of the observers)
  observing
obsess
  obsessed
  obsession
  obsessive
obsolete
  obsolescence
  obsolescent
obstacle
obstetric
  obstetrician
  obstetrics
obstinate
  obstinacy
  obstinately
obstreperous
  obstreperously
  obstreperousness
obstruct

obstruction
obstructive
obstructively
obtain
obtainable
obtrude
obtruder
obtruding
obtrusion
obtrusive
obtuse
obtusely
obtuseness
obverse
obviate
obviating
obvious
obviously
occasion
occasional
occasionally
occident (west)
occidental
occlude
occluding
occlusion
occult (to conceal)
occultation
occult (mysterious)
occupant
occupancy
occupation
occupational
occupy
occupied
occupier
occupier's
(of the occupier)
occupiers'
(of the occupiers)
occupies
occupying
occur
occurred
occurrence

occurring
occurs
ocean
oceanic
ocelot (animal)
ochre
ocher
o'clock
oct- (eight)
octagon
octagonal
octane
octave
octavo
octet
October
octogenarian
octopus
octopuses, octopodes
(*pl.*)
octoroon
ocular
oculist
oculist's (of the oculist)
oculists' (of the oculists)
odd
odder
oddity
oddities (*pl.*)
oddly
oddment
odds
odds-on
ode
odious (hateful)
odiously
odiousness
odium
odour (smell)
odor
odoriferous
odorous
odourless
odorless
oecumenical, ecumenical

ecumenical
oedema
edema
oesophagus
esophagus
oesophageal
off
offing
off-licence
offal
offence
offense
offend
offender
offensive
offensively
offensiveness
offer
offered
offering
offers
offertory
offhand
offhanded
offhandedly
offhandedness
office
officer
officer's (of the officer)
officers' (of the officers)
official
officialese
officially
officiate
officiating
officious
officiously
officiousness
offprint
offset
offsetting
offshoot
offside
offspring
oft

often
oftener
ogle (to make eyes at)
ogling
ogre (giant)
ogress (*fem.*)
ohm
ohmic
ohmmeter
Ohm's Law
oil
oily
ointment
OK, O.K., okay
old
olden
older
old-fashioned
old maid
old maid's
(of the old maid)
old maids'
(of the old maids)
old-maidish
oleander (shrub)
olfaction
olfactory
olig- (few)
oligarch
oligarchy
oligarchies (*pl.*)
oligopoly
oligopolies (*pl.*)
olive
Olympia
Olympian
Olympic
Ombudsman
omega
omelette
omelet
omen
ominous
ominously
omicron

omit
omission
omits
omitted
omitting
omni- (all)
omnibus
omnibuses (*pl.*)
omnipotence
omniscience
omniscient
omnivorous
once
once-over
oncoming
one
oneness
one's (of one)
oneself
onerous
onerousness
one-up
one-upmanship
ongoing
onion
on-line, online
onlooker
only
onomatopoeia
onomatopoeic
onrush
onset
onslaught
onus
onward
onyx
oolite
oolitic
ooze
oozing
opacity
opal
opalescence
opalescent
opaque

opacity
opaquely
open
open-and-shut
opened
open-ended
opener
opening
openly
openness
opera
operatic
operatically
operetta
operate
operability
operable
operating
operation
operational
operationally
operative
operator
ophthalmia
ophthalmic
ophthalmologist
ophthalmology
opiate (drug)
opine
opining
opinion
opinionated
opium
opossum
opossums (*pl.*)
opponent
opportune
opportunely
opportuneness
opportunism
opportunist
opportunity
opportunities (*pl.*)
oppose
opposer

169

opposing
opposite
opposition
oppress
oppression
oppressive
oppressively
oppressor
opprobrious
opprobrium
opt (to choose)
optative
optic (of the eye)
optical
optically
optician
optimum
optimisation
optimization
optimise
optimize
optimising
optimizing
optimism
optimist
optimistic
optimistically
option
optional
optionally
opulence
opulent
opus
opera (*pl.*)
oracle
oracular
oral
orally
orange
orangeade
orang-utan, orang-utang
orate
orating
oration
oratio obliqua

oratio recta
orator (speaker)
oratory (speech-making)
oratorio (sacred opera)
oratorios (*pl.*)
oratory (chapel)
oratories (*pl.*)
orb
orbit
orbital
orbited
orbiting
orbits
orchard
orchestra
orchestras (*pl.*)
orchestra's
    (of the orchestra)
orchestras'
    (of the orchestras)
orchestrate
orchestrating
orchestration
orchestrator
orchid
ordain
ordination
ordeal
order
ordered
ordering
orderliness
orderly
orders
ordinal (number)
ordinance (decree)
ordinary
ordinarily
ordinate (*maths.*)
ordination
ordnance (military stores)
    Ordnance Survey
ordure
ore (mineral)
oregano (herb)

organ
organist
organic
organically
organise
organize
organisation
organization
organiser
organizer
organising
organizing
organism
orgasm
orgy
orgies (*pl.*)
orgiastic
oriel (window)
orient (east)
oriental
orientally
orientate
orientating
orientation
orifice
origami (paper-folding)
origin
original
originality
originally
originate
originating
originator
orison
ormolu
ornament
ornamental
ornamentation
ornate
ornately
ornitho- (bird)
ornithologist
ornithology
orotund
orphan

orphanage
orphaned
orphan's
   (of the orphan)
orphans'
   (of the orphans)
orrery
  orreries (*pl.*)
ortho- (right or straight)
  orthodontics
  orthodontist
  orthodox
  orthodoxy
  orthographic
  orthography
  orthopaedic
  orthopedic
ortolan
oscillate
  oscillating
  oscillation
  oscillator
  oscillatory
  oscillogram
  oscillograph
  oscilloscope
osculate (to kiss)
  osculating
  osculation
osier
osmosis
osprey
  ospreys (*pl.*)
  osprey's (of the osprey)
  ospreys'
    (of the ospreys)
oss- (bone)
  osseous
  ossification
  ossified
  ossify
  ossifying
  ossuary
  ossuaries (*pl.*)
ostensible

ostensibly
ostensive
  ostensively
ostentation
  ostentatious
  ostentatiously
osteo- (bone)
  osteo-arthritis
  osteology
  osteopath
  osteopathic
  osteopathy
ostler
ostracise
  ostracize
  ostracising
  ostracizing
  ostracism
ostrich
  ostriches (*pl.*)
  ostriches'
    (of the ostriches)
  ostrich's (of the ostrich)
other
  otherwise
otiose (lazy)
otitis (ear disease)
otter
ottoman
oubliette
ought
  oughtn't (ought not)
ounce
our
  ours
  ourself
  ourselves (*pl.*)
out
  outage
  outer
  outermost
  outing
outbid
  outbidding
outboard

outbound
outbreak
outburst
outcast
outclass
  outclassed
outcome
outcry
  outcries (*pl.*)
outdo
  outdoing
  outdone
outdoors
outerspace, outer space
outfit
  outfitter
  outfitting
outflank
  outflanked
outgoing
outgrow
  outgrew
  outgrown
  outgrowth
outing
outlandish
outlast
outlaw
  outlawry
outlay
outlet
outline
  outlining
outlive
  outliving
outlook
outlying
outmanoeuvre
  outmaneuver
  outmanoeuvring
  outmaneuvring
outmoded
outmost
outnumber
  outnumbered

171

outnumbering
out-patient
  out-patient's
    (of the out-patient)
  out-patients'
    (of the out-patients)
outpost
outpouring
output
  outputting
outrage
  outrageous
  outrageously
  outraging
outreach
outrider
outrigger
  outrigged
outright
outrun
  outran
  outrunning
outset
outshine
  outshining
  outshone
outside
  outsider
  outsider's
    (of the outsider)
  outsiders'
    (of the outsiders)
outsize
outskirts
outspoken
  outspokenness
outstanding
outstare
  outstaring
out-station
outstay
  outstayed
outstretched
outstrip
  outstripped

outstripping
outstrips
outvote
  outvoting
outward
  outward-bound
  outwardly
outweigh
outwit
  outwits
  outwitted
  outwitting
outworn
oval
ovary
  ovaries (*pl.*)
ovation
oven
over
  overall
overact
overarm
overawe
  overawing
overbalance
  overbalancing
overbearing
overboard
overburden
  overburdened
overcast
overcharge
  overcharged
  overcharging
overcoat
overcome
  overcame
  overcoming
over-confident
overcrowded
overdo
  overdoes
  overdoing
  overdone
  overdid

overdose
  overdosing
overdraft
overdraw
  overdrew
overdress
  overdressed
overdrive
overdue
overeat (to eat too much)
  overate
  overeaten
  overeating
overflow
  overflowed
overground
overgrow
  overgrew
  overgrown
  overgrowth
overhang
  overhanging
  overhung
overhaul
overhead
overhear
  overheard
overheat
  overheated
over-indulgence
overjoy
  overjoyed
overland
overlap
  overlapped
  overlapping
  overlaps
overlay
  overlaid
overleaf
overload
  overloaded
overlook
overnight
overpay

over-paid
over-populate
overpower
overpowered
overpowering
overrate (to over-value)
overrated
overrating
overreach
over-react
override
overridden
overriding
overrode
overripe
overrule
overruled
overruling
overrun
overran
overrunning
overseas
oversee
overseeing
overseen
overseer
overseer's
(of the overseer)
overseers'
(of the overseers)
over-sexed
overshadow
overshadowed
overshoot
overshot
oversight
over-simplify
over-simplification
oversleep
overslept
overspend
over-spent
overstate
overstatement
overstating

overstay
overstep
overstepped
overstepping
over-subscribe
overt
overtly
overtake
overtaking
overtook
overtax
overtaxing
overthrow
overthrew
overthrown
overtime
overtire
overtired
overtiring
overtone
overture
overturn
overturned
overweening
overweight
overwhelm
overwork
overwrought
oviduct
oviparous
ovoid (egg-shaped)
ovulate
ovulation
ovum (egg cell)
ova (*pl.*)
owe
owing
owl
own
owned
owner
owner's (of the owner)
owners' (of the owners)
ownership
ox

oxen (*pl.*)
oxalic
oxalic acid
oxide
oxidise
oxidize
oxidisation
oxidization
oxidising
oxidizing
oxtail
oxtongue
oxy-acetylene
oxygen
oxygenate
oxygenating
oxygenation
oyster
oyster's (of the oyster)
oysters' (of the oysters)
ozone

P

pace
pacing
pachyderm
pachydermatous
pacific (peaceful)
pacifically
Pacific
pacify
pacifiable
pacification
pacified
pacifier
pacifies
pacifism
pacifist
pacifying
pack
package

packaging
packed
packet (parcel)
pact (treaty)
pad
  padded
  padding
  pads
paddle
  paddler
  paddling
paddock
padlock
  padlocked
padre
  padre's (of the padre)
  padres' (of the padres)
padrone (boss)
paean (thanksgiving)
paed- (child)
  paediatrician
  pediatrician
  paediatrics
  pediatrics
pagan
  paganism
page
  pagination
  paging
pageant
  pageantry
  pageantries (*pl.*)
pagoda
  pagodas (*pl.*)
paid (*from* pay)
  paid-up
pail (bucket)
pain
  painful
  painfully
  painless
  painlessly
  painstaking
paint
  painter

painter's (of the painter)
painters'
        (of the painters)
pair
paired
paisley
pal (friend)
  pally
  pal's (of the pal)
  pals' (of the pals)
palace
  palatial
palaeo- (ancient)
  palaeographic
  paleographic
  palaeography
  palaeolithic
  paleolithic
  palaeozoic
palate (of mouth)
  palatable (tasting good)
palatial (*from* palace)
palaver
  palavered
  palavering
  palavers
pale (whitish)
  palely
  paleness
  pallor
pale (stake *or* post)
  paling
palette (artist's)
palindrome
palisade
pall (cloth over coffin)
  pall-bearer
pall (to be boring)
  palled
  palling
Palladium
pallet (tool)
pallet (mattress)
palliasse
  paillasse

palliate
    (to ease pain, etc.)
  palliating
  palliation
  palliative
pallid (pale)
pallor (paleness)
palm
  palmist
  palmistry
palm (tree)
  palmy (flourishing)
palomino
  palominos (*pl.*)
palpable (obvious)
  palpably
palpate
  (to feel with the hand)
  palpating
  palpation
palpitate (to throb)
  palpitating
  palpitation
palsy
  palsied
paltry
  paltrier
  paltriness
pamper
  pampered
  pampering
pamphlet
  pamphleteer
pan
  pancake
Pan (god of nature)
pan- (all)
  panacea
  panchromatic
  pancreas
  pandemic
  pandemonium
  panegyric
  panoply
  panorama

panoramic
pantechnicon
Pantheon
pantomime
panache (swagger)
panda (animal)
pander (to indulge)
  pandered
  pandering
pane (of glass)
panel
  panelist
  panelled
  paneled
  panelling
  paneling
pang
panic
  panicked
  panicking
  panicky
  panics
  panic-stricken
pannier
panorama
  panoramas (*pl.*)
  panoramic
  panoramically
pansy
  pansies (*pl.*)
  pansy's (of the pansy)
  pansies' (of the pansies)
pant (to breathe quickly)
pantaloon
pantechnicon
pantheism
  pantheistic
Pantheon
panther
  panther's
    (of the panther)
  panthers'
    (of the panthers)
pantile (curved tile)
pantomime

pantry
  pantries (*pl.*)
pants (clothes)
papacy
  papal
paper
  paperback
  papered
  papering
  paperweight
papier mâché
papist
  papistry
paprika
papyrus
  papyri (*pl.*)
par (nominal value)
parable (story)
parabola (curve)
  parabolic
  parabolically
parachute
  parachute's
    (of the parachute)
  parachutes'
    (of the parachutes)
  parachuting
  parachutist
parade
  parading
paradise
paradox
  paradoxical
  paradoxically
paraffin
paragon
paragraph
parakeet, parrakeet
parallax
parallel
  paralleled
  paralleling
  parallelism
  parallelogram
parallelepiped

paralyse
  paralyze
  paralysing
  paralyzing
  paralysis
  paralytic
parameter
paramilitary
paramount (supreme)
paramour (lover)
paranoia
  paranoiac
  paranoid
parapet
paraphernalia
paraphrase
  paraphrasing
paraplegia (paralysis)
parasite
  parasitic
  parasitical
parasol
paratroops
  paratrooper
paratyphoid
parboil
parcel
  parcelled
  parceled
  parcelling
  parceling
parched (thirsty)
parchment
pardon
  pardonable
  pardoned
  pardoning
pare (to cut)
  paring
paregoric (pain-killer)
parent
  parentage
  parental
  parentally
  parent's (of the parent)

parents' (of the parents)
parenthesis
parentheses (*pl.*)
parenthetic
par excellence
pariah (outcast)
parish
parishes (*pl.*)
parishioner
Parisian
Parisienne (*fem.*)
parity
parities (*pl.*)
park
parka
parlance
(choice of words)
parley (to discuss)
parleyed
parleying
parleys
parliament
parliamentarian
parliamentary
parlour (room)
parlor
parlous (perilous)
parochial
parochialism
parochially
parody
parodies (*pl.*)
parodied
parodies
parodist
parodying
parole
paroxysm
paroxysmal
parquet
parqueted
parquetry
parrakeet, parakeet
parricide
parricidal

parrot
parrot's (of the parrot)
parrots' (of the parrots)
parry
parried
parries
parrying
parse
parsing
parsimonious
parsimony
parsley
parsnip
parson
parsonage
parson's (of the parson)
parsons'
(of the parsons)
part
partly
partake
partaken
partaker
partaking
partook
parterre
parthenogenesis
parthenogenetic
parthenogenetically
Parthenon
partial
partiality
partially
participate
participant
participating
participation
participator
participle
participial
particle
particular
particularise
particularize
particularising

particularizing
particularity
particularly
partisan
partition
partitioned
partitioning
partner
partnered
partnering
partner's
(of the partner)
partners'
(of the partners)
partnership
partridge
part-time
parturition (giving birth)
parturient
party
parties (*pl.*)
parvenu
parvenus (*pl.*)
parvenue (*fem.*)
parvenues (*pl.*)
paschal (of Easter)
pass
passable
passably
passed
passer-by
passers-by (*pl.*)
passes
passage
passé
passenger
passenger's
(of the passenger)
passengers'
(of the passengers)
passim (at various places)
passion
passionate
passionately
passive

passively
passiveness
passivity
passport
password
past
  past master
paste
  pasteboard
  pasting
pastel (picture)
pasteurise
  pasteurize
  pasteurisation
  pasteurization
  pasteurised
  pasteurized
  pasteurising
  pasteurizing
pastille (lozenge)
pastime
pastor (minister)
  pastoral
  pastorate
  pastor's (of the pastor)
  pastors' (of the pastors)
pastry
  pastries (*pl.*)
pasture (grazing land)
  pasturage
pasty
  pasties (*pl.*)
pat
  pats
  patted
  patting
patch
  patched
  patching
  patchwork
  patchy
pate (head)
pâté de foie gras
patent (open)
  patently

patent (invention, etc.)
  patentable
  patentee
       (holder of patent)
pater- (father)
  paterfamilias
  paternal
  paternalistic
  paternally
  paternity
  paternoster
path
  pathless
  pathway
path- (suffering)
  pathetic
  pathetically
  pathogenic
  pathological
  pathologically
  pathologist
  pathology
  pathos
patient (ill person)
  patient's (of the patient)
  patients'
      (of the patients)
patience (calmness)
  patient
  patiently
patina
patio (open courtyard)
patisserie
patois (dialect)
patriarch
  patriarchal
  patriarchy
patrician
patricide
patrimony
  patrimonies (*pl.*)
  patrimonial
patriot
  patriotic
  patriotically

patriotism
patrol
  patrolled
  patrolling
  patrols
patron
  patronage
  patroness (*fem.*)
  patronise
  patronize
  patroniser
  patronizer
  patronising
  patronizing
  patron's (of the patron)
  patrons'
      (of the patrons)
patronymic
patten (kind of shoe)
patter (to chatter)
  pattered
  pattering
patter (to tap)
  pattered
  pattering
pattern (design)
  patterned
patty
  patties (*pl.*)
paucity
paunch
  paunchy
pauper
  pauperism
  pauper's (of the pauper)
  paupers'
      (of the paupers)
pause
  pausing
pave
  pavement
  paving
  paviour
  pavior
pavilion

paw
  pawed
pawn
  pawnbroker
pay
  paid
  payable
  payee
    (one who gets paid)
  payer (one who pays)
  paying
  paymaster
  payment
  payoff
  payroll
pea
  peas (*pl.*)
  peanut
  pease-pudding
peace
  peaceable
  peaceably
  peaceful
  peacefully
  peacefulness
peach
  peaches (*pl.*)
peacock
  peacock's
    (of the peacock)
  peacocks'
    (of the peacocks)
  peahen (*fem.*)
peak
  (projecting part of cap)
  peaked
peak (top)
  peak-load
peak (to waste away)
  peaky
peal (of bells)
pear
pearl
  pearly
  pearlies (*pl.*)

peasant
  peasantry
  peasant's
      (of the peasant)
  peasants'
      (of the peasants)
peat
pebble
  pebbly
peccadillo
  peccadilloes (*pl.*)
  peccadillos (*pl.*)
  peccant (sinning)
pêche Melba
peck
  pecked
  pecking
  peckish (hungry)
pectoral
peculation (embezzlement)
  peculator
peculiar (odd)
  peculiarity
  peculiarities (*pl.*)
  peculiarly
pecuniary (financial)
peda- (boy, child)
  pedagogue (teacher)
  pedagogy
pedal (of bicycle etc.)
  pedalled
  pedaled
  pedalling
  pedaling
  pedals
pedant
  pedantic
  pedantry
peddle (to sell trifles)
  peddling
  pedlar (hawker)
  peddler
  pedlar's (of the pedlar)
  pedlars' (of the pedlars)
pedestal

pedestrian
pedicure
pedigree
pediment
pedlar (hawker)
  peddler
pedometer
peek (to peep)
  peeked
peel (to remove skin)
peep
peer (to stare)
peer (nobleman)
  peerage
  peeress (*fem.*)
  peeress's
      (of the peeress)
  peeresses'
      (of the peeresses)
  peer's (of the peer)
  peers' (of the peers)
peer (equal)
  peer group
  peerless
peeved
  peevish
  peevishness
peewit, pewit
  pewit
peg
  pegged
  pegging
  pegs
pejorative
  pejoratively
Pekinese, Pekingese
pelagic (of open sea)
pelican
pellet
pell-mell
pellucid (clear)
pelmet
pelt (to rain hard)
pelt (animal skin)
pelt (to throw)

178

pelvis
 pelvic
pen (for cattle)
 penned
 penning
pen (for writing)
penal
 penalisation
 penalization
 penalise
 penalize
 penalised
 penalized
 penalising
 penalizing
 penalty
 penalties (*pl.*)
penance
penchant
pencil
 pencilled
 penciled
 pencilling
 penciling
pendant (hanging jewel)
pendent (hanging)
pending
pendulous (drooping)
pendulum
 pendulums (*pl.*)
penetrate
 penetrability
 penetrable
 penetrating
 penetration
 penetrative
penguin
 penguin's
   (of the penguin)
 penguins'
   (of the penguins)
penicillin
peninsula
 peninsulas (*pl.*)

peninsular
   (of a peninsula)
penis
penitence
 penitent
 penitential
 penitentiary
 penitentiaries (*pl.*)
penknife
 penknives (*pl.*)
pennant
penniless
 pennilessness
pennon
penny
 pennies, pence (*pl.*)
penology (study of crime)
pension
 pensionable
 pensioner
pensive
 pensively
 pensiveness
penta- (five)
 pentagon
 pentagonal
 pentameter
 Pentateuch
 pentathlon
penultimate
 penultimately
penumbra
 penumbrae, penumbras
            (*pl.*)
penury (poverty)
 penurious
peon (labourer)
peony (plant)
 peonies (*pl.*)
people
pep (energy)
pepper
 peppered
 peppering
 peppery

peppermint
pepsin
 peptic
Pepys
 Pepysian
peradventure
perambulate
 perambulating
 perambulation
 perambulator
per annum
per capita
perceive
 perceivable
 perceiving
per cent
 percentage
perception
 perceptible
 perceptibly
 perceptive
perch
perchance
percipience
 percipient
percolate
 percolating
 percolation
 percolator
percuss
 percussed
 percussion
 percussive
perdition
peregrinate (to wander)
 peregrinating
 peregrination
 peregrine
peremptory
 peremptorily
 peremptoriness
perennial
 perennially
perfect
 perfection

perfectionist
perfidy
  perfidious
perforate
  perforating
  perforation
  perforator
perforce
perform
  performance
  performer
  performer's
    (of the performer)
  performers'
    (of the performers)
perfume
  perfumery
  perfumeries (*pl.*)
  perfuming
perfunctory
  perfunctorily
  perfunctoriness
pergola
  pergolas (*pl.*)
perhaps
peri- (around)
  pericardial
  pericardium
  perimeter
  peripatetic
  peripheral
  periphery
  periphrasis
  periscope
  peritoneum
  peritonitis
peril
  perilous
  perilously
period
  periodic
  periodical
  periodically
  periodicity

peripatetic
    (walking about)
periphery
  peripheral
periscope
perish
  perishable
peritonitis
periwinkle
perjure
  perjurer
  perjuring
  perjurious
  perjury
perk
  perkiness
  perky
  perks (perquisites)
permafrost
permalloy
permanence
  permanency
  permanent
  permanently
permanganate
permeable
  permeability
permeate
  permeating
  permeation
permission
  permissible
  permissive
  permissiveness
permit
  permits
  permitted
  permitting
permutation
pernicious (injurious)
  perniciously
  perniciousness
pernickety (fussy)
perorate
    (to end a speech)

perorating
peroration
peroxide
perpendicular
  perpendicularity
  perpendicularly
perpetrate
  (to commit crime, etc.)
  perpetrating
  perpetration
  perpetrator
perpetual
  perpetually
perpetuate
    (to make permanent)
  perpetuating
  perpetuity
perplex
  perplexity
perquisite
per se
persecute
  persecuting
  persecution
  persecutor
persevere
  perseverance
  persevering
persiflage
persimmon
persist
  persistence
  persistency
  persistent
  persistently
person
  personable (handsome)
  personage
  personal
  personality
  personalities (*pl.*)
  personally
  person's (of the person)
  persons'
    (of the persons)

persona grata
  persona non grata
personate
  personating
  personation
  personator
personify
  personification
  personified
  personifies
  personifying
personnel (staff)
perspective
perspicacious (intelligent)
  perspicacity
perspicuous
    (clearly expressed)
  perspicuity
perspire
  perspiration
  perspiring
persuade
  persuadable
  persuader
  persuading
  persuasion
  persuasive
  persuasively
pert
  pertly
  pertness
pertain
pertinacious (persevering)
  pertinaciously
  pertinacity
pertinent (to the point)
  pertinence
perturb
  perturbation
  perturber
peruke (wig)
peruse
  perusal
  perusing
pervious (permeable)

pervade
  pervaded
  pervading
  pervasion
  pervasive
  pervasively
perverse (obstinate)
  perversely
  perversity
pervert (to lead astray)
  perversion
  perverter
  perverting
peseta (Spanish money)
peso (S.American money)
pessary
  pessaries (*pl.*)
pessimism
  pessimist
  pessimistic
  pessimistically
pest
  pesticide
  pestiferous
  pestilence
  pestilent
  pestilential
pester (to annoy)
  pestered
  pesterer
  pestering
pestle
pet
  pets
  pet's (of the pet)
  pets' (of the pets)
  petted
  petting
petal
  petalled
  petaled
petard
peter (to give out)
  petered
  petering

  peters out
petite (small)
petit four (small cake)
petition
  petitioner
petit mal (slight epilepsy)
petit point (embroidery)
petrel (sea-bird)
petr- (stone)
  petrifaction
  petrified
  petrifies
  petrify
  petrifying
  petrol
  petroleum
petticoat
pettifog
  pettifogged
  pettifogger
  pettifoggery
  pettifogging
pettish (sulky)
petty
  pettier
  pettiest
  pettily
  pettiness
petulance
  petulant
  petulantly
pew
pewit, peewit
  pewit
pewter
pfennig (German money)
phagocyte
phalanx
  phalanges, phalanxes
        (*pl.*)
phallus
  phallic
phantasm
  phantasmagoria
  phantasmal

phantasmic
phantom
pharisee
  pharisaic
pharmacy
  pharmacies (*pl.*)
  pharmaceutical
  pharmacist
  pharmacologist
  pharmacology
  pharmacopoeia
pharynx
  pharyngeal
  pharyngitis
phase
  phasing
pheasant
  pheasant's
    (of the pheasant)
  pheasants'
    (of the pheasants)
phenacetin
phenobarbitone
  phenobarbital
phenol (type of benzene)
phenomenon
  phenomena (*pl.*)
  phenomenal
  phenomenally
phenyl
  (formed from benzene)
phial, vial (small bottle)
phil-, philo- (loving)
  philander
  philanderer
  philanthropic
  philanthropically
  philanthropist
  philanthropy
  philatelist
  philately
  philharmonic
  philologist
  philology
  philosopher

philosopher's
  (of the philosopher)
philosophers'
  (of the philosophers)
philosophical
philosophically
philosophy
Philistine
philistinism
philtre (love-potion)
  philter
phlebitis
phlegm
  phlegmatic
  phlegmatically
phlox
phobia
phoenix
phon- (voice)
  phone (telephone)
  phonetic
  phonetically
  phoning
  phonograph
phoney (sham)
  phony
phos- (light)
  phosgene
  phosphate
  phosphorescence
  phosphorescent
  phosphoric
  phosphorus
phot- (light)
  photocopier
  photocopy
  photocopies (*pl.*)
  photocopying
  photogenic
  photograph
  photographer
  photographic
  photography
  photometer
  photometric

photometry
photostat
photosynthesis
phrase
  phraseology
  phrasing
phrenetic, frenetic
phrenology
  phrenologist
phthisis
  phthisical
phylactery
  phylacteries (*pl.*)
phylloxera
phylum
  phyla (*pl.*)
phys- (nature)
  physical
  physically
  physician
  physicist
  physics
  physiognomist
  physiognomy
  physiological
  physiologically
  physiologist
  physiology
  physiotherapist
  physiotherapy
  physique
piano
  pianos (*pl.*)
  pianist
  pianoforte
  pianola
  piano's (of the piano)
  pianos' (of the pianos)
piano (softly)
  pianissimo (very softly)
piastre (Turkish money)
  piaster
piazza
picador (bull-fighter)
picaresque (literary style)

Piccadilly
piccalilli (pickle)
piccaninny (small child)
  pickaninny
  piccaninnies (*pl.*)
  pickaninnies (*pl.*)
piccolo (flute)
  piccolos (*pl.*)
pick
  pickaxe
  pickax
  picker
pick-a-back, piggyback
picket (of strikers)
  picketed
  picketing
picket (long stick)
picket (soldiers or police)
pickle
  pickling
pickpocket
picnic
  picnicked
  picnicker
  picnicking
picric (acid)
pictorial
  pictorially
picture
  picturesque
  picturesquely
  picturesqueness
  picturing
piddle
  piddling
pidgin English
pie
piebald
piece
  piecemeal
  piece-work
  piecing
pièce de résistance
pied-à-terre
pier (at seaside)

pier-head
pierce
  piercing
pierrot
  pierrot's (of the pierrot)
  pierrots'
        (of the pierrots)
  pierrette (*fem.*)
piety
  pietism
  pietist
piezo-electric
  piezo-electricity
piffle
  piffling
pig
  pigged
  piggery
  piggeries (*pl.*)
  pigging
  piggish
  pig-iron
  piglet
  pig's (of the pig)
  pigs' (of the pigs)
  pigsty
  pigsties (*pl.*)
pigeon
  pigeon-hole
  pigeon-holing
  pigeon-toed
piggyback, pick-a-back
pigheaded
  pigheadedness
pigment
  pigmentation
pigtail
  pigtailed
pike (long stick)
  pikestaff
pike (fish)
pilaff, pilaf
pilchard
pile
  pile up

piling
pilfer
  pilferage
  pilfered
  pilferer
  pilfering
pilgrim
  pilgrimage
  pilgrim's
        (of the pilgrim)
  pilgrims'
        (of the pilgrims)
pill
pillage
  pillager
  pillaging
pillar
  pillar-box
pillion
pillory
  pilloried
  pillorying
pillow
pilot
  pilotage
  piloted
  piloting
  pilot's (of the pilot)
  pilots' (of the pilots)
pimpernel
pimple
  pimply
pin
  pinhead
  pinned
  pinning
pinafore
pince-nez
pincers
pinch
  pinched
pinch-hit (baseball)
  pinch-hitter
  pinch-hitting
pincushion

pine (tree)
pine (to waste away)
  pining
pineapple
ping-pong
pinion
  pinioned
  pinioning
pink
pinnace
pinnacle
pinpoint
pint
pin-up
pioneer
  pioneered
  pioneering
  pioneers
pious
  piously
pip
  pipped
  pip-squeak
pipe
  piper
  pipette
  piping
pippin (apple)
piquant
  piquancy
pique (vexation)
piquet (card-game)
pirate
  piracy
  pirate's (of the pirate)
  pirates' (of the pirates)
  piratical
  pirating
pirouette
  pirouetted
  pirouetting
pisc- (fish)
  piscatorial
  piscina (fish pond)
  piscine (bathing pool)

pistachio (nut)
  pistachios (*pl.*)
pistil (of flower)
pistol (fire-arm)
piston (of engine)
pit
  pitted
  pitting
pitch
  pitches (*pl.*)
pitcher (jug)
piteous
  piteously
pitfall
pith
  pithily
  pithiness
  pithy
pittance
pituitary
pity
  pities (*pl.*)
  pitiable
  pitied
  pities
  pitiful
  pitifully
  pitiless
  pitilessly
  pitying
pivot
  pivotal
  pivoted
  pivoting
pixy, pixie
  pixies (*pl.*)
pizza
  pizzeria
  pizzicato
placard
placate
  placability
  placable
  placating
  placation

place
  placement
  placing
placebo
  placebos (*pl.*)
placenta
placid
  placidity
  placidly
placket
plage (beach)
plagiarise
  plagiarize
  plagiarising
  plagiarizing
  plagiarism
  plagiarist
plague
  plaguing
plaice (fish)
plaid
plain
  plainclothed
  plainclothes
  plainer
  plainly
  plainness
  plainsong
  plain-spoken
plaint
  plaintiff (prosecutor)
  plaintiffs (*pl.*)
  plaintiff's
      (of the plaintiff)
  plaintiffs'
      (of the plaintiffs)
plaintive (sad)
  plaintively
  plaintiveness
plait (of hair)
plan
  planned
  planner
  planning
  plans

planchette

plane
  planing

planet
  planetarium
  planetaria,
      planetariums(*pl.*)
  planetary

plank

plankton

plant
  planter

plantain

plantation

plaque

plasma

plaster
  plastered
  plasterer
  plastering

plastic
  plastically
  plasticine
  plasticity

plate
  plateful
  platefuls (*pl.*)
  plate-glass
  plating

plateau
  plateaus, plateaux (*pl.*)

platform

platinum

platitude
  platitudinous

platonic
  platonically

platoon

platter

platypus
  platypuses (*pl.*)

plaudit

plausible
  plausibility
  plausibly

play
  player
  playfellow
  playful
  playfully
  playfulness
  playgoer
  playgoing
  playmate
  play off
  playwright
  playwright's
      (of the playwright)
  playwrights'
      (of the playwrights)

plaza

plea

plead
  pleader

pleasant
  pleasantly
  pleasantness
  pleasantry (joke)
  pleasantries (*pl.*)

please
  pleased
  pleasing

pleasure
  pleasurable
  pleasurably

pleat

plebeian

plebiscite

pledge
  pledging

Pleistocene

plenary

plenipotentiary
  plenipotentiaries (*pl.*)

plenitude

plenteous
  plenteously

plenty
  plentiful
  plentifully

plentifulness

plethora
  plethoric

pleura
  pleural
  pleurisy

pliable
  pliability

pliant
  pliancy

pliers

plight

Plimsoll line

plimsolls (canvas shoes)

plinth

Pliocene

plod
  plodded
  plodder
  plodding
  plods

plonk (cheap wine)

plop
  plopping

plot
  plots
  plotted
  plotter
  plotting

plough
  plow

plover

ploy

pluck
  pluckier
  pluckily
  plucky

plug
  plugged
  plugging
  plugs

plum
  plummy
  plum-pudding

plumage

plumb (to measure depth)
plumbago
plumber
  plumbing
plume
plummet
  plummeted
  plummeting
plump
  plumper
  plumpness
plunder
  plundered
  plunderer
  plundering
plunge
  plunger
  plunging
pluperfect
plural
  pluralism
  plurality
plus
plush
  plushy
plutocracy
  plutocracies (*pl.*)
  plutocrat
  plutocratic
plutonium
ply
  plied
  plies
  plying
  plywood
pneum- (wind, lung)
  pneumatic
  pneumonia
poach (to steal game)
  poached
  poacher
  poacher's
      (of the poaeher)
  poachers'
      (of the poachers)

poaches
poach (to cook)
  poached
  poaches
  poaching
pock
  pockmark
  pock-marked
pocket
  pocket-book (wallet)
  pocketed
  pocketing
pod
podge
  podgy
podium
  podia (*pl.*)
  podiums (*pl.*)
poem
poesy
poet
  poetic
  poetical
  poetically
  poetry
  poet's (of the poet)
  poets' (of the poets)
pogrom
poignant
  poignancy
  poignantly
poinsettia
point
  point-blank
  pointed
  pointedly
  pointless
  pointlessly
poise
poison
  poisoned
  poisoner
  poisoning
  poisonous
poke

poker
poking
poky
polar
  polarisation
  polarization
  polarise
  polarize
  polarising
  polarizing
  polarity
pole
polemic
  polemical
  polemically
police
  policing
  policeman
  policemen (*pl.*)
  policeman's
      (of the policeman)
  policemen's
      (of the policemen)
  policewoman
  policewomen (*pl.*)
  policewoman's
    (of the policewoman)
  policewomen's
    (of the policewomen)
policy
  policies (*pl.*)
poliomyelitis
polish
polite
  politely
  politeness
  politer
politic
  political
  politically
  politician
  politician's
      (of the politician)
  politicians'
      (of the politicians)

polity

polka

poll

  polled

  polling

  polls

  pollster

pollard

pollen

pollinate

  pollinating

  pollination

  pollinator

pollute

  pollutant

  polluting

  pollution

polo

polonaise

polonium

polony

  polonies (*pl.*)

poltergeist

poltroon

poly- (many)

  polyandrous

  polyandry

  polyanthus

  polychrome

  polychromatic

  polyester

  polygamist

  polygamous

  polygamously

  polygamy

  polyglot

  polygon

  polymer

  polymerisation

  polymerization

  polymerise

  polymerize

  polyp

  polyphonic

  polyphony

polypus

polystyrene

polysyllabic

polytechnic

polythene

polyunsaturated

pomade

pomatum

pomegranate

pommel (of saddle)

pomp

  pomposity

  pompous

  pompously

Pompeii

  Pompeian

poncho

  ponchos (*pl.*)

pond

ponder (to consider)

  pondered

  pondering

ponderous (heavy)

poniard

pontiff

  pontiffs (*pl.*)

  pontifical

pontificate

  pontificating

  pontification

pontoon

pony

  ponies (*pl.*)

  ponies' (of the ponies)

  pony's (of the pony)

  pony-tail

poodle

  poodle's (of the poodle)

  poodles'

      (of the poodles)

pooh-pooh

pool

  pooled

poop

poor

poorer

poorly

poorness

pop

popcorn

pop-eyed

popped

popper

popping

pops

pope

  popery

  pope's (of the pope)

  popes' (of the popes)

poplar (tree)

poplin

poppet

poppy

  poppies (*pl.*)

populace

popular

  popularisation

  popularization

  popularise

  popularize

  popularising

  popularizing

  popularity

  popularly

populate

  populating

  population

  populous

porcelain

porch

  porches (*pl.*)

porcupine

pore

  (to look, think intently)

  poring

pore (of skin)

pork

  porker

pornography

  pornographer

187

pornographic
pornographically
porous
  porosity
porphyry
porpoise
  porpoise's
      (of the porpoise)
  porpoises'
      (of the porpoises)
porridge
  porringer
port (harbour)
port (wine)
portable
  portability
portal (gateway)
portcullis
portend (to foreshadow)
portent (omen)
  portentous
porter (for luggage)
  porterage
porter (beer)
portfolio
  portfolios (*pl.*)
porthole
portico
  porticoes, porticos (*pl.*)
portion
portly
  portlier
  portliness
portmanteau
  portmanteaus,
     portmanteaux(*pl.*)
portrait
  portraiture
portray
  portrayal
  portrayed
Portugal
  Portuguese
pose
  poser

posing
posh
position
  positioned
  positioning
positive
  positively
  positivism
  positivist
positron
posse
possess
  possession
  possessive
  possessively
  possessiveness
  possessor
possible
  possibility
  possibilities (*pl.*)
  possibly
post (letters, etc.)
  postage
  postal order
  poste restante
  post-haste
  postman
  postmen (*pl.*)
  postman's
      (of the postman)
  postmen's
      (of the postmen)
  postmark
  postmaster
  postmaster's
      (of the postmaster)
  postmasters'
      (of the postmasters)
  post office
  post-paid
post- (after)
  post-date
  post-dating
  posterior
  posterity

postgraduate
posthumous
posthumously
post-impressionism
post-impressionist
post-mortem
post-natal
postpone
postponement
postponing
postscript
poster
postulate
  postulant
  postulating
  postulation
posture
  postural
  posturer
  posturing
posy
  posies (*pl.*)
pot
  potted
  potter
  potting
potable (drinkable)
  potation
potash
  potassium
potato
  potatoes (*pl.*)
pot-belly
  pot-bellied
pot-boiler
potency
  potent
  potently
potentate
potential
  potentiality
  potentially
potentiometer
pother
pot-hole

pot-holer
pot-holing
potion (drink)
pot-pourri
pottage
potter
  pottered
  potterer
  putterer
  pottering
pottery
  potteries (*pl.*)
potty (crazy)
  pottier
  pottily
pouch
  pouches (*pl.*)
pouffe (hassock)
  pouf
poultice
  poulticing
poultry
  poulterer
pounce
  pouncing
pound
  poundage
pound (to beat)
poundal (unit)
pour
  poured
  pouring
pourboire (tip)
pourparler (discussion)
pout
  pouter
poverty
powder
  powdered
  powdering
  powdery
power
  powered
  powerful
  powerfully

powerless
powerlessness
powwow
pox
practicable (possible)
  practicability
practical (ingenious)
  practicality
  practicalities (*pl.*)
  practically (almost)
practice (doctor's, etc.)
  practitioner
practise (piano, etc.)
  practice
  practising
  practicing
pragmatic
  pragmatical
  pragmatically
  pragmatism
prairie
praise
  praiseworthy
  praising
praline
prance
  prancing
prank
prate
  prating
prattle
  prattler
  prattling
prawn
pray (to say prayers)
  prayed
  prayer
  praying
preach
  preached
  preacher
  preacher's
      (of the preacher)
  preachers'
      (of the preachers)

preaches
preamble
prearrange
  prearrangement
  prearranging
prebend
  prebendary
  prebendaries (*pl.*)
precarious
  precariously
  precariousness
precaution
  precautionary
precede (to go before)
  precedence
  precedent
  preceding
precentor
precept
precession (*from* precede)
precinct
precious
precipice
precipitate
  precipitant
  precipitately
  precipitating
  precipitation
  precipitous
  precipitously
précis (shortened version)
  précis (*pl.*)
precise (exact)
  precisely
  precision
preclude
  precluding
  preclusive
precocious
  precociousness
  precocity
precognition
preconceived
  preconception
precursor

precursory

predator
 predacious
 predatory
predecease (to die before)
 predeceasing
predecessor
predestine
 predestination
predetermined
predicament
predicate (to confirm)
 predicating
 predication
predicate (*grammar*)
predict (to prophesy)
 predictable
 predictably
 prediction
predigest
 predigestion
predilection
predispose
 predisposing
 predisposition
predominant
 predominance
 predominantly
predominate
 predominating
pre-eminent
 pre-eminently
 pre-eminence
pre-empt
 pre-emption
 pre-emptive
preen
pre-exist
 pre-existence
 pre-existent
 pre-existing
prefab
prefabricate
 prefabricating
 prefabrication

preface
 prefacing
 prefatory
prefect
 prefectorial
 prefect's (of the prefect)
 prefects'
  (of the prefects)
 prefecture
prefer
 preferable
 preferably
 preference
 preferential
 preferentially
 preferment
 preferred
 preferring
 prefers
prefix
 prefixes (*pl.*)
 prefixed
pregnant
 pregnancy
 pregnancies (*pl.*)
prehensile
 prehension
prehistoric
 prehistorically
 prehistory
prejudge
 prejudgement
 prejudging
 prejudgment
prejudice
 prejudicial
 prejudicially
 prejudicing
prelate
 prelate's (of the prelate)
 prelates'
  (of the prelates)
 prelacy
 prelacies (*pl.*)
preliminary

preliminaries (*pl.*)
preliminarily
prelude
 preluding
premarital
premature
 prematurely
 prematurity
premeditate
 premeditating
 premeditation
premier (prime minister)
 premiership
premier (most important)
première (first night)
premise, premiss
  (statement in logic)
 premises, premisses (*pl.*)
premises (houses, etc.)
premium
premonition
 premonitory
prenatal
prentice
preoccupy
 preoccupation
 preoccupied
 preoccupying
prepare
 preparation
 preparative
 preparatorily
 preparatory
 preparedness
 preparing
prepay
 prepaid
 prepayable
 prepayment
 prepays
preponderance
 preponderant
 preponderantly
preponderate
 preponderating

preposition
prepossess
  prepossessing
preposterous
  preposterously
prerequisite
prerogative
presage
  presaged
  presaging
presbyter
  Presbyterian
prescience
  prescient
prescribe (medicine, etc.)
  prescribing
  prescription
  prescriptive
present (gift)
present (to give)
  presentation
present (being there)
  presence
present (now)
  presently
present (to introduce)
  presentable
presentiment (expectation)
preserve
  preservation
  preservative
  preserver
  preserving
preside
  presidency
  presidencies (*pl.*)
  president
  presidential
  president's
    (of the president)
  presidents'
    (of the presidents)
  presidial
  presiding
  presidium

press
  pressed
pressure
  pressurisation
  pressurization
  pressurise
  pressurize
  pressurising
  pressurizing
prestidigitator (conjurer)
  prestidigitation
prestige
  prestigious
presto (fast)
  prestissimo (very fast)
pre-stress
  pre-stressed
presume
  presumably
  presuming
  presumption
  presumptive
  presumptuous
presuppose
  presupposing
  presupposition
pretence
  pretense
pretend
  pretender
  pretension
  pretentious
  pretentiously
preterite
  preterit
preternatural
pretext
pretty
  prettier
  prettily
  prettiness
prevail
  prevailing
  prevalence
  prevalent

prevaricate
  prevaricating
  prevarication
  prevaricator
prevent
  preventable,
        preventible
  prevention
  preventive,
        preventative
preview
previous
  previously
pre-war
prey (plunder)
  preyed
  preying
price
  priceless
  pricing
prick
  pricker
prickle
  prickling
  prickly
pride
priest
  priesthood
  priestly
  priest's (of the priest)
  priests' (of the priests)
prig
  priggish
prim
  primly
  primmer
  primmest
primacy
prima donna
  prima donnas (*pl.*)
  prima donna's
    (of the prima donna)
  prima donnas'
    (of the prima donnas)
prima facie

primary
  primarily
primate
  primacy
prime
  prime minister
  priming
primeval
primitive
  primitively
primogeniture
    (being first-born)
  primogenitor
    (earliest ancestor)
primordial
  primordially
primrose
primula
  primulas (*pl.*)
primus (stove)
prince
  princely
  prince's (of the prince)
  princes' (of the princes)
  princess
  princesses (*pl.*)
  princess's
    (of the princess)
  princesses'
    (of the princesses)
  principality
  principalities (*pl.*)
principal (chief)
  principally
principle (moral code)
print
  printable
  printer
  printer's (of the printer)
  printers'
    (of the printers)
prior (before)
  priority
  priorities (*pl.*)
prior (monk)

prioress (*fem.*)
priory
priories (*pl.*)
prise, prize
    (to force open)
prize
prising, prizing
prizing
prism
prismatic
prison
  prisoner
  prisoner's
    (of the prisoner)
  prisoners'
    (of the prisoners)
pristine
private
  privacy
  privateer
  privately
privation
privative
privet (hedge)
privilege
  privileged
privy
Privy Council
Privy Councillor
prize (reward)
  prize fight
  prize fighter
prize (to value)
  prizing
probable
  probability
  probably
probate
probation
  probationer
probe
  probing
probity (integrity)
problem
  problematic

problematical
problematically
proboscis
proboscises,
    proboscides(*pl.*)
proceed
procedural
procedure (method)
proceeding
process
  processes (*pl.*)
  processor
procession
processional
proclaim
  proclaimed
  proclamation
proclivity
  proclivities (*pl.*)
procrastinate
  procrastinating
  procrastination
  procrastinator
procreate
  procreating
  procreative
  procreator
proctor
  proctorial
  proctor's
    (of the proctor)
  proctors'
    (of the proctors)
procure
  procurable
  procuration
  procurator
  procuring
prod
  prodded
  prodding
  prods
prodigal
  prodigality
  prodigally

prodigy
  prodigies (*pl.*)
  prodigious
  prodigiously
  prodigiousness
produce
  producer
  producing
product
  production
  productive
  productively
  productiveness
  productivity
profane
  profanation
  profanely
  profanity
  profanities (*pl.*)
profess
  professed
  professes
  professing
  profession
  professional
  professionalism
  professionally
  professor
  professor's
    (of the professor)
  professors'
    (of the professors)
  professorial
proffer
  proffered
  proffering
proficiency
  proficient
  proficiently
profile
profit
  profitability
  profitable
  profitably
  profited

profiteer
profiteered
profiteering
profiting
profitless
profits
profligate
  profligacy
  profligately
pro forma
profound
  profounder
  profundity
  profoundly
profuse
  profusely
  profusion
progenitor (ancestor)
  progenitrix (*fem.*)
  progeniture
progeny
prognosis
  prognoses (*pl.*)
  prognostic
  prognosticating
  prognostication
program (for a computer)
programme
      (usual spelling)
programmed
programmer
programming
progress
progresses
progression
progressive
progressively
prohibit
  prohibited
  prohibiting
  prohibition
  prohibitionist
  prohibitive
  prohibitively
project

projection
projector
projectile
prolapse
proletarian
  proletariat
proliferate
  proliferating
  proliferation
prolific
  prolifically
  prolification
prolix (long-winded)
  prolixity
prologue
prolong
  prolongating
  prolongation
promenade
  promenader
  promenading
prominence
  prominent
  prominently
promiscuous
  promiscuity
  promiscuously
promise
  promising
  promissory
promontory
  promontories (*pl.*)
promote
  promoter
  promoter's
    (of the promoter)
  promoters'
    (of the promoters)
  promoting
  promotion
prompt
  prompter
  promptitude
  promptly
  promptness

promulgate
  promulgating
  promulgation
  promulgator
prone
prong
  pronged
pronoun
pronounce
  pronounceable
  pronouncement
  pronouncing
  pronunciation
proof
  proof-reader
  proof-reader's
    (of the proof-reader)
  proof-readers'
    (of the proof-readers)
  proof-reading
prop
  propped
  propping
  props
propaganda
  propagandist
propagate
  propagating
  propagation
  propagator
propel
  propellant (rocket fuel)
  propellent
  propelled
  propeller
  propelling
  propels
propensity
  propensities (pl.)
proper
  properly
property
  properties (pl.)
  propertied
prophecy (prediction)

prophecies (pl.)
prophesy (to predict)
  prophesied
  prophesies
  prophesying
prophet
  prophetic
  prophetically
prophylactic
  prophylaxis
propinquity
propitiate
  propitiating
  propitiator
  propitiatory
  propitious
  propitiously
proponent
proportion
  proportional
  proportionally
  proportionate
propose
  proposal
  proposer
  proposing
  proposition
propound
proprietary
        (legally owned)
proprietor (owner)
  proprietor's
    (of the proprietor)
  proprietors'
    (of the proprietors)
  proprietress (fem.)
  proprietress's
    (of the proprietress)
  proprietresses'
    (of the proprietresses)
propriety (decency)
  proprieties (pl.)
propulsion
  propulsive
pro rata

prorogue
  prorogation
  proroguing
prosaic
  prosaically
proscenium
proscribe (to outlaw)
  proscribing
  proscription
  proscriptive
prose
  prosily
  prosiness
  prosy
prosecute
  prosecution
  prosecutor
  prosecutor's
    (of the prosecutor)
  prosecutors'
    (of the prosecutors)
proselyte
  proselytise
  proselytize
  proselytiser
  proselytizer
  proselytising
  proselytizing
  proselytism
prosody
prospect
  prospective
  prospector
  prospectus
  prospectuses (pl.)
prosper
  prospered
  prospering
  prosperity
  prosperous
prostate (gland)
prostitute
  prostituting
  prostitution
prostrate (lying flat)

prostration
protagonist
protean (variable)
protect
  protection
  protective
  protector
  protectorate
protégé
protein (food chemical)
pro tempore, pro tem
protest
  protestation
  protester, protestor
Protestant
  Protestantism
  Protestant's
    (of the Protestant)
  Protestants'
    (of the Protestants)
proto- (first)
  protocol
  proton
  protoplasm
  prototype
  protozoon
  protozoa (*pl.*)
protract
  protractor
protrude
  protruding
  protrusion
protuberance
  protuberant
proud
  prouder
  proudly
prove
  provable
  proved
  proven (in Law)
  proving
provenance
provender
proverb

proverbial
proverbially
provide
  provider
  providing
providence
  provident
  providential
  providentially
province
  provincial
  provincialism
provision
  provisional
  provisionally
proviso
  provisos (*pl.*)
  provisory
provocation
  provocative
  provocatively
provoke
  provoking
provost
prow
prowess
prowl
  prowler
proximate (nearest)
proximity
proxy
  proxies (*pl.*)
prude
  prudery
  prudish
prudent
  prudence
  prudential
  prudentially
prune
(to trim a plant or tree)
  pruner
  pruning
prune (dried plum)
prurience

prurient
prussic
pry
  pried
  pries
  prying
psalm
  psalmist
psalter (book of psalms)
pseudo- (false)
  pseudonym
  pseudonymity
  pseudonymous
  pseudonymously
psittacosis (parrot disease)
psych- (soul)
  psyche
  psychedelic
  psychiatric
  psychiatrist
  psychiatry
  psychic
  psychoanalysing
  psychoanalyzing
  psychoanalysis
  psychoanalyst
  psychoanalytic
  psychoanalytical
  psychological
  psychologist
  psychology
  psychopath
  psychopathic
  psychosis
  psychoses (*pl.*)
  psychosomatic
ptarmigan
pterodactyl
ptomaine
puberty
pubescence
  pubescent
pubis
  pubic
public

publican
publication
publicise
publicize
publicising
publicizing
publicist
publicity
publish
publisher
publisher's
    (of the publisher)
publishers'
    (of the publishers)
puce
puck
puckish
pucker (to wrinkle)
puckered
puckering
pudding
puddle
puerile
puerilely
puerility
puerperal
puff
puffiness
puffy
puffin (sea-bird)
pug
pug's (of the pug)
pugs' (of the pugs)
pugilism
pugilist
pugnacious
pugnaciously
pugnacity
puisne (judge)
pukka
puling (whining)
pull
pulled
pulls
pullet

pulley
pulleys (*pl.*)
pullulate (to sprout)
pullulating
pulmonary
pulp
pulpit
pulsar (star)
pulsate
pulsating
pulsation
pulse
pulseless
pulsing
pulverise
pulverize
pulverisation
pulverization
pulverising
pulverizing
puma
pumas (*pl.*)
pumice
pummel
pummelled
pummeled
pummelling
pummeling
pummels
pump
pumpernickel
pumpkin
pun
punned
puns
punster
punch
punctilious
punctiliously
punctiliousness
punctual
punctuality
punctually
punctuate
punctuating

punctuation
puncture
punctured
puncturing
pundit
pungent
pungency
pungently
punish
punishable
punished
punishes
punishment
punitive
punnet (small basket)
punt
punter
puny
punier
pup
puppy
puppies (*pl.*)
puppy's (of the puppy)
puppies'
    (of the puppies)
pupa
pupae (*pl.*)
pupate
pupating
pupation
pupil (at school)
pupil's (of the pupil)
pupils' (of the pupils)
pupil (of the eye)
puppet
puppeteer
puppetry
puppet's (of the puppet)
puppets'
    (of the puppets)
purblind
purchase
purchasable
purchaser

purchaser's
   (of the purchaser)
purchasers'
   (of the purchasers)
purchasing
purdah
pure
  purely
  purer
purée (food)
purgatory
  purgatorial
purge
  purgation
  purgative
  purged
  purging
purify
  purification
  purified
  purifier
  purifies
  purifying
purism
  purist
Puritan
  puritanic
  puritanical
  puritanism
purity
purl (in knitting)
purloin
purple
purport
purpose
  purposeful
  purposeless
  purposely
purr
  purred
purse
  purser
pursue
  pursuance
  pursuant

pursuing
pursuit
purulence
purulent
purvey (to provide)
  purveyance
  purveyor
purview (scope)
pus (from wound)
push
  pushed
  pusher
  pushes
  push-over
pusillanimity
  pusillanimous
puss (cat)
  pussy
  pussies (*pl.*)
  pussy's (of the pussy)
  pussies' (of the pussies)
pustule
put (to place)
  puts
  putting
putative
putrefy
  putrefaction
  putrefied
  putrefying
  putrescence
  putrescent
putrid
putt (in golf)
  putted
  putter
  putting
  putts
puttee (leggings)
putty (for glazing)
puzzle
  puzzlement
  puzzler
  puzzling
pyelitis

pygmy
  pygmies (*pl.*)
pyjamas
  pajamas
pylon
pyorrhoea
  pyorrhea
pyramid
  pyramidal
pyr- (fire)
  pyre (funeral pile)
  pyrites
  pyrotechnics
python

Q

quack (charlatan)
  quackery
quack (duck's)
quadr- (four)
  quadrangle
  quadrangular
  quadrant
  quadratic
  quadrature
  quadrilateral
  quadrille
  quadruped
  quadruple
  quadruplet
  quadruplex
  quadruplicate
  quadruplicating
  quadruplication
quadrag- (forty)
  quadragenarian
  Quadragesima
quaff
  quaffed
  quaffing
  quaffs

quagmire
quail
  quailed
  quailing
quaint
  quainter
  quaintly
  quaintness
quake
  quaking
Quaker
qualify
  qualification
  qualified
  qualifies
  qualifying
qualitative
  qualitatively
quality
  qualities (*pl.*)
qualm
quandary
  quandaries (*pl.*)
quango
  quangos (*pl.*)
quantify
  quantifiable
  quantification
  quantified
  quantifying
quantity
  quantities (*pl.*)
  quantitative
  quantitatively
quantum
  quanta (*pl.*)
quarantine
quarrel
  quarrelled
  quarreled
  quarrelling
  quarreling
  quarrels
  quarrelsome
quarry (excavation)

quarries (*pl.*)
quarrying
quarry (victim)
quart
quarter
  quartered
  quartering
  quarterly
  quartermaster
  quartermaster's
   (of the quartermaster)
  quartermasters'
   (of the quartermasters)
quartet, quartette
quarto
quartz
  quartzite
quasar (star)
quash
quasi- (almost)
Quaternary
quatrain
quaver (to tremble)
  quavered
  quavering
quaver (musical note)
quay
quean (hussy)
queasy
  queasiness
queen (sovereign)
  queenly
  queen's (of the queen)
  queens' (of the queens)
queer
  queered
  queerer
  queering
  queerly
quell
  quelled
quench
querulous
  querulously
  querulousness

query
  queries (*pl.*)
  queries
  queried
  querying
quest
question
  questionable
  questionably
  questioned
  questioner
  questioning
  questionnaire
queue
  queued
  queuer
  queuing
quibble
  quibbler
  quibbling
quick
  quicker
  quickly
  quickness
  quicksand
  quicksilver
  quicken
quid pro quo
quiescence
  quiescent
quiet
  quieten
  quietened
  quietening
  quieter
  quietly
  quietude
quietus
quiff
quill
quilt
quince
quinine
quinq- (five)
  quinquennial

quinquennium

quinsy

quint- (fifth)

  quintessence

  quintet

  quintette

  quintuple

  quintuplet

quip

  quipped

  quipping

  quips

quire (of paper)

quirk

quisling

quit

  quits

  quitted

  quit (*he,* she)

  quitter

  quitting

quite

quittance

quiver (to shake)

  quivered

  quivers

quiver (arrow case)

qui vive

Quixote

  quixotic

  quixotically

  quixotism

quiz

  quizzes (*pl.*)

  quizzed

  quizzes

  quizzical

  quizzically

  quizzing

quod (prison)

quoit

quorum

  quorums (*pl.*)

quota

  quotas (*pl.*)

quote

  quotable

  quotation

  quoting

quotidian (daily)

quotient

R

rabbi (Jewish preacher)

  rabbis (*pl.*)

  rabbinical

  rabbi's (of the rabbi)

  rabbis' (of the rabbis)

rabbit

rabble (mob)

rabid

  rabidly

rabies (disease of dogs)

race

  racecourse

  racehorse

  racer

  race-track

  racily

  racing

  racy

raceme (of flowers)

racial

  racialism

  racialist

  racially

  racism

  racist

rack

racket (disturbance)

racket, racquet (tennis)

racket (swindle)

  racketeer

raconteur

racoon, raccoon

radar

radial

  radially

radiant

  radiance

  radiantly

radiate

  radiating

  radiation

  radiator

radical

  radicalism

  radically

radio

  radios (*pl.*)

  radioactive

  radioactivity

  radioed

  radioes

  radiogram

  radiographer

  radiography

  radioisotope

  radiologist

  radiology

radish

  radishes (*pl.*)

radium

radius

  radii, radiuses (*pl.*)

raffia

raffish

raffle

  raffling

raft

rafter (of a roof)

rag

  ragged

rag (to tease)

  ragged

  ragging

  rags

ragamuffin

  ragamuffin's

    (of the ragamuffin)

ragamuffins'
  (of the ragamuffins)
rage
  raging
raglan
ragout
ragtime
raid
  raider
rail
  railroad
  railway
rail (to scold)
  railing
  raillery (teasing)
raiment
rain (wet weather)
  rainbow
  rain-check
  raincoat
  rainfall
  rainless
  rainy
raise
  raising
raisin (dried grape)
raison d'être
rajah, raja
rake
  raking
  rakish
rallentando
    (becoming slower)
rally
  rallies (*pl.*)
  rallied
  rallies
  rallying
ram
  rammed
  rammer
  ramming
  ramrod
  rams
ramble

rambler
rambling
ramekin, ramequin
ramify
  ramification
  ramified
  ramifies
ramp
rampage
  rampaging
rampant
  rampancy
rampart
ramshackle
ran (*from* run)
ranch
  ranches (*pl.*)
  rancher
rancid
rancour
  rancor
  rancorous
random
  randomly
rang (*from* ring)
range
  ranging
  rangy
rank
  ranker
rankle
  rankling
ransack
  ransacked
ransom
  ransomed
  ransoming
rant
rap (to knock)
  rapped
  rapping
  raps
rapacious
rapacity
rape (to violate)

raping
rapist
rape (plant)
rapid
  rapidity
  rapidly
rapier
rapine (robbery)
rapport (close connection)
rapprochement
rapscallion
rapt (enraptured)
rapture
  rapturous
  rapturously
rare
  rarefaction
  rarefied
  rarefy
  rarefying
  rarer
  rarely
  rarity
  rarities (*pl.*)
rare (underdone)
rarebit (Welsh)
rascal
  rascality
  rascal's (of the rascal)
  rascals' (of the rascals)
rase, raze (to destroy)
  rasing, razing
rash (reckless)
  rashly
rash (on skin)
  rashes (*pl.*)
  rasher (bacon)
rasp
raspberry
  raspberries (*pl.*)
rat
  rats
  ratted
  ratting
ratchet

rate
  ratable
  rateable
  ratepayer
  rating
rather
ratify
  ratification
  ratified
  ratifies
  ratifying
ratio
  ratios (*pl.*)
ratiocinate
  ratiocinating
  ratiocination
ration
  rationed
  rationing
rational (reasonable)
  rationale (basic reason)
  rationality
  rationally
rationalise
  rationalize
  rationalisation
  rationalization
  rationalising
  rationalizing
  rationalism
rattan
  ratan
rattle
  rattlesnake
  rattling
raucous
  raucously
  raucousness
ravage
  ravager
  ravaging
rave
  raving
ravel
  ravelled

raveled
ravelling
raveling
raven
  raven's (of the raven)
  ravens' (of the ravens)
ravenous
  ravenously
ravine (gorge)
ravioli
ravish
raw
  raw-boned
  rawer
  rawness
ray
rayon
raze, rase (to destroy)
  razing, rasing
razor
  razor's (of the razor)
  razors' (of the razors)
razzle-dazzle
reach
  reached
  reaches
react
  reactance
  reaction
  reactionary
  reactive
  reactor
reactivate
  reactivating
read
  readable
  reader
  reader's (of the reader)
  readers' (of the readers)
readdress
  readdressed
readjust
  readjustment
readmit
  readmission

readmittance
readmitted
readmitting
ready
  readily
  readiness
  ready-made
reagent
real
  realism
  realist
  realistic
  realistically
  reality
  realities (*pl.*)
  really
realise
  realize
  realisable
  realizable
  realisation
  realization
  realising
  realizing
realm
ream (of paper)
reap
  reaped
  reaper
reappear
  reappearance
  reappeared
rear
  rearguard
rear
  (to raise children, etc.)
rearm
  rearmament
rearrange
  rearrangement
  rearranging
reason
  reasonable
  reasonableness
  reasonably

reassemble
  reassembling
reassess
  reassessed
  reassesses
  reassessment
reassure
  reassurance
  reassured
  reassuring
  reassuringly
rebate
rebel
  rebelled
  rebelling
  rebellion
  rebellious
  rebel's (of the rebel)
  rebels' (of the rebels)
  rebels
rebirth
rebound
rebuff
  rebuffed
rebuild
  rebuilt
rebuke
  rebuking
rebut
  rebuts
  rebuttal
  rebutted
  rebutting
recalcitrant
  recalcitrance
recall
  recalled
recant
  recantation
recap
  recapping
recapitulate
  recapitulating
  recapitulation
recapture

recapturing
recede
  receding
receipt
receive
  receivable
  receiver
  receivership
  receiving
recent
  recently
receptacle
reception
  receptionist
  receptive
recess
  recesses (*pl.*)
  recessed
  recession
  recessive
recession
  recessional
  recessive
recharge
  rechargeable
  recharging
recherché
recidivism
  recidivist
recipe
recipient
  recipient's
      (of the recipient)
  recipients'
      (of the recipients)
reciprocal
  reciprocally
reciprocate
  reciprocating
  reciprocation
  reciprocity
recite
  recital
  recitation
  recitative

reciter
  reciting
reckless
  recklessly
  recklessness
reckon
  reckoner
reclaim
  reclamation
recline
  reclining
recluse
  reclusion
recognise
  recognize
  recognisable
  recognizable
  recognisance
  recognizance
  recognising
  recognizing
  recognition
recoil
recollect
  recollection
recommend
  recommendation
recommit
  recommitment
  recommittal
  recommitted
  recommitting
recompense
  recompensing
reconcile
  reconcilable
  reconcilement
  reconciliation
  reconciling
recondite
recondition
  reconditioned
reconnaissance
reconnoitre
  reconnoiter

reconnoitred
reconnoitered
reconnoitring
reconnoitering
reconquer
  reconquered
  reconquering
  reconquest
reconsider
  reconsideration
  reconsidered
  reconsidering
reconstruct
  reconstruction
record
  recorder
  record-player
re-count (to count again)
recount (to tell)
recoup
  recouped
recourse
recover (to get better)
  recovered
  recovering
  recovery
recover (to cover again)
  recovered
  recovering
recreant
re-create (create again)
  re-creating
recreation
  recreative
recriminate
  recriminating
  recrimination
  recriminatory
recrudescence
  recrudescent
recruit
  recruit's (of the recruit)
  recruits' (of the recruits)
rectangle
  rectangular

rectify
  rectifiable
  rectification
  rectified
  rectifier
  rectifies
  rectifying
rectilinear,
                rectilineal
rectitude
rector
  rectorial
  rector's (of the rector)
  rectors' (of the rectors)
  rectory
  rectories (*pl.*)
rectum
  rectal
recumbent
recuperate
  recuperating
  recuperation
  recuperative
recur
  recurred
  recurrence
  recurrent
  recurring
  recurs
recusant
  recusancy
recycle
  recycling
red
  redbreast
  redden
  reddened
  reddening
  redder
redeem
  redeemable
  redeemer
  redemption
redeploy
  redeployment

redevelop
  redeveloped
  redevelopment
rediffusion
redirect
  redirected
  redirection
redistribute
  redistributed
  redistributing
  redistribution
redo
  redid
  redoing
  redone
redolent
  redolence
redouble
  redoubling
redoubt (type of fortress)
redoubtable (formidable)
redound
redress
  redressment
reduce
  reducible
  reducing
  reduction
reductio ad absurdum
redundant
  redundancy
  redundancies (*pl.*)
reduplicate
  reduplicating
  reduplication
re-echo
  reecho
  re-echoed
  re-echoes
  re-echoing
reed (water plant)
reef
reek (smell)
reel (to stagger)
reel (of cotton, etc.)

reel (dance)
re-elect
  reelect
  re-election
re-enter
  reenter
  re-entered
  re-entering
  re-entrant
  re-entry
re-establish
  reestablish
  re-establishment
re-examine
  reexamine
  re-examination
  re-examining
re-export
  reexport
  re-exportation
refectory (dining-hall)
  refectories (*pl.*)
refer
  referable
  reference
  referred
  referring
  refers
referee
  referees (*pl.*)
  refereed
  refereeing
  referee's (of the referee)
  referees'
    (of the referees)
referendum
  referenda,
    referendums(*pl.*)
refill
  refillable
refine
  refinement
  refinery
  refineries (*pl.*)
  refining

refit
  refits
  refitted
  refitting
reflate
  reflating
  reflation
  reflationary
reflect
  reflection
  reflective
  reflector
reflex
  reflexive (*grammar*)
refloat
reform
  reformation
  reformatory
  reformatories (*pl.*)
  reformed
  reformer
  reformer's
    (of the reformer)
  reformers'
    (of the reformers)
refract
  refraction
    (bending of light)
  refractive
refractory (stubborn)
  refractoriness
refrain
refresh
  refresher
  refreshment
refrigerate
  refrigerant
  refrigerating
  refrigeration
  refrigerator
refuel
  refuelled
  refueled
  refuelling
  refueling

refuels
refuge
  refugee
  refugee's
    (of the refugee)
  refugees'
    (of the refugees)
refulgence
  refulgent
refund
refurbish
refuse (to say no)
  refusal
  refusing
refuse (rubbish)
refute (to prove wrong)
  refutable
  refutal
  refutation
  refuting
regain
regal (royal)
  regalia
  regally
regale (to entertain)
  regaling
regard
  regardless
regatta
  regattas (*pl.*)
regenerate
  regeneration
  regenerative
  regenerator
regent
  regency
  regencies (*pl.*)
regicide
  regicidal
regime
  (method of government)
  regimen (strict routine)
  regiment (soldiers)
  regimental
  regimentation

region
  regional
  regionally
register
  registered
  registering
  register office
  registers
  registration
registrar (of college, etc.)
registry
  registries (*pl.*)
regress
  regression
  regressive
regret
  regretful
  regretfully
  regrets
  regrettable
  regrettably
  regretted
  regretting
regular
  regularity
  regularly
regularise
  regularize
  regularisation
  regularization
  regularising
  regularizing
regulate
  regulating
  regulation
  regulator
regurgitate
  regurgitating
  regurgitation
rehabilitate
  rehabilitating
  rehabilitation
rehearse
  rehearsal
  rehearsing

reign (to rule)
  reigned
  reigning
  reigns
reimburse
  reimbursement
  reimbursing
rein (of horse)
reincarnation
reindeer
reinforce
  reinforceable
  reinforcement
  reinforcing
reinstate
  reinstatement
  reinstating
reiterate
  reiterating
  reiteration
reject
  rejection
rejoice
  rejoicing
rejoinder
rejuvenate
  rejuvenating
  rejuvenation
relapse
  relapsing
relate
  relating
  relation
  relationship
relative (connected with)
  relatively
  relativity
relative (relation)
relax
  relaxation
  relaxed
relay
  relayed
release
  releasing

relegate
  relegating
  relegation
relent
  relentless
  relentlessly
relevance
  relevant
reliable
  reliability
  reliably
reliance
reliant
relic
relief
relieve
  relieving
religion
  religious
  religiously
relinquish
reliquary
relish
reluctance
  reluctant
  reluctantly
rely
  reliable
  relied
  relies
  relying
remain
  remainder
  remaindered
remand
remark
  remarkable
  remarkably
remedy
  remedies (*pl.*)
  remediable
  remedial
  remedied
  remedying
remember

remembered
remembering
remembrance
remind
reminder
reminisce
reminiscence
reminiscent
reminiscing
remiss (careless)
remissness
remissible
(may be remitted)
remission
remit (to pardon or pay)
remits
remittal
remittance
remitted
remitting
remnant
remonstrate
remonstrance
remonstrant
remonstrating
remonstration
remonstrator
remorse
remorseful
remorseless
remorselessly
remote
remotely
remotest
remount
remove
removable
removal
remover
removing
remunerate
remunerating
remuneration
remunerative
Renaissance

rend
rent (torn)
render
rendered
rendering
rendition
rendezvous
rendezvous (*pl.*)
renegade (turncoat)
renege, renegue (to deny)
renege
renegation
reneging, renegueing
renew
renewable
renewal
renewed
rennet
renounce
renounceable
renouncement
renouncing
renovate
renovating
renovation
renovator
renown
renowned
rent
rental
rentier
renunciate
renunciating
renunciation
reopen
reopened
reopening
reorganise
reorganize
reorganisation
reorganization
reorganising
reorganizing
repair
repaired

repairer
repairs
reparable
reparation
repartee
repartees (*pl.*)
repast (meal)
repatriate
repatriating
repatriation
repay
repaid
repayable
repayment
repays
repeal
repealed
repeat
repeatedly
repeater
repel
repelled
repellent
repelling
repels
repent
repentance
repentant
repercussion
repertoire (list of plays)
repertory (theatre)
repetition
repetitious
repetitive
rephrase
rephrasing
repine
repining
replace
replaceable
replacement
replacing
replay
replayed
replenish

replenishment
replete
  repletion
replica
  replicas (*pl.*)
reply
  replies (*pl.*)
  replied
  replying
report
  reportable
  reportedly
  reporter
  reporter's
      (of the reporter)
  reporters'
      (of the reporters)
  reporting
repose
  reposing
repository
  repositories (*pl.*)
repossess
  repossession
reprehend
  reprehensible
  reprehension
represent
  representation
  representative
repress
  repression
  repressive
reprieve
  reprieving
reprimand
reprint
reprisal
reproach
  reproaches (*pl.*)
  reproached
  reproaches
  reproachful
  reproachfully
reprobate (to condemn)

reprobating
reprobation
reprobate (sinner)
reproduce
  reproducible
  reproducing
  reproduction
  reproductive
reproof (blame)
  reproofs (*pl.*)
reprove (to scold)
  reproval
  reproving
  reprovingly
reptile
  reptilian
republic
  republican
  republicanism
  republish
  republication
repudiate
  repudiating
  repudiation
repugnance
  repugnant
repulse
  repulsing
  repulsion
  repulsive
repute
  reputable
  reputation
  reputedly
request
requiem
requiescat in pace (R.I.P.)
require
  requiring
requisite
  requisition
requite
  requital
  requited
re-route

re-routeing
rerun
  reran
  rerunning
rescind
  rescission
rescript
rescue
  rescuer
  rescuer's
      (of the rescuer)
  rescuers'
      (of the rescuers)
  rescuing
research
  researches (*pl.*)
  researcher
  researching
resemble
  resemblance
  resembling
resent
  resentful
  resentment
reserve
  reservation
  reservedly
  reserving
  reservist
reservoir
reset
  resets
  resetting
resettle
  resettlement
  resettling
reside
  residence
  residency
  residencies (*pl.*)
  residential
  residing
residue
  residual
  residuary

residuum
      (chem. residue)
resign
  resignation
resilience
  resilient
  resiliently
resin
  resinous
resist
  resistance
  resistant
  resister (person)
  resistive
  resistor (*electr.*)
resit
  resat
  resitting
resole (shoes)
  resoling
resolute
  resolutely
  resolution
resolve
  resolving
resonance
  resonant
resonate
  resonating
  resonator
resort (to turn to)
resort (holiday place)
resound
resource
  resourceful
respect
  respectability
  respectable
  respectful
  respectfully
respective
  respectively
respire
  respiration
  respirator

respiratory
respiring
respite
resplendence
  resplendent
  resplendently
respond
  respondent
  response
  responsive
responsible
  responsibility
  responsibly
rest
restaurant
  restaurateur
restful
  restfully
  restfulness
restitution
restive
  restively
  restiveness
restless
  restlessly
  restlessness
restore
  restoration
  restorative
  restorer
  restoring
restrain
  restraint
restrict
  restriction
  restrictive
restructure
  restructuring
result
  resultant
resume
  résumé (summary)
  resuming
  resumption
resurgence

resurgent
resurrect
  resurrection
resuscitate
  resuscitating
  resuscitation
retail
  retailer
  retailer's (of the retailer)
  retailers'
      (of the retailers)
retain
  retainer
  retention
  retentive
retaliate
  retaliating
  retaliation
  retaliatory
retard
  retardation
retch (to vomit)
  retched
  retches
retention
  retentive
rethink
  rethought
reticence
  reticent
reticule
retina (of the eye)
retinue (of people)
retire
  retirement
  retiring
retort (to answer back)
retort (for distillation)
retouch
  retouched
  retouches
retrace
  retracing
retract
  rectractable

retractile

retraction

retractor

retread

retreat

retrench

retrenchment

retribution

retributive

retrieve

retrievable

retrieval

retriever

retrieving

retro- (back)

retroactive

retrograde

retrogression

retrogressive

retrospect

retrospection

retrospective

retrospectively

return

returnable

reunion

reunite

reuniting

reuse

reusable

rev (to speed up)

revs

revved

revving

revalue

revaluation

revaluing

revamp

revamping

reveal (to disclose)

revelation

reveille

revel (to make merry)

revelled

reveled

reveller

reveler

revelling

reveling

revelry

revelries (*pl.*)

revels

revenge

revengeful

revenging

revenue

reverberate

reverberating

reverberation

reverberator

revere

reverence

reverend (clergyman)

reverent (respectful)

reverential

revering

reverie

revers (turned back cloth)

reverse

reversal

reversible

reversing

reversion

revert

revetment

review

    (to examine critically)

reviewer

revile

reviling

revise

Revised Version

revising

revision

revitalise

revitalize

revitalising

revitalizing

revive

revival

reviving

revoke

revocable

revocation

revoking

revolt

revolution

revolutionary

revolutionaries (*pl.*)

revolutionise

revolutionize

revolutionising

revolutionizing

revolve

revolver

revolving

revue (entertainment)

review

revulsion

reward

rewrite

rewriting

rewritten

rewrote

rhapsody

rhapsodies (*pl.*)

rhapsodical

rhapsodise

rhapsodize

rhapsodising

rhapsodizing

rheostat

rhesus

rhetoric

rhetorical

rhetorically

rheumatic

rheumatism

rheumatoid

rheumy

rhinoceros

rhinoceroses (*pl.*)

rhinoceros's

    (of the rhinoceros)

rhinoceroses'
  (of the rhinoceroses)
rhizome
rhododendron
  rhododendrons (*pl.*)
rhombus
  rhomboid
rhubarb
rhyme
  rhyming
rhythm
  rhythmic
  rhythmical
  rhythmically
rib
  ribbed
  ribbing
ribald
  ribaldry
ribbon
rice
rich
  riches (*pl.*)
  richer
  richly
  richness
rick (of hay)
rick, wrick (to sprain)
  ricked, wricked
rickets
rickety
rickshaw, ricksha
ricochet
  ricocheted,
         ricochetted
  ricocheted
  ricocheting,
         ricochetting
  ricocheting
rid
  riddance
riddle
ride
  ridable
  ridden

rider
  rider's (of the rider)
  riders' (of the riders)
  riding
  rode
ridge
  ridging
ridicule
  ridiculing
  ridiculous
  ridiculously
rife (widespread)
riff-raff
rifle (gun)
rifle (to steal)
  rifling
rift
rig
  rigged
  rigging
right
  right angle
  right-angled
  righteous
  righteousness
  rightful
  rightfully
  rightly
rigid
  rigidity
  rigidly
rigmarole
rigor (stiffness)
  rigor mortis
    (stiffness after death)
rigour (severity)
  rigor
  rigorous
  rigorously
rile
  riling
rim
  rimmed
rime (frost)
rind

ring (to sound)
  rang
  ringer
  rung
ring (jewel)
ring (circle)
ring
  (combine of firms, etc.)
  ringleader
  ringlet (of hair)
rink
rinse
  rinsing
riot
  rioted
  rioter
  riotous
  riotously
  riotousness
rip
  ripped
  rips
ripe
  ripely
  ripen
  ripened
  ripeness
  ripening
  ripens
  riper
R.I.P.
riposte
ripping (excellent)
ripple
  rippling
rise
  risen
  riser
  rising
  rose
risible
risk
  riskier
  riskily
  riskiness

risky

risotto

risqué

rissole

rite (ceremony)

ritual

  ritualism

  ritualist

  ritualistic

  ritually

rival

  rivalled

  rivaled

  rivalling

  rivaling

  rivalry

  rivals

river

  river's (of the river)

  rivers' (of the rivers)

rivet

  riveted

  riveter

  riveting

Riviera

rivulet

roach

  roach (*pl.*)

  roaches (*pl.*)

road

  road-hog

  road sense

  roadway

  roadworthiness

  roadworthy

roam (to wander)

roan

roar

  roared

  roars

roast

rob

  robbed

  robber

  robbery

robberies (*pl.*)

robber's (of the robber)

robbers'

      (of the robbers)

robbing

robs

robe (dress)

  robing

robin

  robin redbreast

  robin's (of the robin)

  robins' (of the robins)

robot

robust

  robustly

  robustness

rock (stone)

  rockery

  rockeries (*pl.*)

  rocky

rock (to swing)

  rock and roll

  rocking-horse

rocket

  rocketed

  rocketing

  rocketry

rococo

rod

rode (*from* ride)

rodent

rodeo

  rodeos (*pl.*)

roe (deer)

roe (of fish)

rogation

rogue

  roguery

  rogue's (of the rogue)

  rogues' (of the rogues)

  roguish

roisterer

role (actor's part)

roll

  roll-call

rolled

roller

roller-skate

rolling

roll (of bread)

rollick

roly-poly

romance

  romancer

  romancing

romantic

  romantically

  romanticise

  romanticize

  romanticising

  romanticizing

  romanticism

romp

  romper

rondo

  rondos (*pl.*)

rood (crucifix)

roof

  roofs (*pl.*)

rook

  rookery

  rookeries (*pl.*)

rookie

room

  roomful

  roominess

  room-mate

  roomy

roost

  rooster (hen)

root

  rootless

rope

  roping

rosary

  rosaries (*pl.*)

rose (flower)

  roseate

  rose-leaf

  rose-leaves (*pl.*)

rosily
rosy
rose (*from* rise)
rosé (wine)
rosemary
rosette
rosin
  rosined
roster (list of duties, etc.)
rostrum
  rostra, rostrums (*pl.*)
  rostra (*pl.*)
rot
  rots
  rotted
  rotten
  rottenness
  rotter
  rotting
rota
  rotas (*pl.*)
Rotarian
rotary
rotate
  rotatable
  rotating
  rotation
rote (procedure)
rotisserie
rotor (of electr. motor)
rotund
    (round and plump)
  rotundity
rotunda (circular building)
rouble (Russian money)
  ruble
roué
rouge
rough
  roughage
  roughen
  roughened
  roughening
  rougher
  roughly

roughness
rough-hew
  rough-hewed
  rough-hewing
  rough-hewn
roughshod
roulette
round
  roundabout
  rounder
  roundness
roundelay
rounders
rouse
  rousing
rout (to defeat)
route (road taken)
  route march
routine (procedure)
rove
  rover
  roving
row (a boat)
  rower
row (line of things, etc.)
row (noise)
rowdy
  rowdies (*pl.*)
  rowdily
  rowdiness
  rowdyism
rowlock
royal
  royalist
  royally
  royalty
  royalties (*pl.*)
rub
  rubbed
  rubber
  rubbing
  rubs
  rubbish
  rubbishy
rubble (broken bricks)

rubicund
rubric
ruby
  rubies (*pl.*)
ruche
  ruching
ruck (crease)
  rucked
  ruckle
  ruckling
rucksack
ruction
rudder
ruddy
  ruddiness
rude
  rudely
  rudeness
  ruder
rudiment
  rudimentary
rue
  rueful
  ruefully
  rueing
  ruing
ruff (collar)
ruffian
ruffle
  ruffling
rug
rugby, rugger
rugged
  ruggedness
ruin
  ruination
  ruinous
  ruinously
rule
  ruler
  ruler's (of the ruler)
  rulers' (of the rulers)
  ruling
rum
  rumble

rumbling
ruminate
  ruminant
  ruminating
rummage
  rummaging
rummy (game)
rummy (queer)
rumour
  rumor
  rumoured
  rumored
rump
rumple
  rumpling
rumpus
  rumpuses (*pl.*)
run
  ran
  runabout
  runaway
  runner
  runner-up
  running
  runny
  runs
  runway
rune (early Norse letter)
  runic
rung (*from* ring)
rung (of ladder)
rupee (Indian money)
rupture
  rupturing
rural
  rurally
ruse
rush
  rush-hour
rusk
russet
rust
  rustier
  rustiness
  rustless

rust-proof
rust-proofed
rust-proofing
rusty
rustic
  rusticate
  rusticating
  rustication
  rusticity
rustle
  rustler
  rustling
rut (track in ground)
  rutted
rut (of deer)
  ruts
  rutted
  rutting
ruthless (pitiless)
  ruthlessly
  ruthlessness
rye (corn)

S

sabbath
  Sabbatarian
  sabbatical
sable
sabotage
  sabotaged
  sabotaging
  saboteur
sabre
  saber
sac (pouch)
saccharin
sacerdotal
sachet
sack
  sacked
sacrament

sacramental
sacred
  sacredly
  sacredness
sacrifice
  sacrificial
  sacrificing
sacrilege
  sacrilegious
sacrosanct
sad
  sadden
  saddened
  sadder
  sadly
  sadness
saddle
  saddler
  saddlery
  saddling
sadism
  sadist
  sadistic
safari
  safaris (*pl.*)
safe
  safe conduct
  safe deposit
  safe keeping
  safely
  safer
  safety
safeguard
saffron
sag
  sagged
  sagging
  sags
saga
  sagas (*pl.*)
sagacious
  sagaciously
  sagacity
sage (wise)
  sagely

sage (herb)
sago
sahib
said (*from* say)
sail (of ship)
  sailer (ship)
  sailor (man)
  sailor's (of the sailor)
  sailors' (of the sailors)
saint
  sainthood
  saintliness
  saintly
  saint's (of the saint)
  saints' (of the saints)
sake
salaam (low bow)
  salaamed
salacious
  salacity
salad
salamander
salami (sausage)
salary
  salaries (*pl.*)
  salariat
  salaried
sale (at shop)
  saleability
  salability
  saleable
  salable
  salesman
  salesman's
    (of the salesman)
  salesmen's
    (of the salesmen)
  saleswoman
  saleswomen (*pl.*)
  saleswoman's
    (of the saleswoman)
  saleswomen's
    (of the saleswomen)
salicin
  salicylic

salient
saline
  salinity
saliva
  salivary
  salivate
  salivating
  salivation
salle à manger
    (dining-room)
sallow
  sallowness
sally
  sallies (*pl.*)
  sallied
  sallies
  sallying
salmon
salmonella (bacterium)
salon (drawing-room)
saloon (of pub)
salsify (vegetable)
salt
  salt-cellar
  saltiness
  salty
  saltpetre
  saltpeter
salubrious
  salubrity
salutary
salute
  salutation
  saluting
salvation
salve (to save)
  salvage
  salvaging
  salving
salve (ointment)
salver (tray)
salvo (from gun)
  salvoes, salvos (*pl.*)
  salvos (pl.)
sal volatile

Samaritan
same
samovar
sample
  sampler
  sampling
sanatorium
  sanitarium
  sanatoriums,
    sanatoria(*pl.*)
  sanitariums,
    sanitaria(pl.)
sanctify
  sanctification
  sanctified
  sanctifies
sanctimonious
  sanctimoniously
  sanctimoniousness
sanction
sanctity
sanctuary (holy place)
  sanctuaries (*pl.*)
sanctum (private room)
  sanctums, sancta (*pl.*)
sand
  sandbag
  sandbagged
  sandbagging
  sandpaper
  sandpapered
  sandpapering
  sandy
sandal (shoe)
sandalwood
sandwich
  sandwiches (*pl.*)
sane
  sanely
  sanity
sang-froid
sanguinary (bloodthirsty)
sanguine (hopeful)
sanitary
sanitation

sanity (*from* sane)
Santa Claus
sap
  sapped
  sapping
sapience
  sapient
sapling
sapper
sapphire
saprophyte
  saprophytic
saraband
sarcasm
  sarcastic
  sarcastically
sarco- (flesh)
  sarcoma
  sarcophagus
  sarcophagi (*pl.*)
sardine
sardonic
  sardonically
sari, saree
sartorial
sash
  sashes (*pl.*)
Satan
  satanic
satchel
sate
  sated (satisfied)
satellite
satiate
  satiable
  satiated (overfull)
  satiating
  satiation
  satiety
satin
  satinette
  satinet
satire
  satirical
  satirically

satirise
satirize
satirising
satirizing
satirist
satisfy
  satisfaction
  satisfactorily
  satisfactory
  satisfiable
  satisfied
  satisfies
  satisfying
satsuma
saturate
  saturating
  saturation
Saturday
saturnine
satyr (forest god)
sauce (cheek)
  saucier
  saucily
  sauciness
  saucy (cheeky)
sauce (gravy)
  saucepan
  saucer
sauerkraut
sauna (steam bath)
saunter
  sauntered
  sauntering
sauté (fried)
sausage
savage
  savagely
  savagery
  savage's (of the savage)
  savages'
      (of the savages)
savant
save
  saver
  saving

save (except)
saveloy
saviour (rescuer)
  savior
savoir faire
savour (taste)
  savor
  savoriness
  savouring
  savoring
  savoury
  savory
saw (to cut)
  sawed
  sawing
  sawn
saw (*from* see)
saxifrage (rock plant)
saxophone
  saxophonist
say
  said
  saying
  says
scab
scabbard
scabies
scaffold
scald
scale (to climb)
  scaling
scale (of fish)
  scaly
scale (music)
scale (size)
scale (weighing)
scallop, scollop
scallywag
  scalawag
scalp
scalpel
scamp
scamper
  scampered
  scampering

scampi (prawns)
scan (*grammar*)
  scanner
  scanning
  scans
  scansion
scan (to look at)
  scanned
  scanning
  scans
scandal
  scandalise
  scandalize
  scandalising
  scandalizing
  scandalmonger
  scandalous
  scandalously
scant
  scantier
  scantily
  scantiness
  scanty
scapegoat
scapegrace (rascal)
scapula (shoulder-blade)
scar (mark of wound)
  scarred
  scarring
scarce
  scarcely
  scarcity
  scarcities (*pl.*)
scare
  scarecrow
  scaring
scarf
  scarfs, scarves (*pl.*)
scarify
  scarification
  scarified
  scarifying
scarlatina
scarlet
scarp (steep slope)

scat
  scatted
scathe
  scatheless
  scathing
scatter
  scatter-brain
  scattered
  scattering
scavenge
  scavenger
  scavenging
scenario
  scenarios (*pl.*)
scene
  scenery
  scenic
scent (perfume)
  scented
scepsis (doubt)
  sceptic (doubter)
  skeptic
  sceptical
  skeptical
  sceptically
  skeptically
  scepticism
  skepticism
sceptre (ceremonial staff)
  scepter
schedule
  scheduled
  scheduling
scheme
  schematic
  schematically
  schemer
  scheming
scherzo
  scherzos (*pl.*)
schism
  schismatic
schist (rock)
schizoid
schizophrenia

schizophrenic
schnapps
schnorkel, snorkel
scholar
scholarly
scholar's
    (of the scholar)
scholars'
    (of the scholars)
scholarship
scholastic
school
schoolboy
schoolboy's
    (of the schoolboy)
schoolboys'
    (of the schoolboys)
schoolgirl
schoolgirl's
    (of the schoolgirl)
schoolgirls'
    (of the schoolgirls)
schooling
schoolmaster
schoolmistress
schoolteacher
school (of fish, etc.)
schooner
sciatica
science
scientific
scientifically
scientist
scientist's
    (of the scientist)
scientists'
    (of the scientists)
scimitar
scintillate
  scintillating
  scintillation
scion
scission (cutting)
scissors
sclerosis

scoff
scoffer
scold
scollop, scallop
sconce
scone
scoop
scoot
scooter
scope
scorbutic
scorch
scorcher
score
score-board
scorer
scoring
scorn
scornful
scornfully
scorpion
Scot
Scotch
Scotland
Scotsman
Scotsmen (*pl.*)
Scotsman's
  (of the Scotsman)
Scotsmen's
  (of the Scotsmen)
Scotswoman
Scottish
scot-free
scotch
 (to prevent or wedge)
scoundrel
scoundrelism
scour
scourer
scourge
scout
scout's (of the scout)
scouts' (of the scouts)
scowl
scrabble

scrabbling
scrag
scraggy
scramble
scrambling
scrap
scrapped
scrapping
scrappy
scrape
scraper
scraping
scratch
scratches (*pl.*)
scratched
scratches
scrawl
scrawny
scream
screech
screeched
screeches
screech-owl
screed
screen
screened
screenplay
screw
screwdriver
screwy
scribble
scribbler
scribbling
scribe
scrimmage
scrimp
scrip (certificate)
script
script-writer
scripture
scriptural
scrofula
scrofulous
scroll
scrotum

scrounge
scrounger
scrounging
scrub
scrubbed
scrubbing
scrubby
scrubs
scruff (of neck)
scruffy
scruffily
scruffiness
scrum
scrummage
scrumptious
scrunch
scruple
scrupulous
scrupulously
scrupulousness
scrutiny
scrutineer
scrutinise
scrutinize
scrutinising
scrutinizing
scuba
scud
scudded
scudding
scuff
scuffed
scuffle
scuffling
scull
sculler
scullery
sculleries (*pl.*)
scullion
sculpture
sculpt
sculptor
sculptor's
  (of the sculptor)

sculptors'
    (of the sculptors)
sculptress
sculptresses (*pl.*)
sculptress's
    (of the sculptress)
sculptresses'
    (of the sculptresses)
scum
  scummy
scupper
  scuppered
scurf
scurrilous
  scurrilously
scurry
  scurried
  scurries
  scurrying
scurvy (mean)
  scurvily
scurvy (deficiency disease)
scutcheon, escutcheon
scuttle (to sink a ship)
  scuttling
scuttle (for coal)
scuttle (to hurry)
  scuttling
scythe
  scything
sea
  seaboard
  sea-borne
  seafarer
  seafaring
  seafood
  seagull
  seagull's (of the seagull)
  seagulls'
    (of the seagulls)
  seakale
  sea-level
  sea-lion
  seaman
  seamen (*pl.*)

seaman's
    (of the seaman)
seamen's
    (of the seamen)
seamanship
seaplane
seascape
sea-serpent
seashore
seasick
seasickness
seaside
seaweed
seaworthiness
seaworthy
seal (to close firmly)
  sealing-wax
seal (animal)
  seal's (of the seal)
  seals' (of the seals)
  sealskin
seam (in sewing)
  seamless
  seamstress, sempstress
  seamy
seance
sear (to scorch)
  seared
search
  searched
  searcher
  searches
  searchlight
season
  seasonable
  seasonably
  seasonal
    (varying by season)
  seasonally
  seasoned
  seasoning
seat
  seat-belt
sebaceous
sec (of wine, dry)

secant, sec (*maths.*)
secateurs
secede
  seceding
  secession
seclude
  secluding
  seclusion
  seclusive
second (of time)
  second hand (of watch)
second
  (to support a motion)
  seconded
  seconder
second
  (to transfer an officer)
  secondment
second (after first)
  second-guess
  second-hand (not new)
  second-rate
secondary
  secondaries (*pl.*)
  secondarily
  secondary school
secret
  secrecy
  secretive
  secretively
  secretiveness
  secretly
secretary
  secretaries (*pl.*)
  secretaire (desk)
  secretarial
  secretariat
  secretaries'
    (of the secretaries)
  secretary's
    (of the secretary)
secrete (to hide)
  secreting
secrete (from a gland)
  secreting

secretion

sect

  sectarian

section

  sectional

sector

secular

secure

  securely

  securing

  security

  securities (*pl.*)

sedate (dignified)

  sedately

sedate

  (to use drug to calm)

  sedating

  sedation

  sedative

sedentary

sedge

sediment

  sedimentary

  sedimentation

sedition

  seditious

  seditiously

seduce

  seducer

  seducing

  seduction

  seductive

  seductively

sedulous

  sedulity

see

  saw

  seeing

  seen

  seer

see (bishopric)

seed

  seedling

seed (in tennis)

seedy (unwell)

seediness

seek

  seeker

  sought

seem (to appear)

  seemingly

seemly

  seemliness

seen (*from* see)

seep

  seepage

see-saw

seethe

  seething

segment

  segmentation

segregate

  segregating

  segregation

  segregative

seine (fishing net)

seismic

  seismograph

  seismologist

  seismology

seize

  seizing

  seizure

seldom

select

  selection

  selective

  selectively

  selectivity

  selector

selenium

self

  selves (*pl.*)

  self-addressed

  self-assured

  self-centred

  self-centered

  self-conscious

  self-consciously

  self-consciousness

self-defence

self-defense

self-employed

self-esteem

self-evident

self-explanatory

self-image

self-important

self-interest

selfish

selfishly

selfishness

selfless

self-made

self-portrait

self-possessed

self-raising (flour)

self-regulating

self-righteous

self-righteousness

selfsame

self-satisfied

self-service

self-starter

self-styled

self-sufficient

self-taught

sell

  seller

  sellout

  sold

seltzer

selvage, selvedge

semantic

semaphore

semblance

semen

  seminal

semester

semi- (half)

  semi-automatic

  semibreve

  semicircle

  semicircular

  semicolon

semiconductor
semi-conscious
semi-detached
semifinal
semi-precious
semiquaver
semi-skilled
semitone
semitropical
seminar (study group)
seminary
    (college for priests)
seminaries (*pl.*)
semolina
sempstress, seamstress
senate
  senator
  senatorial
  senator's
    (of the senator)
  senators'
    (of the senators)
send
  sender
  sent
senile
  senility
senior
  seniority
  senior wrangler
senna
sensation
  sensational
  sensationalism
  sensationally
sense
  senseless
  senselessly
  senselessness
  sensing
sensible
  sensibility
  sensibly
sensitise
  sensitize

sensitising
sensitizing
sensitive
  sensitively
  sensitivity
sensor (detecting device)
sensory
sensual (self-indulgent)
  sensualist
  sensuality
  sensually
sensuous
  (affected by beauty)
  sensuously
  sensuousness
sent (*from* send)
sentence (of words)
sentence
  (to punish for a crime)
  sentencing
sententious (pompous)
  sententiously
  sententiousness
sentience (feeling)
  sentient
sentiment
  sentimental
  sentimentalise
  sentimentalize
  sentimentalising
  sentimentalizing
  sentimentalist
  sentimentality
  sentimentally
sentinel
sentry
  sentries (*pl.*)
  sentries' (of the sentries)
  sentry's (of the sentry)
separate
  separable
  separating
  separation
  separatism
  separator

sepia
sepoy
  sepoys (*pl.*)
sepsis (infection)
September
septic (infected)
  septicaemia
  septicemia
septuagenarian
septum
sepulchre
  sepulcher
  sepulchral
sequel
sequence
  sequential
sequester (to isolate)
  sequestered
  sequestering
sequestrate (to confiscate)
  sequestrating
  sequestration
  sequestrator
sequin
seraglio
  seraglios (*pl.*)
seraph
  seraphs, seraphim (*pl.*)
  seraphic
serenade
  serenader
  serenading
serendipity
  serendipitous
serene
  serenely
  serenity
serf (land-slave)
  serfdom
sergeant
  sergeant-major
serial
  (story in instalments)
  serialisation
  serialization

serialise
serialize
serialising
serializing
serially
series
  series (*pl.*)
serif
serious
  seriously
  seriousness
serjeant (legal official)
sermon
  sermonise
  sermonize
  sermonising
  sermonizing
serpent
  serpentine
  serpent's
      (of the serpent)
  serpents'
      (of the serpents)
serrated
  serration
serried
serum
  sera, serums (*pl.*)
servant
  servant's
      (of the servant)
  servants'
      (of the servants)
serve
  server
  serving
service
  serviceability
  serviceable
  servicing
serviette
servile
  servility
servitude
sesame

session (academic year)
session (meeting)
set
  setback
  sets
  setter
  setting
settee
settle
  settlement
  settler
  settler's (of the settler)
  settlers' (of the settlers)
  settling
seven
  seventeen
  seventeenth
  seventh
  seventieth
  seventy
  seventies
sever (to cut)
  severance
  severed
  severing
several
  severally
severe (strict)
  severely
  severity
sew (to stitch)
  sewed
  sewing
  sewing-machine
  sewn
sewer (drain)
  sewage
sex
  sexed
  sexier
  sexiness
  sexual
  sexuality
  sexually
  sexy

sexagenarian
sextant
sextet
sexton
sextuple
shabby
  shabbier
  shabbily
  shabbiness
  shabby-genteel
shack
shackle
  shackling
shade
  shading
  shadily
  shady
shadow
  shadowy
shaft
shaggy
shagreen
Shah
  Shah's (of the Shah)
  Shahs' (of the Shahs)
shake
  shaken
  shaker
  shake-up
  shakily
  shakiness
  shaking
  shaky
  shook
shale
shall
  shalt (thou)
  shan't (shall not)
shallot
shallow
  shallower
  shallowness
sham
  shammed
  shammer

shamming
shams
shamble
shambling
shame
shamefaced
shameful
shamefully
shameless
shamelessly
shaming
shampoo
shampooed
shampooing
shamrock
shandy
shandygaff
shanghai
shanghaied
shank
shantung
shanty (hut)
shanties (*pl.*)
shanty town
shanty (song)
shanties (*pl.*)
shape
shapeless
shapeliness
shapely
shaping
shard, sherd (potsherd)
share
shareholder
shareholder's
(of the shareholder)
shareholders'
(of the shareholders)
sharer
sharing
shark
sharp
sharpen
sharpened
sharpener

sharpening
sharper
sharply
sharpshooter
sharp-witted
sharper (cheater at cards)
shatter
shattered
shattering
shatter-proof
shave
shaved
shaven
shaver
shaving
shawl
she
she'd (she had, would)
she's (she is)
she'll (she will)
sheaf
sheaves (*pl.*)
shear (to cut)
sheared
shearer
shearing
shears
shorn
sheath
sheath-knife
sheathe (to encase)
sheathing
shed (hut)
shed (to take off)
shedding
sheds
sheen
sheep
sheep (*pl.*)
sheepish
sheepishly
sheepskin
sheep's (of the sheep)
sheer (absolute)
sheer (to swerve)

sheering
sheer (very steep)
sheet
sheikh, sheik
sheik
shelf
shelves (*pl.*)
shell
shellfish
shellac
shellacked
shellacking
shelter
sheltered
shelterer
sheltering
shelve
shelving
shemozzle
shenanigan
shepherd
shepherded
shepherdess (*fem.*)
shepherdesses (*pl.*)
shepherdess's
(of the shepherdess)
shepherdesses'
(of the shepherdesses)
shepherd's
(of the shepherd)
shepherds'
(of the shepherds)
sherbet
sherd, shard (potsherd)
sheriff
sheriffs (*pl.*)
sheriff's (of the sheriff)
sheriffs' (of the sheriffs)
sherry
sherries (*pl.*)
shield
shift (of workers)
shift (to move)
shifty (deceitful)
shiftily

shiftiness
shilling
shilly-shally
  shilly-shallied
  shilly-shallier
  shilly-shallyer
  shilly-shallies
  shilly-shallying
shimmer
  shimmered
  shimmering
shin
shindy
  shindies (*pl.*)
shine
  shines
  shining
  shiny
  shone
  shined
shingle
  shingled
  shingling
shingles (disease)
ship
  shipmate
  shipment
  shipped
  shipper
  shipping
  ship's (of the ship)
  ships' (of the ships)
  shipshape
  shipwreck
  shipwrecked
  shipwright
shire
shirk
  shirker
shirr
  shirring
shirt
shiver
  shivered
  shivering

shivers
shivery
shoal
shock
  shock-absorber
  shocker
  shocking
shod (fitted with shoes)
shoddy (shabby)
  shoddier
  shoddily
  shoddiness
shoe
  shoes (*pl.*)
  shod
  shoelace
shone (*from* shine)
shoo
  shooed
shook (*from* shake)
shoot
  shot
shop
  shopkeeper
  shoplifting
  shopped
  shopper
  shopping
  shop's (of the shop)
  shops' (of the shops)
shore (to prop up)
  shored
  shoring
shore (seashore)
shorn (cut short)
short
  shortage
  shortbread
  shortcake
  short-change
  short-circuit
  short-circuited
  shortcoming
  short cut
  shorter

short-lived
shortly
shortness
short shrift
short sight
short-sighted
short-sightedness
short-tempered
shorten
  shortened
  shortening
shorthand
shotgun
should (*from* shall)
  shouldn't (should not)
shoulder
  shoulder-blade
  shouldered
  shouldering
shout
shove
  shoving
shovel
  shovelled
  shoveled
  shovelling
  shoveling
show
  showdown
  showed
  showily
  showman
  showmanship
  showmen (*pl.*)
  shown
  show off
  show-piece
  showy
shower
  shower-bath
  showery
shrapnel
shred
  shredded
  shredder

shredding
shrew (witch)
  shrewish
  shrew's (of the shrew)
  shrews' (of the shrews)
shrewd (cunning)
  shrewdly
  shrewdness
shriek
shrift
shrike
shrill
  shriller
  shrilly
  shrillness
shrimp
shrine
shrink
  shrank
  shrinkage
  shrunk
  shrunken
shrivel
  shrivelled
  shriveled
  shrivelling
  shriveling
  shrivels
shroud
shrub
  shrubbery
  shrubberies (*pl.*)
shrug
  shrugged
  shrugging
  shrugs
shudder
  shuddered
  shuddering
shuffle
  shuffling
shun
  shunned
  shunning
  shuns

shunt
shut
  shut-down
  shuts
  shutters
  shutting
shuttle
  shuttlecock
  shuttling
shy (bashful)
  shyer
  shier
  shyly
  shyness
shy (to throw)
  shied
  shies
  shying
shy (of a horse)
  shied
  shies
  shying
sibilant
sibling
sic (thus)
siccative
sick
  sick bay
  sicken
  sickened
  sickening
  sickens
  sickly
  sickness
sickle (for reaping)
side
  sideboard
  sideburns
  sidelight
  sideline
  sidelong
  side-splitting
  side-step
  side-track
  sidewalk

  sideways
  siding
sidle
  sidling
siege
sienna (colour)
siesta
sieve
  sieving
sift
sigh
  sighed
  sighing
sight
  sighted
  sightless
  sightlessness
  sightliness
  sightly
  sightseeing
  sightseer
sign
  signer
  signpost
  sign-writer
  sign-writing
signal
  signalled
  signaled
  signaller
  signaler
  signalling
  signaling
  signally
  signalman
  signalmen (*pl.*)
  signals
signature
signatory
  signatories (*pl.*)
  signatories'
    (of the signatories)
  signatory's
    (of the signatory)
signet (ring)

significance
  significant
  significantly
signify
  signified
  signifies
  signifying
Signor (*Mr.*)
  Signora (*Mrs.*)
  Signorina (*Miss*)
Sikh
silage
silence
  silencer
  silencing
  silent
  silently
silhouette
  silhouetted
  silhouetting
silica (in sand, etc.)
  silicate
  silicon (chem. element)
  silicone
    (compound of silicon)
  silicosis (disease)
silk
  silken
  silkworm
  silky
sill
sillabub, syllabub
            (sweet cream)
silly
  sillier
  sillily
  silliness
silo
  silos (*pl.*)
silt
silvan, sylvan (wooded)
silver
  silvered
  silvering
  silversmith

silver-tongued
silvery
simian
similar (alike)
  similarity
  similarities (*pl.*)
  similarly
simile (comparison)
  similes (*pl.*)
similitude (similarity)
simmer
  simmered
  simmering
simnel
simony
simper
  simpered
simple
  simple-minded
  simpler
  simpleton
  simplex
  simplicity
  simplification
  simplified
  simplifies
  simplify
  simplifying
  simplistic
  simply
simulacrum
  simulacra (*pl.*)
simulate
  simulating
  simulation
  simulator
simultaneous
  simultaneity
  simultaneously
sin
  sinful
  sinfully
  sinfulness
  sinless
  sinned

sinner
sinning
sins
since
sincere
  sincerely
  sincerity
sine (without)
  sinecure
  sine die
  sine qua non
sine, sin (*maths.*)
  sine wave
  sinusoidal
  sinusoidally
sinew
  sinewy
sing
  sang
  singer
  singer's (of the singer)
  singers' (of the singers)
  singing
  singsong
  sung
singe (to scorch)
  singeing
single
  single-minded
  singlet (garment)
  singleton (single thing)
  singling
  singly
singular
  singularity
  singularly
sinister
  sinisterly
sink
  sank
  sinker
  sinking
  sunk (was)
  sunken
sink (in kitchen)

225

Sino- (Chinese)
  sinologist
  sinology
sinuous (with curves)
  sinuously
sinus (cavity)
  sinuses (*pl.*)
  sinusitis
sip
  sipped
  sips
siphon
  siphoned
sir
  sire
siren
  siren's (of the siren)
  sirens' (of the sirens)
sirloin
sirocco
  siroccos (*pl.*)
sisal
sister
  sisterhood
  sister-in-law
  sisters-in-law (*pl.*)
  sister-in-law's
    (of the sister-in-law)
  sisters-in-law's
    (of the sisters-in-law)
  sisterly
  sister's (of the sister)
  sisters' (of the sisters)
sit
  sat
  sit-in
  sit-ins (*pl.*)
  sits
  sitter
  sitting
site (location)
situate
  situating
  situation
sitz-bath

six
  sixteen
  sixteenth
  sixth
  sixthly
  sixtieth
  sixty
  sixties (*pl.*)
size
  sizeable
  sizable
  sizeably
size (glue)
  sizing
size up (to estimate)
sizzle
  sizzling
skate
  skater
  skater's (of the skater)
  skaters' (of the skaters)
  skating
skate (fish)
skedaddle
  skedaddling
skein
skeleton
  skeletal
sketch
  sketcher
  sketchier
  sketchily
  sketchiness
  sketchy
skew
  skew-whiff
skewer
ski
  skied
  skier
  skiing
skid
  skidded
  skidding
  skids

skiff
skill
  skilful
  skillful
  skilfully
  skilled
skillet
skim
  skimmed
  skim milk
skimp
  skimpily
  skimpiness
  skimpy
skin
  skin-deep
  skin-diver
  skin-diving
  skinflint
  skinned
  skinning
  skinny
  skin-tight
skip
  skipped
  skipping
  skips
skip (for rubbish)
skipper (captain)
  skipper's
    (of the skipper)
  skippers'
    (of the skippers)
skirl
skirmish
skirt
skit (satire)
skittish
  skittishly
  skittishness
skittle
  skittle alley
skua (sea-bird)
skulk
skulduggery,

skullduggery

skull (of head)
  skull-cap
skunk
sky
  sky-diving
  sky-high
  skylark
  skylight
  skyscraper
slab
slack (lazy)
  slacker
  slacking
slack (coal-dust)
slacken
  slackened
  slackening
  slackness
slag
slain (*from* slay)
slake
  slaking
slalom
slam
  slammed
  slamming
  slams
slander
  slandered
  slanderer
  slandering
  slanderous
  slanders
slang
  slangy
slang (to abuse)
slant
slap
  slapdash
  slapped
  slapping
  slaps
  slapstick
slash

slat
slate
slattern
  slatternly
slaughter
  slaughtered
  slaughter-house
  slaughtering
slave
  slave's (of the slave)
  slaves' (of the slaves)
  slavery
  slavish
  slavishly
  slavishness
slaver
  slavered
  slavering
slay
  slain
  slaying
  slew
sleazy
sled, sledge, sleigh
sledge-hammer
sleek
  sleekness
sleep
  sleeper
  sleepier
  sleepily
  sleepiness
  sleeping
  sleeping-draught
  sleeping partner
  sleepless
  sleeplessness
  sleep-walker
  sleep-walking
  sleepy
  slept
sleet
sleeve
  sleeveless
  sleeving

sleigh (*see* sledge)
sleight (cunning)
  sleight of hand
            (conjuring)
slender
  slenderness
slept (*from* sleep)
sleuth
slew (*from* slay)
slew, slue
      (to swing round)
  slue
  slewed
  slued
  slewing
  sluing
slice
  slicing
slick
  slicker
slide
  slid
  slide-rule
  sliding
slight (small)
  slighter
  slightest
  slightly
slight (to insult)
slim (thin)
  slimmed
  slimmer
  slimming
  slimness
  slims
slime (dirt)
  slimy
sling
  slung
slink
  slunk
slip
  slip-knot
  slipped
  slipperiness

slippery
slipping
slips
slipshod
slip-stream
slipper
slit
  slitting
  slits
slither (to slide)
  slithered
  slithering
  slithers
sliver (to break up)
  slivered
  slivering
  slivers
slobber
  slobbered
  slobbering
sloe (fruit)
  sloe-eyed
  sloe gin
slog
  slogged
  slogger
  slogging
  slogs
slogan
sloop (ship)
slop
  slopped
  sloppier
  sloppily
  sloppiness
  sloppy
  slops
slope
  sloping
slosh
  sloshed
  sloshes
  sloshing
slot
  slotted

sloth (laziness)
  slothful
sloth (animal)
slouch
  slouched
  slouches
slough (marsh)
slough (to discard skin)
sloven
  slovenliness
  slovenly
slow
  slower
  slowly
sludge
slue, slew
          (to swing round)
  slue
  slewed
  slued
  slewing
  sluing
slug (animal)
slug (to hit)
  slugged
  sluggard
  sluggish
  sluggishly
  sluggishness
sluice
  sluicing
slum
  slumming
slumber
  slumbered
  slumbering
  slumbrous
  slumberous
slump
slung (*from* sling)
slunk (*from* slink)
slur
  slurred
  slurring

slurry
  (liquid mud or cement)
slush
slut
  sluttish
sly
  slyer
  slyly
  slyness
smack (to hit)
smack (boat)
small
  smaller
  smallness
smart (neat)
  smarten
  smartened
  smartening
  smarter
  smartly
  smartness
smart (to be painful)
smash
smattering
smear
  smeared
smell
  smelled
  smellier
  smelliest
  smells
  smelly
  smelt
smelt (to melt metal)
smelt (fish)
smidgen, smidgin
smile
  smiling
smirch (to soil)
  smirched
smirk (to grin)
smite
  smiting
  smitten (was)
  smote

smith
  smithy
  smithies (*pl.*)
smithereens
smock
  smocking
smog
smoke
  smokable
  smokeless
  smoker
  smokier
  smoking
  smoky
smooth
  smoother
  smoothly
  smoothness
smorgasbord
smother
  smothered
  smothering
smoulder
  smolder
  smouldered
  smoldered
  smouldering
  smoldering
smudge
  smudging
smug
  smugger
  smugly
  smugness
smuggle
  smuggler
  smuggling
smut
  smuttiness
  smutty
snack
snaffle
  snaffling
snag
snail

snail's (of the snail)
snails' (of the snails)
snake
snap
  snapdragon
  snapped
  snapper
  snappily
  snapping
  snappish
  snappy
  snaps
  snapshot
snare
  snaring
snarl
snatch
  snatched
  snatches
sneak
sneer
  sneered
  sneers
sneeze
  sneezing
snicker
  snickered
  snickering
  snickers
snide
sniff
sniffle
  sniffling
snifter
snigger
  sniggered
  sniggering
  sniggers
snip (to cut)
  snipped
  snippet
  snipping
  snips
snipe (bird)
snipe (to shoot)

  sniping
snivel
  snivelled
  sniveled
  sniveller
  sniveler
  snivelling
  sniveling
  snivels
snob
  snobbery
  snobbish
  snobbishly
  snobbishness
  snob's (of the snob)
  snobs' (of the snobs)
snooker
  snooker pool
snoop
  snooper
snooze
  snoozing
snore
  snorer
  snoring
snorkel, schnorkel
snort
snot
  snotty
snout
snow
  snowball
  snowballed
  snowballing
  snowdrop
  snowfall
  snowflake
  snowmobile
  snow-plough
  snowplow
  snow-shoe
snub
  snubbed
  snubbing
  snub-nosed

snubs

snuff

snuffers

snuffle

  snuffling

snug

  snuggery

  snuggeries (*pl.*)

  snugly

snuggle

  snuggling

soak

soap

  soap-flakes

  soaping

  soap-suds

  soapy

soar (to fly high)

  soared

  soaring

  soars

sob

  sobbed

  sobbing

  sobs

sober

  sobered

  sobering

  sobriety

sobriquet (nickname)

soccer

sociable

  sociability

  sociably

social

  socialisation

  socialization

  socialise

  socialize

  socialising

  socializing

  Socialism

  Socialist

  socialite

  socially

Social Security

society

  societies (*pl.*)

socio-economic

sociology

  sociological

  sociologist

sock

socket

sod (turf)

soda

  soda-water

sodden (wet)

sodium

sodomy

sofa

soft

  softball

  soften

  softened

  softening

  softens

  softer

  softly

  softness

  software

soggy

soil (to dirty)

  soiled

soil (ground)

soirée

sojourn

solace

  solacing

solar

  solarium

  solar system

sold (*from* sell)

solder

  soldered

  soldering iron

soldier

  soldiering

  soldier's (of the soldier)

soldiers'

  (of the soldiers)

sole (alone)

  solely

sole (fish)

sole (of shoe)

  soling

solecism

solemn

  solemnisation

  solemnization

  solemnise

  solemnize

  solemnising

  solemnizing

  solemnity

  solemnly

solenoid

solicit

  solicitation

  soliciting

  solicitor

  solicitor's

  (of the solicitor)

  solicitors'

  (of the solicitors)

  solicitous (sympathetic)

  solicitously

  solicitude

solid

  solidarity

  solider

  solidification

  solidified

  solidifies

  solidify

  solidifying

  solidity

  solidly

  solid-state

soliloquise

  soliloquize

  soliloquising

  soliloquizing

  soliloquy

soliloquies (*pl.*)
solitaire (single gem)
solitary
  solitarily
  solitariness
solitude
solo
  solos (*pl.*)
  soloist
  soloist's (of the soloist)
  soloists' (of the soloists)
solstice
  solstitial
soluble
  solubility
solution
solve
  solvable
  solving
solvent
  solvency
soma- (body)
  somatic
sombre
  somber
  sombrely
  somberly
  sombreness
  somberness
sombrero
  sombreros (*pl.*)
some
  somebody
  somebody's
    (of somebody)
  somehow
  someone
  somewhat
  somewhere
somersault
somn- (sleep)
  somnambulism
  somnambulist
  somnolence
  somnolent

son
  son-in-law
  sons-in-law (*pl.*)
  son-in-law's
    (of the son-in-law)
  sons-in-law's
    (of the sons-in-law)
  sonny
  son's (of the son)
  sons' (of the sons)
sonar
sonata
  sonatina
song
  songster
sonic
  sonic boom
sonnet
sonorous
  sonorously
  sonority
soon
  sooner
soot
soothe
  soothing
soothsayer
sop
  sopping
soph- (wisdom)
  sophism
  sophist
  sophisticated
  sophistry
  sophomore
soporific
soprano
  sopranos, soprani (*pl.*)
  soprano's
    (of the soprano)
  sopranos'
    (of the sopranos)
sorcerer
  sorceress (*fem.*)
  sorcery

sordid
  sordidly
  sordidness
sore (painful)
  sorely
  soreness
  sorer
sorority
sorrel
sorrow
  sorrowful
  sorrowfully
  sorrowfulness
sorry
  sorrier
sort
  (to arrange in groups)
  sorter
sort (kind)
sortie
sot
  sottish
sotto voce (in a whisper)
soubrette
soufflé
sought (*from* seek)
soul
  soulful
  soulfully
  soulless
sound (low noise)
  sounder
  soundless
  soundlessly
  soundproof
  soundproofed
sound (in good condition)
  soundly
  soundness
sound (to measure depth)
soup
soupçon
sour
  sourer
  sourly

sourness
source (of river)
source (origin)
souse
  sousing
south
  southerly
  southern
  southerner
  southward
  sou'-wester
souvenir
sovereign (ruler, coin)
  sovereign's
      (of the sovereign)
  sovereigns'
      (of the sovereigns)
  sovereignty
sovereign (excellent)
soviet
sow (pig)
sow (to plant seeds)
  sowed
  sown
soya
  soya bean
  soybean
spa
space
  spacecraft
  spaceship
  spacesuit
  spacing
  spacious
  spaciousness
spade
spaghetti
span
  spanned
  spanning
  spans
span (spick and span)
spangle
spaniel
spank

spanner
spar (to box)
  sparred
  sparring
  spars
spar (pole on ship)
spare
  sparing
  sparingly
spark
  sparkle
  sparkler
  sparkling
sparrow
  sparrow's
      (of the sparrow)
  sparrows'
      (of the sparrows)
sparse
  sparsely
spasm
  spasmodic
  spasmodically
spastic
spat (*from* spit)
spate
spatial
spatter
  spattered
spatula
spavin
  spavined
spawn
spay
  spayed
speak
  speaker
  speaker's
      (of the speaker)
  speakers'
      (of the speakers)
  spoke
  spoken
spear
  speared

spearhead
special
  speciality
  specialty
  specialities (*pl.*)
  specialties (*pl.*)
  specially
specialise
  specialize
  specialisation
  specialization
  specialising
  specializing
specialist
  specialist's
      (of the specialist)
  specialists'
      (of the specialists)
specie (money in coins)
species
  species (*pl.*)
specify
  specific
  specifically
  specification
  specified
  specifies
  specifying
specimen
specious (plausible)
speck
  speckled
spectacle
  spectacles
  spectacular
  spectacularly
spectator
  spectator's
      (of the spectator)
  spectators'
      (of the spectators)
spectre (ghost)
  specter
  spectral
spectroscope

spectroscopic

spectrum
  spectra (*pl.*)
speculate
  speculating
  speculation
  speculative
  speculatively
  speculator
speech
  speeches (*pl.*)
  speechified
  speechify
  speechifying
  speechless
  speechlessly
speed
  sped
  speeded
  speedier
  speedily
  speedometer
  speedy
spell
  spelled
  speller
  spelling
  spelt
spell (a charm)
  spell-binding
  spellbound
spelt (kind of wheat)
spelter (zinc or pewter)
spend
  spender
  spendthrift
  spent
sperm
  spermaceti
  sperm-whale
spew
sphagnum
sphere
  spherical
  spherically

spheroid
sphincter
sphinx
  sphinxes (*pl.*)
sphygm- (pulse)
  sphygmomanometer
spice
  spicier
  spicily
  spiciness
  spicy
spick and span
spider
  spider's (of the spider)
  spiders' (of the spiders)
  spidery
spigot
spike
  spiking
  spiky
spill (of wood)
  spillikin
spill (to upset)
  spilled
  spillage
  spills
  spilt
spin
  spin-bowler
  spin-drier
  spinner
  spinneret
  spinning
  spinning-wheel
  spin-off
  spins
  spinster
  spun
spinach
spindle
  spindly
spine
  spinal
  spinal column
  spineless

spinet
spinnaker
spinney
  spinneys (*pl.*)
spinster
  spinsterhood
spiraea
spiral
  spiralled
  spiraled
  spiralling
  spiraling
  spirally
spire
spirit
  spirited
  spiritedly
  spiriting
  spiritless
  spirituous
spiritual
  spiritualism
  spiritualist
  spiritualistic
  spiritually
spirt, spurt
spit
  spat
  spitfire
  spits
  spitter
  spitting
  spittle
  spittoon
spit (of earth)
spit (likeness)
spit (promontory)
spite
  spiteful
  spitefully
  spitefulness
spiv
splash
  splash-down
  splashed

splashes
splatter
splay
spleen
 splenetic
splendid
 splendidly
 splendour
 splendor
splice
 splicing
splint
 splinter
 splintered
 splintering
split
 splits
 splitting
splurge
 splurging
splutter
 spluttered
 spluttering
spoil
 spoiled
 spoilt
spoke
 spokeshave
spoke (*from* speak)
 spoken
 spokesman
 spokesmen (*pl.*)
spoliation (*from* spoil)
 spoliator
sponge
 sponger
 sponging
 spongy
sponsor
 sponsored
 sponsoring
 sponsor's
    (of the sponsor)
 sponsors'
    (of the sponsors)

spontaneous
 spontaneity
 spontaneously
spoof
 spoofer
spool
spoon
 spoon-fed
 spoon-feeding
 spoonful
 spoonfuls (*pl.*)
spoonerism
spoor (track)
sporadic
 sporadically
spore
sporran
sport
 sportive
 sportively
 sportsman
 sportsmen (*pl.*)
 sportsman's
    (of the sportsman)
 sportsmen's
    (of the sportsmen)
 sportsmanship
spot
 spot-check
 spotless
 spotlessness
 spotlight
 spotlighting
 spotlit
 spots
 spotted
 spotter
 spotting
 spotty
spouse
spout
sprain
 sprained
sprat
sprawl

spray
 sprayer
spread
 spread-eagle
 spread-eagled
spree
sprig
sprightly
 sprightlier
 sprightliness
spring (to jump)
 sprang
 springboard
 springing
 sprung
spring (season)
 spring-clean
 spring-cleaned
 spring-cleaning
 springtime
spring (of water)
spring (of watch, etc.)
sprinkle
 sprinkler
 sprinkling
sprint
 sprinter
sprite
sprocket
sprout
spruce
 sprucely
 spruceness
sprue
sprung (*from* spring)
spry
 spryer
 spryly
 spryness
spud (potato)
spud (small spade)
spume
spun (*from* spin)
spunk
spur (to encourage)

spurred
spurring
spurs
spur (in horse's side)
spur (side-road)
spurious
spurn
spurt, spirt
sputnik
sputter
  sputtered
  sputtering
  sputters
sputum
spy
  spies (*pl.*)
  spied
  spies' (of the spies)
  spying
  spy's (of the spy)
squabble
  squabbling
squad
  squadron
  squadron-leader
squalid
  squalidly
  squalor
squall (to cry)
  squalled
  squalling
squall (of wind)
  squally
squalor
squander
  squandered
  squandering
square
  squarely
  squaring
squash
squat (dumpy)
squat (to sit down)
  squats
  squatted

squatter
squatting
squaw
squawk
  squawker
squeak
squeal
squeamish
  squeamishness
squeegee
squeeze
  squeezing
squelch
squib (firework)
squid (sea-animal)
squiggle
  squiggling
squill
squint
squire
  squirarchy
  squirearchy
  squireen
  squire's (of the squire)
  squires' (of the squires)
  squiring
squirm
squirrel
  squirrel's
     (of the squirrel)
  squirrels'
     (of the squirrels)
squirt
stab
  stabbed
  stabs
  stabbing
stable (fixed)
  stabilisation
  stabilization
  stabilise
  stabilize
  stabiliser
  stabilizer
  stabilising

  stabilizing
  stability
stable (for horses)
  stabling
staccato
stack
stadium
  stadiums, stadia (*pl.*)
staff (people)
  staffed
  staff officer
staff (rod)
stag
  stag's (of the stag)
  stags' (of the stags)
stage (of theatre)
  stagecraft
  stage fright
  stage manager
  stagey, stagy
  staging
stage (progress)
stagger
  staggered
  staggering
  staggers (sheep disease)
stagnate
  stagnating
  stagnation
  stagnant
staid (steady)
  staidly
  staidness
stain
  stainless
stair (step)
  staircase
stake (post)
stake (to bet)
  stakeholder
  staking
stalactite
    (from roof of cave)
  stalagmite
    (pillar of deposit)

stale (not fresh)
 staleness
stale (to urinate)
 staling
stalemate (in chess)
stalk (to chase)
 stalker
stalk (stem)
stall (of engine, to stop)
 stalled
stall (theatre-seat)
stallion
stalwart
stamen
stamina (strength)
stammer
 stammered
 stammerer
 stammering
stamp (with foot)
 stamped
stamp (postage)
 stamp-album
 stamp book
 stamp-collecting
 stamp-collector
stampede
 stampeding
stance
stanch (to stop bleeding)
stanchion
stand
 stand-by
 stood
stand (for spectators)
standard
 standardisation
 standardization
 standardise
 standardize
 standardising
 standardizing
stanza
staple (most important)
staple (for fixing)

stapler
stapling
star (in the sky)
 starless
 starry
star (famous performer)
 stars
 stardom
 starlet
 starred
 starring
 star-turn
starboard (right-hand side)
starch
stare (to gaze)
 staring
stark
 stark naked
start
 starter
startle
 startling
starve
 starvation
 starveling
 starving
state (country)
 stateless
 statesman
 statesmen (*pl.*)
 statesmanship
state (to say)
 statement
 stating
state (condition)
 stately (dignified)
 statelier
 stateliness
static (not moving)
static (*electr.*)
station (position)
 stationary (not moving)
 stationed
 stationing
station (railway)

stationmaster
stationmaster's
 (of the stationmaster)
stationmasters'
 (of the stationmasters)
stationer
stationery (paper)
Stationery Office
statistics
 statistical
 statistically
 statistician
statue (of marble, etc.)
 statuary
 statuesque
 statuette
 stature
 (tallness, importance)
status
 status quo
statute (law)
 statutory
staunch (loyal)
 staunchly
 staunchness
stave (to make a hole)
 staved
 staving
 stove
stave (step of ladder)
stave
 staved
 stave-off (to postpone)
stay (support)
stay (to remain)
 stayed
 staying
steadfast
 steadfastly
 steadfastness
steady
 steadied
 steadier
 steadies
 steadily

steadiness
steadying
steak (meat)
steal (to rob)
stealing
stole
stolen
stealth
stealthily
stealthiness
stealthy
steam
steamed
steam-engine
steamer
steamroller
steamrollered
steamrollering
steed
steel (metal)
steely
steep
steeper
steeply
steepness
steep (to soak)
steeple
steeplechase
steeplejack
steer (to guide a boat)
steerable
steerage
steered
steering
steersman
steer (bullock)
stele, stela
   (Greek gravestone)
stellar
stem
stemmed
stemming
stems
stench
stencil

stencilled
stenciled
stencilling
stenciling
stenography
stenographer
stenographic
stenotype
stentorian
step
stepfather
stepmother
step
stepped
stepping
steps
steppe (plain)
stereo- (three-dimensional)
stereophonic
stereoscope
stereoscopic
stereotype
sterile
sterilisation
sterilization
sterilise
sterilize
steriliser
sterilizer
sterilising
sterilizing
sterility
sterling
stern (strict)
sternly
sterner
sternness
stern (ship's)
sternum (breastbone)
steroid
stertorous
stet (let it stand)
stethoscope
stevedore
stew

stewed
steward
steward's
   (of the steward)
stewards'
   (of the stewards)
stewardess (*fem.*)
stewardess's
   (of the stewardess)
stewardesses'
   (of the stewardesses)
stick
sticker
sticks
stuck
stickleback
stickler
sticky
stickier
stickily
stickiness
stiff
stiffen
stiffened
stiffener
stiffening
stiffer
stiffly
stiff-necked
stifle
stifling
stigma
stigmata (*pl.*)
stigmatise
stigmatize
stigmatising
stigmatizing
stile (over a hedge)
stiletto
stilettos (*pl.*)
still
stillbirth
stillborn
stillness
still (for distilling)

237

stilt (pole for walking)
stilted (solemn)
stimulate
  stimulating
  stimulation
  stimulative
  stimulus
  stimuli (*pl.*)
sting (insect's)
  stinger
  stinging
  stingless
  stung
stingy (mean)
  stingier
  stingily
  stinginess
stink
  stank
  stinker
  stunk
stint
stipend
  stipendiary
  stipendiaries (*pl.*)
stipple
  stippling
stipulate
  stipulating
  stipulation
stir
  stirred
  stirring
  stirs
stirrup
stitch
  stitches (*pl.*)
  stitched
  stitches
stoat
stock
  stockbroker
  stockbroker's
    (of the stockbroker)

stockbrokers'
  (of the stockbrokers)
stocked
Stock Exchange
stockholder
stockist
stockpile
stockpiling
stock-still
stocktaking
stockyard
stockade
stocking
stockinet
stockinette
stocky (short and fat)
  stockier
  stockiness
stodge
  stodgily
  stodging
  stodgy
stoic
  stoical
  stoically
  stoicism
stoke
  stoker
  stoking
stole (robe)
stole (*from* steal)
  stolen
stolid
  stolidity
  stolidly
stomach
  stomach-ache
stone
  stone-deaf
  stonemason
  stone's throw
  stonewalling
  stonier
  stonily
  stoning

stony
stood (*from* stand)
stooge
  stooging
stook (of corn)
stool
stoop
  stooped
stop
  stopcock
  stopgap
  stopover
  stoppage
  stopped
  stopper
  stopping
  stop-press
  stops
  stop-watch
store
  storage
  storekeeper
  store's (of the store)
  stores' (of the stores)
  storing
storey (of a building)
  story
  storeys (*pl.*)
  stories (*pl.*)
stork (bird)
storm
  storm-bound
  stormiest
  stormily
  stormy
story (tale)
  stories (*pl.*)
  story-teller
stoup (flagon)
stout (beer)
stout (fat, determined)
  stouter
  stout-hearted
  stoutly
  stoutness

stove
stove (*from* stave)
stow
  stowage
  stowaway
straddle
  straddling
strafe
  strafing
straggle
  straggler
  straggling
straight (direct)
  straighten
  straightened
  straightening
  straighter
  straightforward
strain
  strained
strain (to sieve)
  strainer
strait (narrow)
  straiten
  straitened (hard up)
  strait-jacket
  strait-laced
  straits (difficulties)
  Straits of Dover
strand (shore)
strand (thread)
stranded (abandoned)
strange
  strangely
  stranger
strangle
  strangling
  stranglehold
strangulate
  strangulating
  strangulation
strap
  straphanger
  strapped
  strapping

stratagem (trickery)
strategy (war tactics)
  strategies (*pl.*)
  strategic
  strategically
  strategist
stratify
  stratification
  stratified
  stratifying
stratosphere
  stratospheric
stratum (layer)
  strata (*pl.*)
stratus (cloud)
  strati (*pl.*)
straw
  strawberry
  strawberries (*pl.*)
stray
  strayed
streak
  streaky
stream
  streamlined
  streamlining
street
  streetcar
strength
  strengthen
  strengthened
  strengthening
strenuous
  strenuously
  strenuousness
streptococcus
  streptococci (*pl.*)
  streptococcal
streptomycin
stress
stretch
  stretcher
strew
  strewed
  strewn

striate
  striated
  striation
stricken (struck down)
strict
  stricter
  strictness
  strictly
stricture (scolding)
stride
  stridden
  striding
  strode
strident (noisy)
  stridency
  stridently
strife
strike
  strikebound
  strike-breaker
  strike-breaking
  striker
  striking
  struck
string
  stringed (with strings)
  stringy
  strung
stringent (very strict)
  stringency
  stringently
strip
  stripped
  stripper
  stripping
  strip-tease
stripe
  stripling
strive
  striven
  striving
  strove
stroboscope
  stroboscopic
stroke

stroking
stroll
  stroller
strong
  stronger
  stronghold
  strongly
strontium
strop
  stropped
  stropping
  strops
struck (*from* strike)
structure
  structural
  structurally
strudel
struggle
  struggling
strum
  strummed
  strummer
  strumming
  strums
strumpet
strung (*from* string)
strut
  struts
  strutted
  strutting
strychnine
stub
  stubbed
  stubbing
  stubs
stubble
stubborn
  stubbornly
  stubbornness
stucco
  stuccoed
stuck (*from* stick)
stud (for collar)
stud (horses)
  stud-farm

student
  student's
    (of the student)
  students'
    (of the students)
studio
  studios (*pl.*)
study
  studied
  studies
  studious
  studiously
  studying
study (room)
  studies (*pl.*)
stuff (fabric)
stuff (to fill tightly)
  stuffed
stuffy (lacking fresh air)
  stuffier
  stuffiness
stultify
  stultification
  stultified
  stultifying
stumble
  stumbling
  stumbling-block
stump
  stumped
stun
  stunned
  stunning
stung (*from* sting)
stunt (unusual action)
stunted (undersized)
stupefy
  stupefaction
  stupefied
  stupefies
  stupefying
stupendous
  stupendously
stupid
  stupider

stupidity
stupor
sturdy
  sturdier
  sturdily
  sturdiness
sturgeon
stutter
  stuttered
  stutterer
  stuttering
  stutters
sty (for pigs)
  sties (*pl.*)
sty, stye (on eyelid)
  sties (*pl.*)
style (method, elegance)
  stylish
  stylishly
  stylishness
  stylist
  stylise
  stylize
  stylised
  stylized
stylus
  (gramophone needle)
  styluses, styli (*pl.*)
stymie
  stymied
styptic
styrene
suave
  suavely
  suavity
subaltern
  subaltern's
    (of the subaltern)
  subalterns'
    (of the subalterns)
subcommittee
subconscious
  subconsciously
  subconsciousness
subcontract

subcontractor

subdivide
  subdividing
  subdivisible
  subdivision
subdue
  subdual
  subdued
  subduing
subedit
  subedited
  subediting
  subeditor
  subeditor's
    (of the subeditor)
  subeditors'
    (of the subeditors)
  subedits
subject (citizen)
  subject's
    (of the subject)
  subjects'
    (of the subjects)
subject
  (matter for discussion)
  subjective
  subjectively
  subjectivity
subject (to subdue)
  subjection
sub judice
subjugate
  subjugating
  subjugation
subjunctive
sublet
  sublets
  subletting
sublime
  sublimity
  sublimely
sublimate (physics)
  sublimating
  sublimation
subliminal

submarine
  submarine's
    (of the submarine)
  submarines'
    (of the submarines)
submerge
  submergence
  submerging
  submersible
  submersion
submit
  submission
  submissive
  submissively
  submissiveness
  submits
  submitted
  submitting
subnormal
  subnormality
  subnormally
subordinate
  subordinating
  subordination
suborn
  subornation (bribing)
  suborner
sub-plot
subpoena
  subpoenaed
sub rosa
subscribe
  subscriber
  subscriber's
    (of the subscriber)
  subscribers'
    (of the subscribers)
  subscribing
  subscription
subsequent
  subsequently
subservient
  subservience
subside
  subsidence

subsiding
subsidiary
  subsidiaries (*pl.*)
subsidise
  subsidize
  subsidising
  subsidizing
subsidy
  subsidies (*pl.*)
subsist
  subsistence
subsoil
subsonic
substance
  substantial
  substantially
substandard
substantiate
  substantiating
  substantiation
substantive (noun)
substantive (permanent)
substation
substitute
  substituting
  substitution
substratum
  substrata (*pl.*)
substructure
subtenant
  subtenancy
  subtenancies (*pl.*)
subtend
subterfuge
subterranean
sub-title
subtle
  subtler
  subtlety (ingenuity)
  subtleties (*pl.*)
  subtly (craftily)
subtract
  subtraction
subtropical
suburb

suburban
suburbanite
suburbia
subvention
subversion
subversive
subvert
subverter
subway
succeed (to be successful)
succeeded
success
successful
successfully
succeed (to follow)
succeeding
succession
successive
successively
successor
succinct
succour
succor
succoured
succored
succouring
succoring
succulence
succulent
succumb
succumbed
such
suck
sucker
suckle
suckling
sucrose
suction
sudden
suddenly
suddenness
suds
sue
sued
sues

suing
suede (kind of leather)
suet
suet pudding
suffer
sufferance
suffered
sufferer
suffering
suffice
sufficiency
sufficient
sufficiently
sufficing
suffix
suffixes (*pl.*)
suffocate
suffocating
suffocation
suffragan (bishop)
suffrage
suffragette
suffuse
suffusing
suffusion
sugar
sugared
sugary
suggest
suggestion
suggestive
suggestively
suicide
suicidal
suit (to be convenient)
suitability
suitable
suitably
suit (clothes)
suitcase
suite (attendants)
suite (of furniture)
suite (of rooms)
suitor
sulk

sulkily
sulkiness
sulky
sullen
sullenly
sullenness
sully
sullied
sullying
sulphur
sulfur
sulphate
sulfate
sulphide
sulfide
sulphuretted
sulfuretted
sulphuric acid
sulfuric acid
sultan (emperor)
sultana (*fem.*)
sultanate
sultana (dried fruit)
sultry
sultrier
sultrily
sultriness
sum
summation
summed
summing
sums
summary
    (short description)
summaries (*pl.*)
summarise
summarize
summarising
summarizing
summariness
summary (without delay)
summarily
summer
summertime
summery (weather)

summit
summitry
summon
summons
summonses (*pl.*)
sump
sumptuary
(legal expression)
sumptuous (luxurious)
sumptuously
sumptuousness
sun
sunbathe
sunbathing
sunbeam
sunburn
sunburnt
Sunday
sundial
sunflower
sunless
sunlight
sunned
sunnier
sunning
sunny
sunrise
sun's (of the sun)
sunspot
sunstroke
sun-tan
sun-tanned
sundae (ice-cream)
Sunday
sundry
sundries (*pl.*)
sung (*from* sing)
sunk (*from* sink)
sunken
sup
supped
supper (meal)
supping
sups
super- (above, more, etc.)

superabundance
superabundant
superannuate
superannuated
superannuation
superb
superbly
supercargo
supercargoes (*pl.*)
supercharge
supercharging
supercilious
superciliously
superciliousness
superconductor
superconductivity
superficial
superficiality
superficially
superfluous
superfluity
superfluously
superheterodyne
superhuman
superimpose
superimposing
superimposition
superintend
superintendence
superintendent
superintendent's
(of the superintendent)
superintendents'
(of the superintendents)
superior
superiority
superlative
superlatively
superman
supermen (*pl.*)
supermarket
supernatural
supernaturalism
supernaturally
supernumerary

supernumeraries (*pl.*)
superpose
superposing
superposition
supersaturate
supersaturating
supersaturation
supersede
supersedence
superseding
supersedure
supersonic
superstition
superstitious
superstructure
supervene
supervening
supervention
supervise
supervising
supervision
supervisor
supervisor's
(of the supervisor)
supervisors'
(of the supervisors)
supervisory
supine (lying flat)
supine (*grammar*)
supper
supperless
supplant
supplanter
supple
supplely
suppleness
supplement
supplementary
supplementation
suppliant
supplicate
supplicating
supplication
supply
supplied

supplier
supplier's
    (of the supplier)
suppliers'
    (of the suppliers)
supplies (*pl.*)
supplies
support
  supporter
suppose
  supposedly
  supposing
  supposition
suppository
  suppositories (*pl.*)
suppress
  suppressible
  suppression
  suppressor
suppurate
  suppurating
  suppuration
supreme
  supremacy
  supremely
surcharge
  surcharging
sure
  surely
  surer
surety
  sureties (*pl.*)
surf
  surf-board
  surfer
surface
  surfacing
surfeit
  surfeited
surge
  surging
surgeon
  surgeon's
    (of the surgeon)

surgeons'
    (of the surgeons)
surgery
surgeries (*pl.*)
surgical
surgically
surly
surlier
surlily
surliness
surmise
surmising
surmount
surname
surpass
surpasses
surplice (clergyman's)
surplus (excess)
surpluses (*pl.*)
surprise
surprising
surrealism
surrealist
surrender
surrendered
surrendering
surreptitious
surreptitiously
surrogate
surround
surtax
surtaxes (*pl.*)
surveillance
survey
surveyor
surveyor's
    (of the surveyor)
surveyors'
    (of the surveyors)
survive
survival
surviving
survivor
survivor's
    (of the survivor)

survivors'
    (of the survivors)
susceptible
susceptibility
suspect
suspect's
    (of the suspect)
suspects'
    (of the suspects)
suspend
suspender
suspension
suspense
suspicion
suspicious
suspiciously
sustain
sustenance
suture
svelte
swab
swabbed
swabbing
swaddle
swaddling-clothes
swag
swagger
swaggered
swaggerer
swaggering
swain
swallow (food, etc.)
swallow (bird)
swallow's
    (of the swallow)
swallows'
    (of the swallows)
swam (*from* swim)
swamp
swampy
swan
swan's (of the swan)
swans' (of the swans)
swank
swanky

swap, swop (to exchange)
  swapped
  swapping
  swaps, swops
sward (of grass)
swarm
swarthy
  swarthier
  swarthily
  swarthiness
swash
  swashbuckler
swastika
swat (a fly)
  swatted
  swatter
  swatting
swath, swathe (strip)
swathe (to bandage)
  swathing
sway
swear
  swearing
  swore
  sworn
sweat
  sweater
  sweaty
swede (kind of turnip)
Swede
  (person from Sweden)
  Swedish
sweep
  sweeper
  swept
sweeping (comprehensive)
sweepstake
sweet
  sweetbread
  sweeten
  sweetened
  sweetening
  sweeter
  sweetheart
  sweetly

sweetmeat
sweet pea
swell (to get bigger)
  swelled
  swelling
  swollen
swell (dandy)
swelter
  sweltered
  sweltering
swept (*from* sweep)
swerve
  swerving
swift (fast)
  swifter
  swiftly
  swiftness
swift (bird)
swig
  swigged
  swigging
  swigs
swill
  swilled
swim
  swam
  swimmer
  swimmer's
    (of the swimmer)
  swimmers'
    (of the swimmers)
  swimming
  swimmingly
  swims
  swum
swindle
  swindler
  swindling
swine
  swine (*pl.*)
  swinish
swing
  swinging
  swings
  swung

swingeing (huge)
swipe
  swiping
swirl
switch
  switches (*pl.*)
  switchback
  switchboard
  switched
swivel
  swivelled
  swiveled
  swivelling
  swiveling
  swivels
swizzle
  swizzling
swollen (*from* swell)
swoon
swoop
swop, swap (to exchange)
  swopped
  swopping
sword
swore (*from* swear)
  sworn
swot (to study hard)
  swots
  swotted
  swotter
  swotting
sybarite
  sybaritic
sycamore
sycophant
syllable (part of word)
  syllabic
syllabub, sillabub
    (sweet cream)
syllabus (course of study)
  syllabuses, syllabi (*pl.*)
syllogism
sylph
sylvan, silvan
sym- (together)

symbiosis
symbol
  symbolic
  symbolical
  symbolically
  symbolise
  symbolize
  symbolising
  symbolizing
  symbolism
symmetry
  symmetrical
  symmetrically
sympathy
  sympathetic
  sympathetically
  sympathise
  sympathize
  sympathiser
  sympathizer
  sympathising
  sympathizing
symphony
  symphonies (*pl.*)
  symphonic
symposium
  symposia (*pl.*)
symptom
  symptomatic
syn- (together)
synagogue
synchromesh
synchronism
  synchronisation
  synchronization
  synchronise
  synchronize
  synchronising
  synchronizing
  synchronous
  synchronously
syncopate
  syncopating
  syncopation
syncope (fainting)

syndic
  syndicalism
  syndicate
  syndication
syndrome
synod
synonym
  synonymous
synopsis
  synopses (*pl.*)
syntax
  syntactic
synthesis
  syntheses (*pl.*)
  synthesise
  synthesize
  synthesising
  synthesizing
  synthetic
  synthetically
syphilis
  syphilitic
syringe
  syringing
syrup
  syrupy
system
  systematic
  systematically
  systematise
  systematize
  systematising
  systematizing
systole (heart function)

T

tab
  tabbed
tabby (cat)
  tabbies (*pl.*)
tabernacle

table
  table d'hôte
  tablespoon
  tablespoonful
  tablespoonfuls (*pl.*)
tableau
  tableaux (*pl.*)
tablet
  tabloid
taboo, tabu
  taboos, tabus (*pl.*)
  tabooed
  tabooing
tabulate
  tabulating
  tabulation
  tabulator
tachycardia
tacit
  tacitly
  taciturn
  taciturnity
tack (nail)
tack
(to change ship's course)
tackle
  tackler
  tackling
tacky (sticky)
  tackiness
tact
  tactful
  tactfully
  tactless
  tactlessly
tactics
  tactical
  tactician
tactile
tadpole
taffeta
tag
  tagged
tagliatelle
tail (of animal)

tailed
tailless
tailor
  tailored
  tailor-made
  tailor's (of the tailor)
  tailors' (of the tailors)
taint
  tainted
take
  taken
  take-off
  take-over
  taker
  takes
  taking
  took
talc
  talcum
tale (story)
talent
  talented
talisman
  talismans (*pl.*)
talk
  talkative
  talkativeness
  talked
  talker
tall
  taller
  tallness
tallow
tally
  tallied
  tallies (*pl.*)
  tallies
  tallying
tally-ho
talon
tambourine
tame
  tameable
  tamable
  tamed

tameness
tamer
taming
tam-o'-shanter
tamp (to plug)
tamper (to interfere with)
  tampered
  tampering
  tampon
tan
  (to convert into leather)
  tanned
  tanner
  tannery
  tanneries (*pl.*)
  tanning
tan (colour)
tandem
tang
tangent, tan (*maths.*)
  tangential
  tangentially
tangerine
tangible
  tangibility
  tangibly
tangle
  tangling
tango
  tangos (*pl.*)
  tangoed
  tangoing
tank
  tankage
  tanker
  tankful
  tankfuls (*pl.*)
  tankard
  tannin
  tannic
tantalise
  tantalize
  tantalising
  tantalizing
  tantalisingly

  tantalizingly
tantalum (metal)
tantalus (stand for wine)
tantamount
tantrum
tap
  tapped
  tapping
  taproom
  tap-root
  tapster
tape
  tapeworm
  tape-measure
  tape-recorder
  taping
taper
  tapered
  tapering
tapestry
  tapestries (*pl.*)
tapioca
tappet
tar
  tarred
  tarring
tarantella (dance)
tarantula (spider)
tardy
  tardier
  tardily
  tardiness
tare (weight)
target
tariff
  tariffs (*pl.*)
tarmac
tarn
tarnish
  tarnished
tarot (cards)
tarpaulin
tarragon
tarry (to delay)
  tarried

tarries
tarrying
tart (pastry)
tart (bitter)
  tartness
tart (prostitute)
tartan (cloth)
tartar (*chem.*)
  tartaric (acid)
  tartrate
tartar (violent person)
task
  task force
  taskmaster
tassel
  tasselled
  tasseled
taste
  tasteful
  tastefully
  tastefulness
  tasteless
  taster
  tastier
  tasting
  tasty
tatter
  tatterdemalion
  tattered
tattle (chatter)
  tattling
tattoo
  tattooed
  tattooer
  tattooing
tattoo (military display)
taught (*from* teach)
taunt
taupe
taut (tight)
  tauten
  tautened
  tautly
  tautness
tautology

tautologic
tautological
tavern
tawdry
  tawdrily
tawny
tax
  taxable
  taxation
  tax-collector
  tax-deductible
  taxed
  taxpayer
taxi
  taxis (*pl.*)
  taxicab
  taximeter
taxi (to move aircraft)
  taxied
  taxiing
taxidermy
      (stuffing animals)
  taxidermist
tea
  tea-bag
  teacup
  tea-leaf
  tea-leaves (*pl.*)
  tea-party
  tea-parties (*pl.*)
  teapot
  teaspoon
  teaspoonful
teach
  taught
  teacher
  teacher's
      (of the teacher)
  teachers'
      (of the teachers)
  teaches
teak
team (of players, etc.)
  team-mate
  team's (of the team)

teams' (of the teams)
teamster
team-work
tear (from weeping)
  tearful
  tearfully
  tearfulness
  tearless
tear (to pull apart)
  tearing
  tears
  tore
  torn
tease
  teased
  teaser
  teasing
teat
technical
  technicality
  technicalities (*pl.*)
  technically
  technician
  technicolor
  technique
  technocracy
  technocracies (*pl.*)
  technological
  technologically
  technology
  technologies (*pl.*)
Teddy-bear
Te Deum (hymn)
tedium
  tedious
  tediously
  tediousness
tee (in golf)
  teed
  teeing
teem (to be abundant)
  teeming
teens (age)
  teenage
  teenager

teenager's
(of the teenager)
teenagers'
(of the teenagers)
teeth (*from* tooth)
teethe
teething
teetotal
teetotaller
teetotaler
teetotalism
tele- (far, distant)
telecommunications
telegram
telegraph
telegraphic
telemeter
telepathy
telepathic
telephone
telephonic
telephoning
telephonist
telephony
telephoto
teleprinter
teleprompter
telescope
telescopic
telescoping
telescopy
teletype
televise
televising
television
telex
telexed
teletex (supertelex)
teletext (data by TV)
tell
tells
tell-tale
told
temerity
temper (to harden metal)

tempered
tempering
temper (anger)
tempera
temperament (character)
temperamental
temperamentally
temperance (soberness)
temperate (mild)
temperature
tempest
tempestuous
template
temple
temple's (of the temple)
temples'
(of the temples)
tempo
tempi, tempos (*pl.*)
temporal (worldly)
temporally
temporary
(not permanent)
temporarily
temporise
temporize
temporiser
temporizer
temporising
temporizing
tempt
temptation
tempter
temptress
tempus fugit
ten
tenfold
tenth
tenthly
tenable
tenability
tenacity
tenacious
tenaciously
tenant

tenancy
tenancies (*pl.*)
tenantry
tenant's (of the tenant)
tenants' (of the tenants)
tend (to be likely)
tend (to look after)
tendency
tendencies (*pl.*)
tendentious
tender (soft)
tenderer
tender-hearted
tenderly
tender (to offer)
tendered
tenders
tender (small ship)
tenderise
tenderize
tenderised
tenderized
tenderising
tenderizing
tendon
tendril
tenement
tenet (belief)
tennis
tennis-court
tennis-racket
tenon
tenon-saw
tenor (procedure)
tenor (singer)
tenor's (of the tenor)
tenors' (of the tenors)
tense (tight)
tensely
tenseness
tense (*grammar*)
tensile
tension
tent
tent's (of the tent)

tents' (of the tents)
tentacle (of animals)
tentative (experimental)
    tentatively
tenterhook
tenuous (thin)
    tenuously
    tenuity
tenure (holding property)
tepid
    tepidly
tercentenary
    tercentennial
term (of school, etc.)
term (word)
termagant
terminal (final)
    terminally
terminal (at airport)
terminal (*electr.*)
terminate
    terminable
    terminating
    termination
terminology
    terminologies (*pl.*)
    terminological
terminus (end of railway)
    termini, terminuses (*pl.*)
termite (white ant)
tern (bird)
tern (set of three)
terrace
    terracing
terracotta
terra firma
terrain
terrapin
terrestrial
terrible
    terribly
terrier
    terrier's (of the terrier)
    terriers' (of the terriers)
terrify

terrific
terrifically
terrified
terrifies
terrifying
territory
    territories (*pl.*)
    territorial
    territorially
terror
terrorisation
terrorization
terrorise
terrorize
terrorising
terrorizing
terrorism
terrorist
terse
    tersely
    terseness
tertian (fever)
Tertiary (third)
test
    test-tube
testament
    testamentary
testate
testator
    testatrix (*fem.*)
testicle
testify
    testified
    testifies
    testifying
testimony
    testimonial
testy (irritable)
    testily
    testiness
tetanus
    tetany
tetchy (irritable)
    tetchily
    tetchiness

tête-à-tête
tether
    tethered
    tethering
tetra- (four)
    tetragon
    tetragonal
    tetrahedral
    tetrahedron
    tetralogy
    tetrarch
    tetrarchy
    tetrode
Teuton
    Teutonic
text
    textual
    textually
textile (cloth)
texture
than
thank
    thankful
    thankfully
    thankfulness
    thankless
    thank-offering
    thanksgiving
that
    that's (that is)
thatch
    thatcher
thaw
    thawed
theatre
    theater
    theatrical
    theatrically
thee (*from* thou)
theft
their (of them)
    theirs
theism
    theist
them (*from* they)

themselves

theme
  thematic

then

thence
  thenceforth
  thenceforward

theo- (God)
  theocracy
  theologian
  theological
  theologist
  theology
  theosophical
  theosophist
  theosophy

theodolite

theorem
  theoretic
  theoretical
  theoretically
  theoretician

theory
  theories (*pl.*)
  theorise
  theorize
  theorising
  theorizing

therapy
  therapeutic
  therapist

there (at that place)
  thereabouts
  thereafter
  thereby
  therefore
  there's (there is)
  thereupon

therm- (heat)
  therm (unit)
  thermal
  thermally
  thermionic
  thermite
  thermocouple

thermodynamic
thermometer
Thermos
thermostat
thesaurus
  thesauri (*pl.*)
these (*pl.* of this)
thesis
  theses (*pl.*)
they
  them
  they'd
      (they had, would)
  they'll (they will)
  they're (they are)
  they've (they have)
thick
  thicken
  thickened
  thickener
  thickening
  thicker
  thicket
  thick-headed
  thickly
  thickness
  thickset
  thick-skinned
thief
  thief's (of the thief)
  thieves (*pl.*)
  thieves' (of the thieves)
  thieving
thigh
thimble
thin
  thinned
  thinner
  thinning
  thin-skinned
thine
thing
think
  thinker
  thinking

thought
third
  thirdly
thirst
  thirstily
  thirsty
thirteen
  thirteenth
thirty
  thirties (*pl.*)
  thirtieth
this
  these (*pl.*)
thistle
thither
thong
thorax
  thoracic
thorn
  thornless
  thorny
thorough
  thoroughbred
  thoroughfare
  thoroughgoing
  thoroughly
  thoroughness
those
thou (you)
though (in spite of)
thought
  thoughtful
  thoughtfully
  thoughtfulness
  thoughtless
  thoughtlessness
  thought-reader
  thought-reading
thousand
  thousandth
thrash (to beat)
  thrashed
  thrashes
thread
  threadbare

threat
  threaten
  threatened
  threatening
three
  three-cornered
  three-dimensional
  threefold
  three-quarters
  three-ply
  threescore
thresh (corn)
  thresher
threshold
threw (*from* throw)
thrice
thrift
  thriftier
  thriftily
  thriftless
  thrifty
thrill
  thrilled
  thriller
  thrilling
thrive
  thrived
  thriven
  thriving
  throve
throat
throb
  throbbed
  throbbing
  throbs
throe (suffering)
  throes (*pl.*)
thrombosis
throne
throng
  thronged
throttle
  throttling
  throttler

through
        (from end to end)
  throughout
throw (to fling)
  threw
  thrown
thrush
  thrush's (of the thrush)
  thrushes'
        (of the thrushes)
thrust
thud
  thudded
  thudding
thug
  thuggery
thumb
  thumbed
thump
thunder
  thunderbolt
  thundered
  thunderer
  thunderstorm
  thunderstruck
  thundery
Thursday
thus
thwart
  thwarted
thy
  thine
  thyself
thyme (herb)
thyroid
tiara
  tiaras (*pl.*)
tibia
tic (twitch)
tick (like a clock)
  ticked
  ticker
tick (on tick, credit)
tick (insect)
ticker-tape

ticket
  ticket collector
ticking (fabric)
tickle
  tickling
  ticklish
tidbit, titbit
tiddler
tiddly-winks (game)
tide
  tidal
  tideless
tidings
tidy
  tidied
  tidier
  tidies
  tidily
  tidiness
  tidying
tie
  tied
  tying
tie-dye
  tie-dyeing
tier (row of seats)
  tiered
tierce (set of three)
tiff
tiffin (lunch)
tiger
  tiger's (of the tiger)
  tigers' (of the tigers)
  tigress (*fem.*)
  tigresses (*pl.*)
  tigresses'
        (of the tigresses)
  tigress's (of the tigress)
tight
  tighten
  tightened
  tightening
  tighter
  tight-laced
  tight-lipped

tightly
tightrope
tights
tike, tyke (dog)
tile
  tiling
till (for money)
till (to cultivate)
  tillable
  tillage
  tilth
till (until)
tiller (of a boat)
tilt
timber (wood)
  timbered
timbre (quality of sound)
time
  time-honoured
  time-honored
  timekeeper
  timeless
  timely
  timepiece
  timer
  timing
timid
  timider
  timidity
  timidly
timorous
  timorously
  timorousness
timpano (drum)
  timpani (*pl.*)
  timpanist
tin
  tinfoil
  tinned
  tinning
  tinny
  tinplate
  (steel coated with tin)
  tintack
tincture

tinder
tinge
  tingeing
tingle
  tingling
tinker
  tinkered
  tinkering
  tinker's (of the tinker)
  tinkers' (of the tinkers)
tinkle
  tinkling
tinnitus (ringing in ears)
tinsel
  tinselled
  tinseled
tint
  tinted
tiny
  tinier
tip
  tipped
  tipper
  tipping
  tips
tip (top)
  tiptop
tip (suggestion)
  tip-off
  tipped-off
  tipster
tip (for rubbish)
  tipped
tippet
tipple
  tippler
  tippling
tipstaff
  tipstaffs, tipstaves (*pl.*)
tipsy
  tipsily
  tipsiness
tiptoe
  tiptoed
  tiptoes

  tiptoeing
tirade
tire
  tired
  tiredness
  tireless
  tirelessly
  tiresome
  tiresomely
  tiring
tiro, tyro (beginner)
  tiros, tyros (*pl.*)
tissue
tit (bird)
tit (nipple)
titan (strong man)
  titanic
titbit
tit for tat
tithe
Titian (painter)
titillate (to stimulate)
  titillating
  titillation
titivate (to smarten)
  titivating
  titivation
title
titmouse
  titmice (*pl.*)
titrate
  titrating
  titration
titter (to giggle)
  tittered
  titters
tittle-tattle
titular (*from* title)
toad
  toadied
  toadstool
  toady
  toadies (*pl.*)
  toadying
to and fro

toast
  toaster
tobacco
  tobacconist
  tobacconist's
    (of the tobacconist)
  tobacconists'
    (of the tobacconists)
toboggan
  tobogganed
  tobogganer
  tobogganist
  tobogganing
toccata
tocsin (alarm bell)
today
  today's (of today)
toddle
  toddler
  toddling
toddy (drink)
to-do (fuss)
toe
  toe-hold
  toeing
toff
toffee
tog
  togs (clothes)
  togged
  togged up (well-dressed)
  toggery
together
toggle
toil
  toiler
toilet
  toiletry
token
tolerate
  tolerable
  tolerably
  tolerance
  tolerant
  tolerantly

tolerating
toleration
toll
  (to ring a church bell)
  tolled
toll (tax)
toll call (telephone)
toll (damage)
tomahawk
tomato
  tomatoes (*pl.*)
  tomato-sauce
tomb
  tombstone
tombola
tomboy
tom-cat
tome (volume)
tomfoolery
tomorrow
tomtit
ton (weight)
  tonnage
  tonne (metric ton)
tone
  tonal
  tonality
  toneless
tongs
tongue
  tongue-tied
  tonguing
tonic
tonight
tonnage (*from* ton)
tonsil
  tonsillectomy
  tonsillitis
tonsure
  tonsorial
too (also)
tool
tooth
  teeth (*pl.*)
  toothache

toothless
toothsome
tootle
  tootling
top
  top-heavy
  topknot
  topmost
  top-notch
  topped
  topping
top (for spinning)
toper (drinker)
topiary
topic
  topical
  topically
topography
  topographer
  topographic
topper (top hat)
topple
  toppling
topsy-turvy
toque (small hat)
torch
  torches (*pl.*)
toreador
torment
  tormentor
tornado
  tornadoes (*pl.*)
torpedo
  torpedoes (*pl.*)
  torpedoed
  torpedoing
torpid
  torpidity
  torpidly
  torpidness
torpor
torque (twisting)
torrent
  torrential
torrid

torsion

torso

  torsos (*pl.*)

tort (wrong-doing)

tortoise

  tortoise-shell

tortuous

    (not straightforward)

  tortuosity

  tortuously

  tortuousness

torture

  torturer

  torturing

tosh (nonsense)

toss

  tossed

  toss-up

tot

total

  totalisator

  totalizator

  totalitarian

  totality

  totalled

  totaled

  totalling

  totaling

  totally

  tote

totem

totter

  tottered

  tottering

touch

  touched

  touches

  touchier

  touchiness

  touchy

touché

tough

  toughen

  toughened

  toughening

tougher

toughly

toughness

toupee

tour

  tourism

  tourist

  tourist's (of the tourist)

  tourists' (of the tourists)

tour de force

tournedos (beef)

tournament

tourniquet

tousle

  tousling

tout

  touted

  touter

  touting

tow (to pull a boat)

  towage

  towed

  towing

  tow-path

tow (fibre)

toward

  towards

towel

  towelling

  toweling

tower

  towered

  towering

town

  townee

  Town Hall

  township

  townspeople

toxaemia

  toxemia

toxic

  toxicologist

  toxicology

  toxin (poison)

toy

toyed

toying

toyshop

trace

traceable

tracer

tracery

tracing

trachea (windpipe)

tracheitis

trachoma

track

tract

  tractable

traction

  traction engine

  tractor

trade

  trade mark

  trader

  tradesman

  tradesmen (*pl.*)

  tradesman's

    (of the tradesman)

  tradesmen's

    (of the tradesmen)

  trade unionist

  trading

tradition

  traditional

  traditionally

traduce

  traducer

  traducing

traffic

  trafficker

  trafficking

tragedy

  tragedies (*pl.*)

  tragedian

  tragedienne (*fem.*)

tragic

  tragically

  tragicomedy

  tragicomic

trail
trail-blazer
trailer
train (railway)
train (of dress)
train (sequence of events)
train (to make efficient)
trainee
trainer
traipse
traipsed
traipsing
trait
traitor
traitorous
traitor's (of the traitor)
traitors' (of the traitors)
traitress (*fem.*)
trajectory
trajectories (*pl.*)
tram
tramcar
trammel
trammelled
trammeled
tramp
tramp's (of the tramp)
tramps' (of the tramps)
trample
trampling
trampoline
trance
tranquil
tranquillisation
tranquilization
tranquillise
tranquilize
tranquilliser
tranquilizer
tranquillising
tranquilizing
tranquillity
tranquilly
transact
transaction

transatlantic
transceiver
transcend
transcendent
transcendental
transcontinental
transcribe
transcribing
transcript
transcription
transept
transfer
transferable
transference
transferred
transferring
transfers
transfigure
transfiguration
transfiguring
transfix
transform
transformation
transformer
transfuse
transfusing
transfusion
transgress
transgressing
transgression
transgressor
tranship
transhipment
transhipped
transhipping
transient
transience
transistor
transistorisation
transistorization
transistorise
transistorize
transit
transition
transitional

transitorily
transitory (temporary)
transitive (*grammar*)
translate
translatable
translating
translation
translator
translator's
    (of the translator)
translators'
    (of the translators)
transliterate
transliterating
transliteration
translucence
translucent
transmigrate
transmigrating
transmigration
transmit
transmission
transmits
transmitted
transmitter
transmitting
transmute
transmutation
transmuting
transoceanic
transom
transpacific
transparence
transparency
transparent
transparently
transpire
transpiration
transpiring
transplant
transplantation
transport
transportable
transportation
transporter

transpose
  transposing
  transposition
transubstantiate
  transubstantiation
transverse
  transversely
transvestite
  transvestism
trap
  trapped
  trapper
  trapping
  traps
trapeze
  trapezium
trash
trauma
  traumas, traumata (*pl.*)
  traumatic
travail (painful effort)
travel
  travelled
  traveled
  traveller
  traveler
  traveller's
      (of the traveller)
  travellers'
      (of the travellers)
  travelling
  traveling
  travelogue
traverse
  traversing
travesty
  travesties (*pl.*)
  travestied
trawl
  trawler
  trawler's
      (of the trawler)
  trawlers'
      (of the trawlers)
tray

treachery
  treacherous
  treacherously
treacle
  treacly
tread
  treadle
  trod
  trodden
tread (of tyre)
treason
  treasonable
  treasonably
treasure
  treasurer
  treasuring
  Treasury
treat
  treatable
  treatment
treatise (literary article)
treaty
  treaties (*pl.*)
treble
  trebly
tree
  tree's (of the tree)
  trees' (of the trees)
trefoil
trek
  trekked
  trekker
  trekking
  treks (he, she)
trellis
tremble
  trembling
tremendous
  tremendously
tremolo (in music)
tremor
  tremulous
  tremulously
  tremulousness
trench

trenches (*pl.*)
trenchant
  trenchancy
  trenchantly
trencher
      (for serving food)
trend
  trendy
trepan
  trepanned
  trepanning
  trepans
trepidation
trespass
  trespassed
  trespasser
  trespasses
trestle
trial
triangle
  triangular
  triangulate
  triangulating
  triangulation
tribe
  tribal
  tribalism
tribulation (distress)
tribune
  tribunal
tributary
  tributaries (*pl.*)
tribute
trice
trick
  trickery
  trickier
  trickily
  trickster
  tricky
trickle
  trickling
tricycle
trident
tried (*from* try)

trier
triennial
trifle
  trifler
  trifling
trigger
  triggered
trigonometry
  trigonometric
  trigonometrical
trill
trilogy
trim
  trimmed
  trimmer
  trimming
Trinity
trinket
trio
triode
trip
  tripped
  tripper
  tripping
  trips
tripartite
tripe
triphthong
triple
  triplet
  triplicate
  triplicating
  triplication
  triply
tripod
  tripodal
tripos
triptych (picture)
triptyque
    (travel document)
trite
  tritely
triumph
  triumphal
  triumphant

triumphantly
triumvirate
trivial
  trivia
  trivialise
  trivialize
  trivialising
  trivializing
  triviality
  trivialities (*pl.*)
  trivially
trod (*from* tread)
  trodden
troll (giant)
troll (to sing)
trolley
  trolleys (*pl.*)
trollop
trombone
troop
  trooper
trophy
  trophies (*pl.*)
tropic
  tropical
  tropism
troposphere
  tropospheric
trot
  trots
  trotted
  trotter
  trotting
troubadour
trouble
  troublesome
  troubling
trough
trounce
  trouncing
troupe (actors)
  trouper
trousers
trousseau
trout

trowel
truant
  truancy
truce
truck
truckle
  truckling
truculence
  truculent
  truculently
trudge
  trudging
true
  true-blue
  truer
truism
truly
truffle
trump
  trumped up
  trumpery
trumpet
  trumpeter
  trumpeting
truncate
  truncating
  truncation
truncheon
trundle
  trundling
trunk
trunnion
truss
  trusses (*pl.*)
  trussed (tied up)
trust
  trustee
  trustee's (of the trustee)
  trustees'
    (of the trustees)
  trusteeship
  trustful
  trustfully
  trustworthiness
  trustworthy

truth
  truthful
  truthfully
  truthfulness
try
  tried
  trier
  tries
  trying
  try-out
try (in football)
  tries (*pl.*)
tryst
tsetse fly
tub
  tubbiness
  tubby
tuba (wind instrument)
  tubas (*pl.*)
tube
  tubing
  tubular
tuber (swelling)
  tubercle
  tubercular
  tuberculosis
  tuberculous
tuck
Tuesday
tuft
  tufted
tug
  tugged
  tugging
  tugs
tug (boat)
  tug's (of the tug)
  tugs' (of the tugs)
tuition
tulip
tumble
  tumbler
  tumbling
tumescent
  tumescence

tumour
  tumor
tumult
  tumultuous
tun (barrel)
tuna, tunny (fish)
  tuna, tunas, tunny,
                tunnies(*pl.*)
tundra
tune
  tuneful
  tunefully
  tunefulness
  tuner
  tune up
  tuning
tungsten
tunic
tunnel
  tunnelled
  tunneled
  tunneller
  tunneler
  tunnelling
  tunneling
  tunnels
tunny, tuna (fish)
  tunny, tunnies, tuna,
                tunas(*pl.*)
turban
  turbaned
turbid
  turbidity
turbine
turbo-alternator
turbo-generator
turbo-jet
turbo-prop
turbot
turbulence
  turbulent
tureen
turf
  turfs, turves (*pl.*)
  turfed

turgid
turkey
  turkeys (*pl.*)
  turkey's (of the turkey)
  turkeys' (of the turkeys)
turmeric
turmoil
turn
  turncoat
  turner
  turnstile
  turntable
turnip
turpentine, turps
turpitude (wickedness)
turquoise
turret
  turreted
turtle
tusk
tussle
  tussling
tussore, tussah, tusseh,
                tusser(fabric)
tutelage
  tutelary
tutor
  tutorial
  tutor's (of the tutor)
  tutors' (of the tutors)
tutti-frutti
tutu
tuxedo
  tuxedoes, tuxedos (*pl.*)
twaddle
twain
tweak
tweed
tweezers
twelve
  twelfth
twenty
  twenties (*pl.*)
  twentieth
twice

twiddle
  twiddling
twig
twilight
  twilighted
  twilit
twill (fabric)
'twill (it will)
twin
  twinned
  twinning
twine (thread)
twine (to twist)
  twining
twinge
twinkle
  twinkling
twirl
twist
  twister
twit (silly person)
twit (to jeer at)
  twits
  twitted
  twitting
twitch
twitter
  twittered
  twittering
  twitters
two
  twofold
tycoon
tying (*from* tie)
tyke, tike (dog)
tympanum (eardrum)
type
  typical
  typically
  typify
  typified
type
  typescript
  typewriter
  typewriting

typewritten
typing
typist
typist's (of the typist)
typists' (of the typists)
type-cast
  type-casting
typhoid
typhoon
typhus
typography
  typographic
tyrant
  tyrannical
  tyrannically
  tyrannise
  tyrannize
  tyranniser
  tyrannizer
  tyrannising
  tyrannizing
  tyrannous
  tyranny
tyre (on car)
  tire
tyro, tiro (beginner)
tzar, tsar, czar
tzigane (gipsy)

U

ubiquity
  ubiquitous
udder
ugly
  uglier
  ugliness
ukase (order)
ukulele
ulcer
  ulcerated
  ulceration

ulcerous
ulster
ulterior
ultimate
  ultimately
ultimatum
  ultimatums,
        ultimata(*pl.*)
ultra- (beyond)
  ultra-conservative
  ultramarine
  ultramicroscopic
  ultra-modern
  ultrasonic
  ultraviolet
umber (colour)
umbilicus
  umbilical
umbrage
umbrella
umpire
  umpire's (of the umpire)
  umpires'
      (of the umpires)
  umpiring
umpteen
  umpteenth
unable
unabridged
unacceptable
unaccompanied
unaccountable
  unaccountably
unaccustomed
unacquainted
unaffected
unafraid
unalterable
un-American
unanimous
  unanimity
  unanimously
unanswerable
  unanswered
unapproachable

unarmed

unashamed

unasked

unassisted

unassuming

unattached

unattainable

unattended

unauthorised

  unauthorized

unavailable

  unavailing

unavoidable

unaware

  unawares

unbalanced

unbearable

  unbearably

unbeaten

  unbeatable

unbecoming

unbeknown

unbelievable

  unbelievably

  unbeliever

unbend

  unbent

unbiased, unbiassed

  unbiased

unbidden

unblemished

unblushing

unborn

unbosom

unbounded

unbowed

unbroken

unburdened

unburied

unbuttoned

uncalled-for

uncanny

  uncannily

  uncanniness

uncared-for

unceremonious

uncertain

  uncertainty

  uncertainties (*pl.*)

unchangeable

uncharitable

uncharted

unchristian

uncivilised

  uncivilized

unclaimed

uncle

  uncle's (of the uncle)

  uncles' (of the uncles)

unclean

uncomfortable

  uncomfortably

uncommitted

uncommon

  uncommonly

uncommunicative

uncompleted

uncompromising

unconcern

unconditional

  unconditionally

unconfirmed

uncongenial

unconnected

unconquerable

unconscionable

unconscious

  unconsciously

  unconsciousness

unconstitutional

  unconstitutionally

uncontrollable

  uncontrollably

  uncontrolled

unconventional

  unconventionally

unco-operative

unco-ordinated

uncorroborated

uncouple

uncoupling

uncouth

  uncouthly

  uncouthness

uncover

  uncovered

uncritical

  uncritically

unction

  unctuous

  unctuously

  unctuousness

uncultivated

undated

undaunted

undeceive

  undeceived

undecided

undefended

undeniable

  undeniably

under

underarm (bowling)

undercarriage

underclothes

  underclothing

undercover

undercurrent

undercut

  undercuts

  undercutting

underdeveloped

underdog

underdone

undergo

  undergoes

  undergoing

  undergone

  underwent

undergraduate

  undergraduate's

  (of the undergraduate)

  undergraduates'

  (of the undergraduates)

underground

undergrowth
underhand
underlie
  underlay
  underlain
  underlies
  underlying
underline
  underlining
underling
undermanned
  undermanning
undermine
  undermining
underneath
undernourishment
  undernourished
underpass
underprivileged
underrate
  underrating
undersigned
understand
  understandable
  understanding
  understood
understatement
understrapper
understudy
  understudies (*pl.*)
  understudies
  understudied
  understudying
undertake
  undertaker
  undertaking
  undertook
underwater
underwear
underweight
underworld
underwrite
  underwriter
  underwriting
  underwritten

underwrote
undeserved
undesirable
  undesirably
undetermined
undeterred
undigested
undignified
undisciplined
undo
  undoes
  undoing
  undone
undoubted
  undoubtedly
undress
  undressed
  undresses
  undressing
undue
  unduly
undulate
  undulating
  undulation
  undulatory
undying
unearned
unearth
  unearthly
  unearthing
uneasy
  uneasily
uneatable
uneconomic
  uneconomical
  uneconomically
uneducated
unemployed
  unemployable
  unemployment
unenterprising
unequal
  unequalled
  unequaled
  unequally

unerring
uneven
  unevenly
  unevenness
uneventful
unexceptionable
      (satisfactory)
unexpected
unfailing
unfair
  unfairly
  unfairness
unfaithful
  unfaithfully
  unfaithfulness
unfashionable
unfasten
  unfastened
unfavourable
  unfavorable
  unfavourably
  unfavorably
unfeeling
  unfeelingly
unfeigned
unfit
  unfitness
  unfitted
  unfitting
unfold
unforeseen
unforgettable
  unforgettably
unfortunate
  unfortunately
unfounded
unfriendly
  unfriendliness
unfurl
  unfurled
unfurnished
ungainly
ungodly
ungovernable
ungrammatical

ungrammatically
ungrateful
  ungratefully
unguarded
unguent
unhappy
  unhappier
  unhappily
  unhappiness
unhealthy
unheard-of
unhinge
  unhinged
unhoped for
unicellular
unicorn
unidentified
  unidentifiable
uniform
  uniformity
  uniformly
unify
  unification
  unified
  unifying
unilateral
  unilaterally
unimpeachable
  unimpeachably
uninhabited
uninhibited
unintelligible
  unintelligibility
  unintelligibly
union
  unionisation
  unionization
  unionise
  unionize
  unionised
  unionized
  unionising
  unionizing
  unionism
  unionist

unique
  uniquely
  uniqueness
unison
unit
  unitary
  unit's (of the unit)
  units' (of the units)
unite
  united
  uniting
unity
  unities (*pl.*)
universe
  universal
  universality
  universally
university
  universities (*pl.*)
unjust
unjustifiable
  unjustifiably
  unjustified
unkempt
unkind
  unkindly
  unkindness
unknowing
  unknown
unlawful
  unlawfully
unleavened
unless
unlettered
unlicensed
unlike
  unlikelihood
  unlikely
unlimited
unload
unlock
  unlocked
unlucky
  unluckier
  unluckily

unmanageable
unmarried
unmask
unmentionable
unmistakable
  unmistakably
unmitigated
unmoved
unnamed
unnatural
  unnaturally
unnecessary
  unnecessarily
unnerved
  unnerving
unnumbered
unobservant
unobtrusive
  unobtrusively
  unobtrusiveness
unoccupied
unofficial
  unofficially
unopened
unpack
  unpacked
unpaid
unparalleled
unparliamentary
unpleasant
  unpleasantly
  unpleasantness
unpractical
unprecedented
unprejudiced
unprepared
unprincipled
unprintable
unprofessional
  unprofessionally
unqualified
unquestionable
  unquestionably
unravel
  unravelled

unraveled
unravelling
unraveling
unravels
unreadable
unready
unreadiness
unreal
unrealistic
unrealistically
unreasonable
unreasonably
unrecognised
unrecognized
unrecognisable
unrecognizable
unreliable
unreliably
unreserved
unreservedly
unresponsive
unrest
unrestrained
unrighteous
unripe
unrivalled
unrivaled
unruffled
unruly
unsafe
unsaid
unsatisfactory
unsatisfactorily
unsatisfactoriness
unsatisfied
unsavoury
unsavory
unsavouriness
unsavoriness
unscathed
unscientific
unscientifically
unscrupulous
unscrupulously
unscrupulousness

unseasonable
unseasonably
unseeing
unseen
unseemly
unseemliness
unserviceable
unsettle
unsettling
unsightly
unsightliness
unskilled
unskilful
unskillful
unskilfully
unskillfully
unsociable
unsociably
unsophisticated
unspeakable
unspeakably
unspoiled
unstable
unstably
unsteady
unsteadily
unsteadiness
unsubstantiated
unsuccessful
unsuccessfully
unsuitable
unsuitably
unsupported
unsurmountable
unsuspected
untactful
untactfully
untenable
unthinkable
untidy
untidier
untidily
untidiness
untie
untied

unties
untying
until
untimely
unto
untold
untouchable
untoward
untraceable
untrue
untruth
untruthful
untruthfully
unusual
unusually
unveil
unveiled
unwanted
unwarranted
unwary
unwarily
unwell
unwholesome
unwholesomeness
unwieldy
unwieldily
unwieldiness
unwilling
unwillingly
unwillingness
unwind
unwinding
unwound
unwise
unwisely
unwitting
unwittingly
unwonted (unusual)
unworkable
unworldly
unworldliness
unworthy
unworthily
unworthiness
unwrap

unwrapped
unwrapping
unwraps
unwritten
upbraid
upbringing
update
updating
upheaval
uphill
uphold
upheld
upholster
upholstered
upholsterer
upholstering
upholstery
upkeep
upon
upper
uppermost
uppish
uppishness
upright
uprightness
uprising
uproar
uproarious
upset
upsets
upsetting
upshot
upside
upside-down
upstairs
upstart
uptight
up to date
upward
upwards
uraemia
uremia
uranium
urban (of a town)
urbane (polite)

urbanely
urbanity
urchin
urea
urge
urgency
urgent
urgently
urging
urine
urinal
urinary
urinate
urinated
urinating
urn
urology
urologist
use
usable
useable
usage
useful
usefully
usefulness
useless
uselessly
uselessness
user
user's (of the user)
users' (of the users)
using
usher
ushered
usherette (*fem.*)
ushering
ushers
usher's (of the usher)
ushers' (of the ushers)
usual
usually
usurp
usurpation
usurper
usury

usurer
usurious
utensil
uterus
uterine
utilise
utilize
utilisable
utilizable
utilisation
utilization
utilising
utilizing
utility
utilitarian
utmost
Utopia
Utopian
utter
utterance
uttered
uttering
utterly
uttermost
uvula
uvular
uxorious

V

vacant
vacancy
vacancies (*pl.*)
vacate
vacating
vacation (holiday)
vaccine
vaccinate (to inoculate)
vaccinating
vaccination
vacillate (to hesitate)
vacillating

vacillation
vacuole
vacuous
  vacuity
vacuum
  vacuums, vacua (*pl.*)
vade-mecum
vagabond
  vagabondage
vagary
  vagaries (*pl.*)
vagina
vagrant
  vagrancy
vague
  vaguely
  vagueness
  vaguer
vain (conceited)
  vainer
  vainglorious
  vainglory
vain (useless)
  vainly
valance (curtain)
vale (farewell)
vale (valley)
valediction
  valedictory
valence (*chem.*)
  valency
valentine
valerian
valet
  valeted
  valeting
  valet's (of the valet)
  valets' (of the valets)
valetudinarian
valiant
  valiantly
valid
  validity
validate
  validating

validation
valise
valley
  valleys (*pl.*)
valour
  valor
valorous
value
  valuable
  valuation
  valueless
  valuer
  valuing
valve
  valve's (of the valve)
  valves' (of the valves)
  valvular
vamp
vampire
van
vandal
  vandalism
vandalise
  vandalize
  vandalised
  vandalized
  vandalising
  vandalizing
vane (weathercock)
vanguard
vanilla
vanish
vanity
vanquish
vantage
vapid
vapour
  vapor
vaporisation
  vaporization
vaporise
  vaporize
vaporiser
  vaporizer
vaporising

  vaporizing
vaporous
variable
  variability
  variance
  variant
  variation
varicoloured
  varicolored
varicose
  varicose veins
variegated
  variegation
varlet
varnish
varsity
vary
  varied
  varies
  variety
  various
  varying
vascular
vase
vaseline
vast
  vaster
  vastly
  vastness
vat (tank)
V.A.T., VAT
    (value-added tax)
vaudeville
vault (cellar)
vault (to jump)
vaunt (to boast)
veal
vector
  vectorial
veer
  veered
vegetable
vegetarian
  vegetarianism
vegetate

vegetating
vegetation
vegetative
vehemence
vehement
vehicle
vehicular
veil
veiled
veiling
vein (blood vessel)
venous
vein (manner)
vein (thin strip)
vellum
velocity
velocities (*pl.*)
velours, velour (fabric)
velvet
velveteen
velvety
venal (corrupt)
venality
venally
vend
vended
vendor (seller)
vender
vendor's (of the vendor)
vendors'
    (of the vendors)
vendetta
vendettas (*pl.*)
veneer
veneered
veneering
venerable
venerate
venerating
veneration
venereal (disease)
vengeance
vengeful
venial (pardonable)
venison

venom
venomous
venous (*from* vein)
vent
ventilate
ventilating
ventilation
ventilator
ventral
ventrally
ventricle
ventricular
ventriloquism
ventriloquist
venture
venturer
venturesome
venturing
venue
veracious
veracity (truthfulness)
veranda, verandah
verb
verbal
verbally
verbatim
verbiage
verbose
verbosity
verbalise
verbalize
verbalising
verbalizing
verbena
verdant
verdancy
verdict
verdigris
verdure
verdurous
verge
verging
verger
verify
verifiable

verification
verified
verifies
verifying
verily
verisimilitude
verity
verities (*pl.*)
veritable
veritably
vermicelli
vermilion
vermin
verminous
vermouth
vernacular
vernal (springlike)
vernier
veronal
versatile
versatility
verse
versed
versification
versified
versifies
versifier
versify
versifying
version
versus (against)
vertebra
vertebrae (*pl.*)
vertebral
vertebrate
vertex (highest point)
vertices, vertexes (*pl.*)
vertical
vertically
vertigo
vertiginous
verve
very
verily
vesper

vessel
vest
vestibule
vestige
  vestigial
vestment
  vesture
vestry
  vestries (*pl.*)
vet (to examine)
  vets
  vetted
  vetting
vetch
veteran (old soldier)
veterinary, vet
  veterinary surgeon
veto
  vetoes (*pl.*)
  vetoed
  vetoing
vex
  vexation
  vexatious
  vexed
via (by way of)
viable
  viability
viaduct
vial (small bottle)
viand
vibrate
  vibrant
  vibrating
  vibration
  vibrato (in music)
  vibrator
  vibratory
vicar
  vicarage
  vicar's (of the vicar)
  vicars' (of the vicars)
vicarious
  (on behalf of another)
vice (depravity)

vicious
viciously
viciousness
vice (tool)
vise
vice- (in place of)
  vice-chancellor
  vice-president
  vice-presidential
  viceregal
  viceroy
  viceroyalty
  vice versa
vichyssoise
vicinity
vicious (*from* vice)
vicissitude
victim
  victimisation
  victimization
  victimise
  victimize
  victimising
  victimizing
  victim's (of the victim)
  victims' (of the victims)
victor
  victorious
  victory
  victories (*pl.*)
victual
  victuals (*pl.*)
  victualled
  victualed
  victualler
  victualer
  victualling
  victualing
video
  video-cassette
  video-disc
  video-frequency
  video-player
  video-recorder
  video-signal

  videotape
  videotext
    (TV plus telephone)
  Viewdata (UK version)
vie (to compete with)
  vied
  vies
  vying
view
  viewer
  viewpoint
vigil
  vigilance
  vigilant
  vigilante
  vigilantly
vignette
vigour
  vigor
  vigorous
  vigorously
  vigorousness
vile (very bad)
  vilely
  vileness
  viler
vilify
  vilification
  vilified
  vilifier
  vilifies
  vilifying
villa
village
  villager
villain (wrong-doer)
  villainous
  villainously
  villain's (of the villain)
  villains' (of the villains)
  villainy
villein (serf)
vim
vinaigrette
vindicate

vindicating
vindication
vindicator
vindictive
vindictively
vindictiveness
vine
vinery
vineyard
vinous
vinegar
vinegary
viniculture
vintage
vintner
vinyl
viol
viola
viola da gamba
violin
violinist
violinist's
        (of the violinist)
violinists'
        (of the violinists)
violoncello
violoncellos (*pl.*)
viola (flower)
violate
violating
violation
violator
violence
violent
violently
violet
V.I.P., VIP
  (very important person)
viper
  viper's (of the viper)
  vipers' (of the vipers)
virago
  viragos (*pl.*)
  viragoes (pl.)
virgin

virginity
virgin's (of the virgin)
virgins' (of the virgins)
virginal (harpsichord)
virile
virility
virtu, vertu (love of art)
virtual
virtually
virtue (goodness)
virtuous
virtuously
virtuoso
virtuosi, virtuosos (*pl.*)
virtuosity
virulence
virulent
virulently
virus
viral
viruses (*pl.*)
visa
visas (*pl.*)
visa'd
visaed
visaing
visage
vis-à-vis
viscera
visceral
viscid
viscidity
viscosity
viscous
viscount
viscount's
        (of the viscount)
viscounts'
        (of the viscounts)
viscountess (*fem.*)
viscountesses (*pl.*)
viscountess's
        (of the viscountess)
viscountesses'
        (of the viscountesses)

visible
visibility
visibly
vision
visionary
visit
visitation
visited
visitor
visitor's (of the visitor)
visitors' (of the visitors)
visits
visor, vizor
vista
vistas (*pl.*)
visual
visualisation
visualization
visualise
visualize
visualising
visualizing
visually
vital
vitalisation
vitalization
vitalise
vitalize
vitalising
vitalizing
vitality
vitally
vitals
    (vital parts of body)
vitamin
vitiate
vitiating
vitiation
viticulture
vitreous
vitrify
vitrification
vitrified
vitriol
vitriolic

269

vituperate
  vituperating
  vituperation
  vituperative
vivace (lively music)
vivacity
  vivacious
viva voce
vivid
  vividly
  vividness
vivify
  vivified
  vivifying
viviparous
vivisect
  vivisection
  vivisector
vixen
vizier
vocabulary
  vocabularies (*pl.*)
vocal
  vocal cord
  vocalisation
  vocalization
  vocalise
  vocalize
  vocalising
  vocalizing
  vocalist
  vocalist's
      (of the vocalist)
  vocalists'
      (of the vocalists)
  vocally
vocation
  vocational
vocative (*grammar*)
vociferate
  vociferating
  vociferation
  vociferous
  vociferously
  vociferousness

vodka
vogue
voice
  voiceless
  voice-print
  voicing
void
  voidable
voilà
voile
volatile
  volatilise
  volatilize
  volatilising
  volatilizing
  volatility
vol-au-vent
volcano
  volcanoes, volcanos (*pl.*)
  volcanic
volition
volley
  volley-ball
volt
  voltage
  voltaic
  voltmeter
  volte-face
voluble
  volubility
  volubly
volume
  volumetric
  voluminous
voluntary
  voluntarily
volunteer
  volunteered
  volunteering
  volunteers
voluptuary
  voluptuaries (*pl.*)
  voluptuous
  voluptuously
  voluptuousness

vomit
  vomited
  vomiting
voodoo
voracious
  voraciously
  voracity (greediness)
vortex (whirlwind)
  vortexes, vortices (*pl.*)
votary
  votaries (*pl.*)
vote
  voter
  voter's (of the voter)
  voters' (of the voters)
  voting
votive
vouch
  voucher
vouchsafe
  vouchsafing
vow
  vowed
vowel
voyage
  voyager
  voyaging
voyeur
vulcanise
  vulcanize
  vulcanisation
  vulcanization
  vulcanising
  vulcanizing
vulgar
  vulgarisation
  vulgarization
  vulgarise
  vulgarize
  vulgarising
  vulgarizing
  vulgarism
  vulgarity
vulnerable
  vulnerability

vulture
vulva
vying (*from* vie)

W

wad
  wadding
waddle
  waddling
wade
  wader
  wading
wafer
waffle
waft
wag
  (to move to and fro)
  wagged
  wagging
  wags
  wagtail
wag (joker)
  waggish
wage (war)
  waging
wage (pay)
  wages
wager (to bet)
  wagered
  wagering
  wagers
waggle
  waggling
wagon, waggon
  wagon
  wagoner
  waggoner
  wagonette, waggonette
  wagon-lit
waif
  waifs (*pl.*)

wail (to cry)
  wailing
wainscot
  wainscoting
waist (round the body)
  waistcoat
wait (to postpone)
wait (at table)
  waiter
  waiter's (of the waiter)
  waiters' (of the waiters)
  waitress (*fem.*)
  waitresses (*pl.*)
  waitress's
        (of the waitress)
  waitresses'
        (of the waitresses)
waits (street singers)
waive (to forgo)
  waiver
  waiving
wake
  wakeful
  wakefulness
  waking
  woke
  waked
  woken
  waked
wake (of ship)
wake
  (lamentation or holiday)
  wakes
walk
  walker
  walker's (of the walker)
  walkers'
        (of the walkers)
  walkie-talkie
  walking-stick
  walk-over
wall
  walled
  wallflower
  wallpaper

wallaby
  wallabies (*pl.*)
wallah, walla
wallet
wallop
  walloped
  walloping
wallow
walnut
walrus
  walruses (*pl.*)
waltz
wan
  wanness
wand
wander
  wandered
  wanderer
  wandering
  wanderlust
  wanders
wane
  waning
wangle
  wangler
  wangling
want
  wanting
wanton (free and easy)
  wantonly
  wantonness
war
  warfare
  warmonger
  warmongered
  warmongering
  warred
  warring
warble
  warbler
  warbling
ward (of hospital)
warder (of prison)
  wardress (*fem.*)
  wardresses (*pl.*)

ward (off)
warden (church, etc.)
  warden's
      (of the warden)
  wardens'
      (of the wardens)
wardrobe
ware (china, etc.)
warehouse
warm
  warmer
  warmth
  warm-hearted
  warmly
  warm-up
warn
  warning
warp
  warped
warrant
  warrant-officer
  warranty
  warranties (*pl.*)
warren
warrior
  warrior's
      (of the warrior)
  warriors'
      (of the warriors)
wart
wary
  warier
  warily
  wariness
wash
  washable
  washed out
  washed up
  washer
  washerwoman
  washerwomen (*pl.*)
  wash out
wasn't (was not)
wasp
  waspish

wassail (to make merry)
waste (to squander)
  wastage
  wasteful
  wastefully
  wastefulness
  waste-pipe
  waster
  wasting
  wastrel
watch (to look at)
  watcher
  watchful
  watchfully
  watchfulness
watch (for telling time)
  watchmaker
watch (sentry)
  watchword
water
  water-borne
  water-closet (W.C.)
  water-colour
  watercolor
  watercress
  watered
  waterfall
  watering
  waterlogged
  watermark
  waterproof
  water-ski
  water-skied
  water-skiing
  watertight
  waterworks
watt
  wattage
  wattmeter
wattle
wave
  waveform
  wavelength
  waving
  wavy

waver (to hesitate)
  wavered
  waverer
wax
  waxwork
wax (to grow)
way
  wayfare
  wayfarer
  wayfaring
  waylay
  waylaid
  waylays
  wayside
  wayward
  waywardness
we
  we'd (we had, would)
  we'll (we will)
  we're (we are)
  we've (we have)
weak (feeble)
  weakened
  weakening
  weaker
  weak-kneed
  weakling
  weakly
  weak-minded
  weakness
weal (scar)
weal (welfare)
weald (former forest)
wealth
  wealthier
  wealthy
wean
  weaned
weapon
  weaponry
wear (clothes)
  wearable
  wear and tear
  wore
  worn

worn-out
weary
  wearied
  wearier
  wearily
  weariness
  wearisome
weasel
weather
  weather-beaten
  weathercock
  weathered
  weathering
weave
  weaver
  weaving
  wove
  woven
web
  webbed
  webbing
  web-footed
wed
  wedded (married)
  wedding
  wedlock
  weds
wedge
  wedging
we'd (we had, would)
Wednesday
wee (tiny)
weed
week (seven days)
  weekday
  week-end
  weekly
  weeklies (*pl.*)
weep
  wept
weevil
weft
weigh
  weighbridge
  weighed

weight
  weightier
  weightily
  weightless
  weightlessness
  weighty
weir (across a river)
weird
  weirder
  weirdly
  weirdness
welcome
  welcoming
weld
  welder
welfare
welkin
well
  well-being
  well-born
  well-bred
  well-known
  well-made
  well-meant
  well-nigh
  well-read
  well-to-do
well (of water)
we'll (we will, shall)
wellingtons
Welsh
  welsher
Welsh rabbit,
        Welsh rarebit
welt (of shoe)
welter (confusion)
welter-weight
wen (tumour)
wench
  wenches (*pl.*)
  wench's (of the wench)
  wenches'
      (of the wenches)
went (*from* go)
wept (*from* weep)

were (*pl.* of *was*)
  weren't (were not)
we're (we are)
werewolf
  werewolves (*pl.*)
west
  westerly
  western
  westernisation
  westernization
  westernise
  westernize
  westernising
  westernizing
  westward
wet
  wet blanket
  wetness
  wets
  wetted
wether (sheep)
whack
  whacked
whale
  whalebone
  whaler
  whaling
wharf
  wharfs, wharves (*pl.*)
  wharfage
  wharfinger
what
  whatever
  whatnot
  whatsoever
wheat
  wheaten
  wheatmeal
wheedle
  wheedling
wheel
  wheelbarrow
  wheelwright
wheeze
  wheezily

wheezing

whelk

whelp

when

  whenever

  whensoever

whence

where

  whereabouts

  whereas

  whereat

  wherefore

  whereupon

  wherever

  wherewithal

wherry

  wherries (*pl.*)

whet (to sharpen)

  whetstone

  whetted

  whetting

whether (...or)

whey (from milk)

which

  whichever

whiff

Whig

while

  whilst

while (away)

  whiling

whim

  whimsical

  whimsy

  whimsies (*pl.*)

whimper

  whimpered

  whimpering

  whimpers

whine (to cry)

  whining

whinny

  whinnied

  whinnies

  whinnying

whip

whipcord

whip-hand

whipped

whipping

whippet (dog)

whirl

  whirligig

  whirlpool

  whirlwind

whirr

  whir

whisk

whisker

  whiskered

whisky (Scotch)

whiskey (other makes)

  whiskeys, whiskies (*pl.*)

  whiskies (*pl.*)

whisper

  whispered

  whisperer

  whispering

whist

whistle

  whistler

  whistling

whit (small amount)

Whit

  Whitsun

white

  whitebait

  white-haired

  whiten

  whitened

  whitening

  whiter

  whitewash

whither (where to)

whiting (fish)

whitlow

whittle

  whittling

whizz, whiz

  whiz

whizzed

whizzes

whizzing

who

  whoever

  whom

  who's (who is *or* has)

  whose

whole

  whole-hearted

  wholesale

  wholesaler

  wholly

  wholesome

  wholesomely

  wholesomeness

whoop (to shout)

  whoopee

  whooping-cough

whopper

whore

  whoremonger

  whoring

whorl

whortleberry

  whortleberries (*pl.*)

why

wick

wicked (bad)

  wickeder

  wickedly

  wickedness

wicker

  wickerwork

wicket (cricket)

  wicket-keeper

  wicket-keeper's

   (of the wicket-keeper)

  wicket-keepers'

   (of the wicket-keepers)

wide

  wide awake

  widely

  widen

  widened

wider
widespread
width
widow
  widowed
  widower
  widower's
        (of the widower)
  widowers'
        (of the widowers)
  widow's (of the widow)
  widows' (of the widows)
wield
wife
  wives (*pl.*)
  wifely
  wife's (of the wife)
  wives' (of the wives)
wig (false hair)
wig (to scold)
  wigged
  wigging
wiggle
  wiggling
wigwam
wild
  wildebeest
  wilder
  wildfire
  wild-goose chase
  wildly
  wildness
wilderness
  wildernesses (*pl.*)
wile (trick)
  wiliness
  wily
wilful
  willful
  wilfully
  willfully
  wilfulness
  willfulness
will
  willing

willingly
willingness
willpower
wilt (thou)
will-o'-the-wisp
willow
willowy
willy-nilly
wilt (to droop)
wimple
win
  winner
  winner's (of the winner)
  winners'
        (of the winners)
  winning
  wins
  won
wince
  wincing
winch
wind
  windier
  windfall
  windless
  windmill
  windward
  windy
wind (to twist)
  winder
  winding
  windlass
  wound
window
  window-pane
  window-shopping
  window-sill
wine
  wine-cellar
  winy
wing
  wing-span
  wing-spread
wink
  winkle

winkling
winner
winnow
winsome
  winsomely
  winsomeness
winter
  wintered
  wintering
  wintry
wipe
  wiping
wire
  wireless
  wiriness
  wiring
  wiry
wisdom
wise
  wiseacre
  wisely
  wiser
wish
  wishful
  wishfully
  wishy-washy
wisp
wistaria, wisteria (shrub)
wistful
  wistfully
  wistfulness
wit
  witless
  witticism
  wittier
  wittily
  wittiness
  witty
witch
  witches (*pl.*)
  witchcraft
  witchery
  witcheries (*pl.*)
  witches' (of the witches)
  witch's (of the witch)

with
  withal
withdraw
  withdrawal
  withdrawn
  withdrew
wither (to shrivel)
  withered
  withering
withers (of a horse)
withhold
  withheld
  withholding
within
without
withstand
  withstood
witness
  witnesses (*pl.*)
  witness-box
  witnessed
  witnessing
  witness's
      (of the witness)
  witnesses'
      (of the witnesses)
wizard
  wizardry
wizened
woad
wobble
  wobbling
woe
  woebegone
  woeful
  woefully
wold (open hilly country)
wolf
  wolves (*pl.*)
  wolf's (of the wolf)
  wolves' (of the wolves)
woman
  women (*pl.*)
  womankind
  womanly

womenfolk
womb
won (*from* win)
wonder
  wondered
  wonderful
  wonderfully
  wondering
  wondrous
wont (accustomed)
  wonted
won't (will not)
woo
  wooed
  wooer
  wooing
wood
  wooden
  woodenly
  woodenness
  woodland
wool
  woollen
  woolen
  woolliness
  woolly
word
  wordily
  wordy
wore (*from* wear)
work
  workable
  worker
  workman
  workmen (*pl.*)
  workman's
      (of the workman)
  workmanship
  workmen's
      (of the workmen)
  workshop
world
  worldliness
  worldly
  worldly-wise

world's (of the world)
world-wide
worm
  worm-eaten
worn (*from* wear)
  worn-out
worry
  worries (*pl.*)
  worried
  worrier
  worries
  worrying
worse
  worsen
  worsened
  worsening
worst
worship
  worshipful
  worshipped
  worshiped
  worshipper
  worshiper
  worshipping
  worshiping
  worships
worst (to defeat)
  worsted
worsted (cloth)
worth
  worthless
  worthwhile
worthy
  worthier
  worthily
would (*from* will)
  wouldn't
wound (to injure)
  wounded
wound (*from* wind)
  wound-up
wove (*from* weave)
  woven
wrack (seaweed)
wraith (ghost)

wrangle
  wrangler
  wrangling
wrap
  wraparound
  wrapped
  wrapper
  wrapping
  wraps
wrath (anger)
  wrathful
wreak (to inflict)
wreath (of flowers)
  wreaths (*pl.*)
wreathe (twist)
  wreathing
wreck
  wreckage
  wrecked
  wrecker
wren
wrench
wrest (to snatch)
  wrested
wrestle
  wrestler
  wrestler's
      (of the wrestler)
  wrestlers'
      (of the wrestlers)
  wrestling
wretch
  wretches (*pl.*)
  wretched
  wretchedly
  wretchedness
  wretch's (of the wretch)
  wretches'
      (of the wretches)
wrick, rick (to sprain)
wriggle
  wriggling
  wriggler
wring (to twist)
  wrung

wrinkle
  wrinkling
wrist
  wristband
  wristlet
  wrist-watch
writ (legal document)
write
  writer
  write-off (cancellation)
  write off (to cancel)
  writer's (of the writer)
  writers' (of the writers)
  write-up
  writing
  written
  wrote
writhe
  writhing
wrong
  wrongdoer
  wrongdoing
  wronged
  wrongful
  wrongfully
wrote (*from* write)
wrought (shaped)
wrung (*from* wring)
wry (twisted)
  wryly
  wryness

X

xeno- (foreign)
xenophobia
    (dislike of foreigners)
xenophobe
xenophobic
Xerox
Xmas (Christmas)
X-ray

X-rayed
xylophone

Y

yacht
  yacht's (of the yacht)
  yachts' (of the yachts)
  yachtsman
  yachtsmen (*pl.*)
Yankee
yap
  yapped
yard (length)
  yardage
  yardstick
yard (enclosure)
yarn (story)
  yarned
yarn (thread)
yashmak
yawl (boat)
yawn
yea (yes)
year
  yearling
  year-long
  yearly
  year-round
  year's (of the year)
  years' (of the years)
yearn
yeast
yell
yellow
yelp
yen (longing)
yeoman
  yeomen (*pl.*)
  yeomanry
  yeoman's
      (of the yeoman)

yeomen's
(of the yeomen)
yes
yesterday
yesterday's
(of yesterday)
yester-year
yet
yew (tree)
yield
yippie (American hippie)
yodel
yodelled
yodeled
yodeller
yodeler
yodelling
yodeling
yodels
yoga (Hindu religion)
yogi (person)
yogurt, yoghourt,
yoghurt
yoke (fitted on neck)
yokel (peasant)
yolk (of egg)
yonder
yore (long ago)
you
you'd (you had, would)
you'll (you will)
your
you're (you are)
yours
yourself
yourselves (*pl.*)
you've (you have)
young
younger
youngest
youngster
youth
youths (*pl.*)
youthful
youth's (of the youth)

youths' (of the youths)
yowl
yo-yo
yule
yuletide

Z

zany
zanies (*pl.*)
zeal
zealot
zealous
zebra
zebras (*pl.*)
zebra crossing
zen
zenith
zephyr
zephyrs (*pl.*)
zero
zeros (*pl.*)
zest
zestful
zigzag
zigzagged
zigzags
zinc
zinnia
Zion
Zionism
Zionist
zip
zip fastener
zipper
zither
zodiac
zombie
zone
zonal
zoo- (animal)
zoo (zoological gardens)

zoological
zoologist
zoology
zoom
zoom lens